Pitt Series in Policy and Institutional Studies

The Social Construction of Expertise

THE ENGLISH CIVIL SERVICE AND ITS INFLUENCE, 1919–1939

Gail Savage

UNIVERSITY OF PITTSBURGH PRESS

Published by the University of Pittsburgh Press, Pittsburgh, Pa. 15260

Eurospan, London
Manufactured in the United States of America
Printed on acid-free paper

Library of Congress Cataloging-in-Publication Data

Savage, Gail, 1947–
The social construction of expertise : the English civil service and its influence, 1919–1939 / Gail Savage.
p. cm. — (Pitt series in policy and institutional studies)
Includes index.
ISBN 0-8229-3904-5 (alk. paper).—0-8229-5596-2 (pbk.)
1. Civil service—Great Britain. 2. Great Britain—Politics and government—1910–1936. 3. Great Britain—Politics and government—1936–1945. 4. Great Britain—Economic policy—1918–1945. 5. Great Britain—Social policy. I. Title. II. Series.
JN425.S28 1996
331.7′6135441—dc20 95-42006
CIP

A CIP catalogue record for this book is available from the British Library

Contents

Tables and Figures

TABLES

FIGURES

Acknowledgments

This project began with my dissertation, which examined the Board of Education and education policy. As with any research endeavor that stretches out over some years, this one has accumulated numerous professional debts to colleagues and archival institutions. These are imbricated within my argument and among my notes, but I want to express my gratitude for the intellectual communities and academic institutions that make work such as mine possible. I do wish to single out one person in particular. Professor Standish Meacham has staunchly performed the duties of adviser and mentor, providing a much-needed and appreciated thread of continuity to my peripatetic academic career.

The boundary between personal debts and professional ones is not always clear-cut, but I will mention two that fall on the personal side. My mother, Betty Savage, has been an unfailing source of support over the years. In moments of uncertainty, she would always counsel me to follow the riskier and more ambitious path that ultimately allowed me to complete this project and to develop subsequent ones. Also, the historical analysis I have pursued here has been enriched by the contemporary perspective I have gained from watching Larry Tabachnick work with affirmative action programs. This has been a salutary reminder that social policy is more than a theoretical and historical abstraction. Real people, motivated by vision, aspiration, and ambition, develop and implement social policy. Although hemmed in by fiscal, political, and organizational constraints, they can accomplish much, and what they accomplish in turn has a material impact on the lives of other real people. This study, I hope, will make a contribution to our understanding of this process.

Finally, I want to credit Michael Weeks for his able work on the tables. Michael is a man of multiple talents, and these tables represent only the tip of the iceberg.

INTRODUCTION

The English Civil Service and Social Policy

■ *The good Civil Servant, unlike the good child, is heard and not seen.*

—R. W. Harris

Social class and the exercise of power represent two constitutive elements of society, between them providing the mainspring of and the apparatus for political action. Beginning with either of these analytically separable concepts can form the basis for a rich, complex depiction of historical events or circumstances. To pursue one path or the other, however, necessarily neglects the difficult question of their relationship, an issue that I will seek to address in this study by delineating the mechanisms that link class and power. In order to sustain this dual focus, my analysis will examine both the social background and the actions of an English elite in a particular historical context. The formulation of English social policy between the First and Second World Wars provides an appropriate nexus of actors, time, place, and events for such an investigation.

In 1919 the English looked to the future guided by a variety of sentiments. In the aftermath of war, the appealing vision of Lloyd George's promised country "fit for heroes to live in" sat uneasily alongside the pervasive but not always welcome realization that irremediable changes had already taken place, which overwhelmed those returning home from war service.[1] In this atmosphere of heightened but conflicting expectations, the determination to put things back the way they were, manifested in the rapid dismantling of wartime controls, created a powerful political impetus. Varying expectations spawned bitter disagreement about the proper response to the social problems of postwar England. The acrimony that accompanied these controversies and the lack of consensus about their resolution embittered English social relations for years afterward.

The significance of the interwar period thus stems in part from its instability and its potential for change. But these two turbulent decades also merit our attention because in many respects a potential for even greater change remained unfulfilled. The capitalist system did not collapse, although economic cataclysm occasionally appeared imminent. Capitalism emerged from these trials, altered in some significant ways, but still recognizable and for a time seemingly more vigorous than before.[2] Immediately after the end of the war, political leaders feared the outbreak of violent social upheavals, and this fear contributed to the press for the sweeping social measures that were rapidly implemented, and almost as rapidly abandoned, by Lloyd George's coalition.[3]

But no truly revolutionary crisis ever materialized, and the English social structure remained stubbornly intact. The General Strike and massive unemployment certainly traumatized those who experienced them but did not lead to the radical reordering of the social system that many feared and others eagerly looked forward to. Whether the institutions of the British state merely weathered this storm or successfully rallied to meet the challenge remains open to debate.[4] In any case, the prospect (or threat) of radical social change imbued the persistence of political stability throughout the 1920s and 1930s with a nervous, anxious quality.

During the two decades between the First and the Second World Wars, the English grappled with social problems of increasing complexity. Those who had reached maturity during Victoria's declining years or during the Indian summer of Edward VII's reign emerged from the trauma of the Great War only to face financial crisis and then depression and unemployment on an unprecedented scale. Throughout the interwar period, thoughtful people debated the legitimacy of government intervention in social and economic processes. At the same time, stimulated by the persistence of mass unemployment, the demand for social services outstripped the capacity of government to provide them. Social issues such as poor law reform, educational reform, and unemployment relief stirred public feelings deeply.

These issues also generated major policy differences among the Conservative, Labour, and Liberal parties. The Labour party favored the expansion of the state's role in dealing with social problems; the Conservatives, who opposed increased spending for social services, did not. The Liberal party under the leadership of Lloyd George advanced the most innovative proposals, but these went unheeded. The Labour party failed to change the shape of English social policy until after England had fought another world war.

The development of social policy in this atmosphere of crisis and conflict provides a convenient arena within which to consider issues of social change, social class, and political power. Disagreements over social policy would likely bear the imprint of class bias. Their resolution would also reveal the extent to which class bias animated the processes of political power as well as how the structure of the political apparatus mediated the expression of class interests.

Civil servants, by virtue of their position, would necessarily play a pivotal role in this process. The civil servant's contribution to the resolution of controversy has often been understood in terms of English society's capacity to absorb such social conflict without undergoing great social change. Policies formulated and carried out by government officials might work to maintain social and political stability by deflecting or modulating the impetus for change. Labour politicians, disappointed over their party's failure to implement any of their policies during either of the first two Labour governments, fastened onto the influence of the civil service as an explanation for those failures. Hugh Dalton, undersecretary of Foreign Affairs in the second Labour government, blamed Margaret Bondfield's officials at the Ministry of Labour for influencing her to oppose borrowing from the unemployment insurance fund as a solution to the government's financial difficulties. Oswald Mosley, chancellor of the Duchy of Lancaster in the second Labour government, served with George Lansbury and Tom Johnston on a committee chaired by J. H. Thomas and appointed by Ramsay MacDonald to formulate schemes to alleviate unemployment. Mosley later complained that Thomas always sided with his officials in opposition to Mosley's proposals.[5]

Judgments such as Dalton's and Mosley's of their colleagues must be treated with caution. But historians have also tended to agree that civil servants played an important and not necessarily supportive role in the first two Labour governments. Robert Skidelsky in his work on the second Labour government, when describing the crisis that overtook the government, called the actions of the civil servants negative, if not obstructive. A.J.P. Taylor, in his Oxford history of England in the twentieth century, commented that the inexperience of Labour ministers increased their dependence on the officials who staffed the ministries.[6]

Those who have studied the civil service have shared similar views of the nature and extent of official influence on government policy. H. E. Dale, himself a former civil servant, observed that the common social background of civil servants and Conservative ministers contributed to the building of a pleasant working relationship between them. J. Donald Kingsley, arguing from the perspective of an outsider, warned that civil servants, unrepresentative as they were of the English population as a whole, could not be trusted to serve the people's interest.[7]

Despite differences of emphasis, these accounts advance a view of the civil service that implies two linked hypotheses about its role in government. First, civil servants have too much power (the argument runs), and second, they use that power to further particular interests—class interests. These notions continue to have great appeal. Ellen Wilkinson's failure to achieve a more radical reform of the English educational system during her tenure at the Ministry of Education after the Second World War has been attributed to the influence of her official advisers. R. H. Crossman's diaries, which contain a frank (if not necessarily objective and disinterested) assessment of the power of his permanent officials, show that many on the left in England still regard their civil service with suspicion.[8] But the Labour party does not have a monopoly on this suspicion. Conservatives too have held the civil service responsible for disappointing reversals in policy when an elected government failed to implement promised reforms. The Thatcher government identified the entrenched power of the civil service as one threat to its attempts to reshape Britain.[9]

The twenty years between the First and Second World Wars make a good testing ground of this view. These two decades were crucial to the development of both social policy and the civil service. The administrative foundations of the welfare state were put into place during these years. In addition, the reorganization of the civil service at the end of the First World War made the upper levels of the government administration both more centralized and more homogeneous than ever before. Although the government records for the entire interwar period have been open to scholars for over two decades, no systematic effort has yet been made to delineate the extent and nature of the influence of the civil service on social policy.[10]

My purpose here is to assess the role of the civil service in the development of English social policy during the 1920s and the 1930s, and in so doing to weigh the validity of these popular hypotheses concerning the power and social biases of the English civil service. I employ a thoroughly empirical methodology to carry out this task, but I address questions drawing a large measure of their significance from a theoretical terrain bounded by the terms *class, elites,* and *power.*

The Theoretical Setting

Class

The voluminous literature on social class attempting to define this indispensable concept falls into two basic categories. One can employ "class" as an objective or nominal category defined by some attribute or set of attributes. Alternatively, one can regard class as a collectivity with an identity in itself. The latter strategy implies that class is a phenomenon—an entity or process—and that the observer, rather than employ the concept as an analytical construct, discerns class as something that is actually happening.[11]

Both approaches to class have drawbacks. To use class as a nominal category alone permits great rigor but generally restricts the analyst to describing patterns of inequality in society. In contrast, the idea that the material circumstances of society itself generate social divisions continues to have intuitive appeal. This view offers the prospect of greater explanatory power but often proves difficult to apply with the precision necessary to persuade the skeptical. Studies animated by this view and inspired by the example set by E. P. Thompson with his now classic *Making of the English Working Class* have produced powerful portrayals of the life of the working class. However, an emphasis on the instruments of domination (and on the resistance to them) viewed from the perspective of those occupying the lower levels of the social scale has left the inner dynamics of the dominant classes out of the account.[12] As a consequence, the image of an upper class characterized by a monolithic efficiency—too often implied by an analytical approach from the bottom up—continues to handicap our understanding of class society. If class is indeed a social process, as E. P. Thompson so forcefully argues, then we ought to be able to observe that process at work from the top as well as from the bottom.[13] We ought also to be able to identify the mechanisms that sustain that process over time.

The Marxian concept of the relationship between class and power posits a process whereby the economic differentiation inherent in capitalism defines classes in conflict with one another—a conflict in which the state represents "the instrument of class domination."[14] Understood in this way, social policy in general (the British welfare state in particular) becomes a strategy whereby capitalist society preserved its hegemony. John Saville set out precisely this view in an essay written in the late 1950s, citing Joseph Chamberlain's famous dictum that "private property must pay to be tolerated" as a self-conscious articulation of the justification for social services as the price capital paid for social peace.[15] Persuasive defenses of this thesis have been constructed based on analyses of particular social policies.[16]

This approach is open to two criticisms, however. Such a view presumes the essentially malleable and cooperative character of the population; it requires, in short, a subordinate class that can be bought off.[17] This type of analysis also tends to make some unexamined assumptions about the processes by which social policy is formulated, locating the source of the values perpetuated by social policy in the social identity of the individuals who occupy key institutional positions. Victor George and Paul Wilding, for example, argue:

> The major social institutions are staffed and organized by members of the dominant social groups which successfully perpetuate themselves from generation to generation—e.g. the former Administrative Class of the Home Civil Service. Their values are expressed and embodied in such institutions as the civil service, the law and the courts, in the public schools and in the state education system through its imitation of the private sector. Through their expression and embodiment in national institutions, class values become national values.[18]

This statement links the social identity of individuals who occupy these privileged positions with the political domination of one class over another without specifying the nature of the link. Although such a hypothesis makes a strong appeal to commonsense notions of how social identity and interest can influence an individual's behavior, it does not identify the mechanisms necessary to sustain such a process. In the absence of those mechanisms, a potentially powerful explanatory insight remains flawed by the limited vision of individual psychology marked by a reductionism and determinism too crude to be persuasive. My study of the civil service and its influence on the formulation of social policy undertakes to provide a more flexible and sophisticated account of the process of domination by drawing upon the methodologies associated with elite theory as well as those associated with class theory.

Elites and Power

Theories based on the concept of elites rather than on the concept of class stress the division between those who have power and those who do not—the rulers and the ruled—as the key to understanding political processes.[19] An individual's identity is consequently defined (at least for the purpose of study) by the proximity to political power rather than by the relationship to the marketplace or to the means of production. The behavior of both groups and individuals is then understood in terms of the acquisition, exercise, and preservation of that power and need have no other significance. Both theoretical orientations have a measure of plausibility in the abstract, but their very abstraction hampers efforts to employ them as guides for research.

These two theoretical traditions underlie the development of two empirical strategies, each of which entails significant weaknesses. The class structure of a society and the exercise of power in that society (two analytically separable components of a social system) have come to constitute two distinct research problems for scholars. This separation—a division of labor logically feasible but not logically necessary—can result in the assumption of what remains to be proved or demonstrated. The perception that political power embodies social and economic power naturally leads to studies that emphasize the social background of elite groups.[20] Taking this approach assumes that this information, once acquired, reveals something important about how these groups performed their duties. The identification of an elite group with a particular class then presumes that class interests in some way shape that group's actions, a conclusion that only a study of the actions themselves can confirm.

On the other hand, to focus solely on the behavior of a group risks losing sight of the relationship between the individuals in that group and the society of which they form a part. Studies that detail particular policies or the work of a particular organization can overlook the social context of the behavior under scrutiny. Social identity may not determine individual behavior, but individual behavior certainly has social significance, a significance subject to observation and interpretation. Individuals, after all, derive the possibilities for behavior from their society. Although the range of these possibilities may vary, they always remain bounded, never stretching to infinity. To do one thing instead of another involves not only a conscious reaction to a concrete situation but also a sometimes unconscious and sometimes conscious expression of socially learned and socially defined values. Whether those values are class values is an empirical question; a satisfactory answer to such a question must draw upon both these empirical strategies in order to link social identity to behavior.

The importance of civil servants as a subject for study thus rests on the assumption that, in addition to representing a particular class, they form an elite group that occupies a strategic position in government. An elite group comprises the individuals occupying positions at the top of a hierarchy.[21] This definition distinguishes membership in an elite group from membership in the group that forms the recruitment pool for the elite group, but it does not preclude the ranking of elite groups among themselves to construct a comprehensive hierarchy. A government ministry comprises a hierarchy with a politician superior to the civil servants. Civil servants and politicians, taken as separate groups, carry on their work in hierarchies, and the apexes of those hierarchies meet in a ministry. Some civil servants, by virtue of their positions, have the opportunity to participate in the formulation of government policy. A ministry serves as a meeting ground where two distinguishable elite groups continuously engage one another.

The civil service is only one of several groups interested in the shaping of England's social policy. Quite apart from the question of what civil servants wish to accomplish is the question of whether they actually achieve their goals. The formulation of social policy provides a context that allows the evaluation of how much influence the civil service exerts over policy compared to the influence of others (the minister, the Cabinet, Parliament, private groups) interested in the same issue. An analysis of government papers reveals the resources civil servants could command for this purpose. The nature of these resources both provide the base for and establish the limits of their power over the formulation of policy.

A restatement of these issues in theoretical terms necessitates a definition of power. Power, then, is a social relationship meaningful only in a particular context that involves at least three components: two subjects and an object.[22] In exercising power one gains an end with regard to some object—overcoming, if necessary, the opposition of another. Anthony Giddens has put the matter simply: "Power is the capacity to achieve outcomes."[23] Power defined in this way becomes a component of every human relationship. Similarly, elites exist in all organizations. In theory all organizations and all human relationships would engage our interest. But not every organization or human relationship makes palpable the social significance of formal political power.

This Analysis

In practice, the concrete detail necessary to sustain and to specify the theoretical argument must be drawn from the close examination of particular cases. In this study I undertake the essentially empirical enterprise of fleshing out these theoretical bare bones. The ways that an elite group—possessing an important position in government—carried out its duties during a particular twenty-year period occupy the center of our attention. The analysis directly engages the challenge to delineate in detail just how the behavior of officials might be understood as both enacting and perpetuating the relationships of dominance and inequality that form large social processes. The question is, Did the social identity of English civil servants influence their official behavior? The answer proves to be yes, but the affirmative carries with it the burden of numerous qualifications.

Civil servants did not commonly exhibit a self-conscious class identity. Rather, they approached their work within the context of a professional identity that marked them as individuals with special qualities and special skills. These authorized their efforts to direct the course of events. Recruitment and promotion practices largely under their own control sustained and enforced their professional identity, which resonated with social significance. The interaction of departmental recruitment and promotion practices with educational background provided a material link between civil servants' status as experts and a more generalized class identity. Professional identity, which varied in important ways from department to department, in turn delimited the approaches civil servants might bring to the policy questions posed by historical circumstances. Those circumstances also worked in various ways to constrain or to enhance the civil servants' influence over the flow of events, that is, the extent to which the civil servants actually succeeded in shaping policy according to their vision. Civil servants could have a decisive influence on policy, and when they did, that influence might purposefully embody class values. Although contingent in nature, these links nonetheless proved a vital and crucial aspect of the political process.

Structure and Organization

This study falls into two parts. The first section treats the social origins and the career patterns of the civil servants who staffed the Board of Education and the Ministries of Health, Labour, and Agriculture during the interwar years. The first three of these departments of state enjoyed a virtual monopoly in administering the social services provided by English government during the interwar period. Education, public health, housing, poor relief, industrial relations, and social insurance all came under their purview. The Ministry of Agriculture carried out many of these responsibilities for rural areas.

These four ministries provide ample scope to compare and contrast official experience and practice in different settings and circumstances, but they do not make up the totality of the home civil service. The complexity of analysis here means it is impractical to undertake that much larger task, although my study will help to pave the way for a comprehensive examination of the civil service. The Treasury, which represents an important special case, is not included in the analysis here, in part because it has already received a good deal of attention and in part because that very attention has tended to obscure the differences existing between and within other departments.[24]

The first part of this study employs *class* primarily as a nominal category. In the analysis, information concerning civil servants' educational experience is used to indicate and define the social identity of the officials in the administration of these four ministries. Taking only one characteristic of an individual's experience as a surrogate for a phenomenon as complex as class clearly has serious drawbacks. Two considerations—one practical and one theoretical—justify this expedient. First, educational experience often represents the only information obtainable about large numbers of people in past time. Second, educational experience plays a vital role in forming one's consciousness and, in the English case, occupies an especially important place in defining class divisions.[25]

An examination of the educational credentials of the officials who staffed these four social service ministries reveals that, despite the overall homogeneity of the upper levels of the home civil service (designated the administrative class during this period), the interwar social service ministries differed markedly, both in their methods of recruitment and in their patterns of promotion. This variation contributed to the formation of a distinctive professional identity in each ministry, which helps to account for the differences in their approaches to policy. This variation turned out to be a product of the active intervention of departments in the recruitment of junior officials. Promotion then reinforced the departmental preferences established by recruitment.

The analysis of the social background of civil servants thus points to their direct participation in the formation of a professional identity, which manifests a social significance in at least two different ways. Given the close relationship between social class and educational opportunity in England, a professional identity predicated (even in part) on educational credentials would reflect larger patterns of social inequality, tending to close off avenues of social mobility and limiting access to the instruments of political power. The very process of so forming a professional identity would keep the social significance of educational experience present in the life of the adult. Although the actual experience of education would lie in an individual's youth, its significance would continue to affect the course of the adult's career. The analysis in part I of this study, which begins with a straightforward application of the concept of class as category, ends by showing how the ascription of class identity can itself be a constitutive part of social class understood as process.

Part II of the book examines the formulation of policy in the social service ministries. The chief source of information for this analysis is memoranda written by the officials who staffed the upper reaches of these ministries. In the course of their duties civil servants expounded their recommendations about the issues confronting them. These memoranda reveal not only the officials' points of view but also how they tried to shape policy to conform to their vision, which also varied from department to department and which proved a logical extension of the values implicit in departmental personnel practices.

The analysis of memoranda taken up in part II, considered in light of the findings outlined in part I, demonstrates that professional identity coincided with and strengthened the class biases of Board of Education officials but seemingly worked to counter comparable biases among Ministry of Agriculture officials. Civil servants at the Board of Education evinced an attitude toward secondary education policy that was closely related to their own educational experience. Agriculture officials, in contrast, lived out their careers in an organization that placed a higher value on an individual's expert knowledge of the practice of agriculture than on his educational credentials.

The cases of Health and Labour reveal two additional scenarios. The professional identity formed at Health effectively foreclosed the possibility that the civil servants in that department would develop a positive response to the social problems that came under their purview. Without being class conscious in the most obvious way, officials at the Ministry of Health consistently supported policies that underwrote the class divisions aggravated by the economic hardships suffered by so many during the interwar decades. The weak political position of Labour in the Cabinet during the interwar years ensured that civil servants there could have comparatively little influence on policy, whatever their views. The Ministry of Labour's story thus underscores the problematic and contingent nature of the power of civil servants.

Questions of social policy loomed large in English political life during the interwar years. The often heated discussions clearly involved important issues—important not just to those who participated in the struggles and to those who had to live with the consequences, but important also for those who now attempt to understand and interpret these events. Civil servants by virtue of their position necessarily engaged these issues of policy in the course of their work. The contests that went on in this discursive arena make concrete the theoretical problem of whether (and to what degree) the exercise of political power is a function of social structure. A close examination of this process shows that social class did indeed inform elite behavior, although it did so in the company of many other factors.

Within the English civil service, the interplay of institutions and individual experience systematically linked class to power. The ministerial culture that developed within each government office entailed a "normative order" that presumed and drew upon a system of class relations.[26] Official behavior in turn reconstituted and enacted these social relations by the implementation of policies bearing its imprint. Civil servants acted purposefully in this respect, even though their articulation of goals does not reveal anything so arrogant, so grandiose, or so tidy as a self-conscious and class-conscious conspiracy. Nevertheless, government officials cannot be relegated to a mere walk-on role in some elaborate social and political coincidence. Civil servants knew what they were doing, and what they did often made a difference.[27]

Part I

1 The Civil Service and the Social Calculus of English Education

■ *If I and others are worried by the continued predominance of Oxford and Cambridge graduates . . . it is not because of any bias against those universities, or any prejudice in favour of London or anywhere else. It is simply because we can see no reason to believe that administrative talent of the kind required in the Service is concentrated to such a degree in particular types of schools, particular universities and particular social strata.*

—R. K. Kelsall

Graduates of Oxford and Cambridge and of the public schools have always dominated the upper ranks of the civil service.[1] The persistence of this phenomenon has, to say the least, aroused doubts about the accessibility of the civil service to merit, irrespective of social origin. These doubts stem from the long-standing association of "particular types of schools" and "particular universities" with "particular" social strata. Given that association and the restrictive nature of the English educational ladder (where, traditionally, relatively few children pursue an academic course of study in preparation for entrance to university, and even fewer actually go on to university), the mechanisms that determined who advanced from rung to rung also defined the social composition of the university-educated population.

A professional group such as the civil service must necessarily draw upon the university educated for its recruits. Those who possess the requisite credentials constitute a pool of candidates created by the educational system rather than by the civil service. The importance of the educational experience of civil servants as an indication of civil service attitudes thus turns on the degree to which the active intervention of the recruiting process shaped the educational profile of government officials. This would suggest the self-conscious decisions made by civil servants who created and sustained a process by so acting. Alternatively, an educational profile that simply mirrored the educational system would indicate the workings of a process logically inherent in a previously defined structure.

The following quantitative description of the educational experience of the civil servants at the Board of Education and the Ministries of Health, Labour, and Agriculture indicates just such an active, conscious effort on the part of these departments to define their own characters. The description also shows distinctive variation by department. Taking this variation as a point of departure and placing it in the larger context of the English educational system, on the one hand, and of the educational profile of the home civil service, on the other, provide standards of comparison that then allow an assessment of the significance of departmental distinctiveness. Comparing the educational background of civil servants to the structure of educational opportunity available to the contemporary population at large identifies the paths that led individuals to the civil service and shows the extent to which the educational system itself defined those paths. A comparison of the educational background of the civil servants in the different social service ministries to that of the entire home civil service specifies and qualifies the widely held view of the civil service as a homogeneous elite Establishment.

The results of the investigations undertaken in part I of this analysis bear directly on the analysis taken up in part II. Employing different methodological tools (qualitative rather than quantitative), the later chapters examine the impact a "particular" educational experience might have had on the behavior of the civil servants who helped to formulate government policy in the four social service ministries. Together these different analytical foci delineate the ways that educational experience formed a contingent link between class structure and political power during the interwar decades.

Education and English Society

The educational experience of the English has been much studied, and the major features of this experience—the limited opportunities for higher education and the social bias of those opportunities that do exist—have attained the status of truisms. A brief review of the details of this familiar material will allow the formulation of more precise standards by which to judge the educational experience of civil servants. Such standards make possible a systematic evaluation of the popular notion of a class-biased government service dominated by a public school-Oxbridge nexus.

During the nineteenth century, English education developed distinctive features. Bifurcation along class lines became entrenched by 1900. Fee-paying students attended the preparatory and secondary schools that fed the universities, and elementary schools (both free and compulsory after 1891) served the bulk of the population. The 1902 Education Act provided for state grants to secondary schools in return for their allocation of "free places" to qualified graduates of elementary schools, thereby creating a scholarship ladder for students from poorer families. This did not, however, greatly enlarge educational opportunity or alter the social ambience of either the more prestigious secondary schools or Oxford and Cambridge. These educational institutions remained the exclusive province of the middle and upper classes (defined broadly by income and occupation) through the Second World War.[2]

The now classic study of social mobility in Britain conducted by D. V. Glass shortly after the Second World War provided a definitive analysis of the distribution of educational opportunity during the first half of the twentieth century.[3] Based on a large and exhaustive sample, this work convincingly documented the narrowness of the educational ladder in Great Britain before the Second World War. Only 14.4 percent of the prewar cohorts of school-age children attended the secondary grammar or secondary boarding schools that produced the vast majority of students who went on to university. Even those who received a secondary education at a prestigious public school did not invariably go on to obtain a university education. Of men born before 1910, only 9.9 percent of those who attended secondary grammar schools went on to university, whereas 20.5 percent of those who attended an independent boarding school went on to university. Less than 1 percent of those who had a nonacademic secondary education—that is, who went through the postprimary level of the public elementary schools administered by local education authorities (LEAs)—eventually reached a university.

Differential educational opportunity did not decrease for later birth cohorts. The proportions of those who went to university increased in each social category for those born between 1910 and 1929, but the discrepancies between the categories widened. The proportion of males who reached university through a secondary grammar school increased from 9.9 to 12.2 percent, whereas the proportion of those males who attended university in spite of a nonacademic secondary education grew from slightly less to slightly more than 1 percent. In contrast to these small gains, the proportion of those who went to university from the independent boarding schools more than doubled, increasing to 44 percent.[4]

England thus provided a university education to very few (less than 3 percent) of its young adults prior to the Second World War. Only a very small proportion of the British population formed the pool from which civil servants were selected. Those promoted from the lower ranks of the civil service or those specially appointed might lack the usually requisite university education. Promotees, however, formed less than 20 percent of the administrative class of the civil service, and they seldom attained high rank in that class.[5] The Glass study also documented a close relationship between social origin and higher education. Of those who went to university, 77 percent came from the upper and middle classes. In contrast, only 0.5 percent of sons of manual workers born before 1910 entered a university. This latter figure doubled for succeeding generations; thus 1 percent of sons of manual workers born between 1910 and 1929 entered university.[6] In short, the English educational system produced a relatively small university-educated population, and a child's social origin delimited the degree to which the opportunity to attend university represented a realistic option. A profession that demanded a university education as a prerequisite automatically excluded the vast bulk of the population by virtue of that requirement. The eligible few would almost certainly have included no more than a token number from the working classes.

The virtual exclusion of the working class from access to the meritocratic ladder did not, by itself, guarantee an administrative elite dominated by a homogeneous social elite. When defined as a sociological category, by occupation and income, the middle and upper classes together make up a diverse group, encompassing the families of minor civil servants, clerks, and teachers, as well as the wealthy and aristocratic. Nevertheless, even understood in this broad sense, the middle and upper classes represented less than 20 percent of the English population at the turn of the century. Those of middle-class status might exhibit a variety of lifestyles and certainly did not have equal command of the comforts and luxuries of daily life, but they all enjoyed access to the means of upward mobility that distinguished them as a group from the remaining 80 percent of the population.[7]

The university-educated formed a small group, but they did not form an undifferentiated one. The degrees from some institutions commanded more esteem than others. The prestige of the ancient universities of Oxford and Cambridge, for example, far exceeded the prestige of other universities; their mystique has remained virtually unchallenged until the present day. Yet at the beginning of the twentieth century, only 15 percent of Britain's full-time university students were enrolled in Cambridge and only 13 percent in Oxford. Almost 20 percent of university students attended one of the institutions making up the University of London. A full quarter of students were enrolled in Scottish universities; another 20 percent attended English universities other than Oxford, Cambridge, and London; and the remaining 6 percent pursued their studies at one of the constituent colleges of the University of Wales.

This pattern did not change appreciably during the first thirty years of the century. The proportion of students attending Oxford and Cambridge decreased slightly, whereas the proportion of students attending other English institutions increased. Oxford and Cambridge thus accounted for less than one-third of all university students in Britain, even at the turn of the century. In contrast, as we shall see, more than two-thirds of open competition entrants to the home civil service before 1939 had attended Oxford or Cambridge.[8]

The entire university-educated population did not have equal access to a civil service career, however. In general, officials looked for evidence of academic success in prospective candidates, and a first-class degree helped identify administrative class material. In addition, the higher civil service remained essentially a male preserve throughout the interwar period. Women were not permitted even to attempt the Class I examination until 1925. Using these provisos to redefine the pool of prospective civil servants changes the pool's character by increasing the proportion of Oxford and Cambridge graduates among the eligible.

A comparison of the figures for the number of first degrees granted in 1928–1929 to full-time enrollment in 1920–1921 shows that Oxford and Cambridge granted more first degrees, whereas the University of London granted substantially fewer than we might expect given their respective enrollments. Cambridge students, for instance, constituted 10.9 percent of British university students in 1920, but they secured 19.4 percent of first degrees granted in 1928. These figures suggest that more Oxford and Cambridge students distinguished themselves academically. Given the residential character of Oxford and Cambridge as opposed to the fragmented, urban nature of the University of London, such an outcome is not surprising. Still, even when we take the granting of first degrees rather than the presence of full-time students as a measure of a university's contribution to the pool from which civil servants were selected, the proportion of all such degrees awarded by Oxford and Cambridge together did not exceed 31 percent of the pool during the 1920s and 1930s.

The consideration that only men were appointed again increases the numerical dominance of Oxford and Cambridge. Oxford and Cambridge enrolled one-quarter of the male full-time students in 1930–1931 and granted 35 percent of the first degrees granted to men in 1934–1935. If those who received honors degrees constituted the true population of prospective higher civil servants, then Oxford and Cambridge produced an even greater proportion of the university graduates who formed the civil service's recruitment pool. In 1934–1935 Oxford and Cambridge together granted almost half (47 percent) of honors degrees granted to men throughout Britain.[9]

The educational system itself thus conferred substantial advantages on Oxford and Cambridge graduates. They could easily represent nearly half the entrants to any field that required outstanding academic credentials without any additional bias introduced by the recruiting or selection process. Even if Oxford and Cambridge graduates accounted for between one-third and one-half of any university-educated group, that would point to nothing more than the structure of higher education in England. On the other hand, if more than 50 percent of such a group came from Oxford and Cambridge together, this would imply some positive biases at work. For Oxford graduates alone to represent more than 15 or 20 percent of any group of university graduates would also indicate that preferential selection shaped that group's composition.

Oxford and Cambridge are usually considered together as the universities of the elite. But this conflates their differential contribution to the university-educated population. Cambridge had a larger student body and granted more degrees, both ordinary and honors, than Oxford. Oxford's share of students decreased during the first half of the twentieth century, dropping from 13.7 percent of the national total in 1900 to less than 10 percent by 1920. The continued domination of government service by Oxford graduates thus takes on additional significance in light of Oxford's relatively small share of the university population.

Secondary education in England, like university education, never represented an automatic stage in a child's development. In 1911 only 4.7 percent of all thirteen-year-olds (4 percent of girls and 5.5 percent of boys) attended a selective secondary school. In 1938 this proportion had increased to 12.1 percent (11.5 percent for girls and 12.8 percent for boys).[10] In addition, social origin significantly affected a child's opportunity to enter such a school. Of sons of manual workers born prior to 1910, for instance, only 2 percent obtained a secondary education in a grammar school or independent school. In contrast, almost 40 percent of the children of the upper and middle class entered secondary school.[11] Even during the nineteenth century, an exceptional child from a working-class home might achieve success within the framework of the English educational system. By and large, however, secondary education like university education remained a privilege of the upper and middle class until after the Second World War.

Secondary education also exhibited a hierarchy of prestige. As a group, public schools (identifiable by their membership in the Headmasters' Conference, an organization that conferred elite status upon those institutions belonging to it) constituted the most esteemed type of secondary school. In addition, particular public schools have long been regarded as veritable factories of the British elite. Eton, Harrow, Westminster, Winchester, Charterhouse, St. Paul's, Merchant Taylors', Rugby, and Shrewsbury (known as the Clarendon schools because they were singled out for special study by the Clarendon Commission in the 1860s) are the schools most often identified in this way.

How large a share of secondary school enrollment did these institutions represent? Table 1 shows the distribution of secondary school enrollment in 1930. At that time, the Clarendon schools accounted for nearly 10 percent

TABLE 1
Enrollment in Headmasters' Conference Schools, 1930 (England, Scotland, Wales)

	No. of Students	*% HMC Enrollment*	*% Secondary School Enrollment*
Clarendon schools			
Eton	1,125		
Harrow	670		
Westminster	365		
Winchester	470		
Charterhouse	614		
St. Paul's	680		
Merchant Taylors'	460		
Rugby	630		
Shrewsbury	500		
Total Clarendon schools	5,514	9.2	2.3
Other well-known schools			
Cheltenham	710		
Clifton	785		
Fettes	264		
Haileybury	530		
Loretto	170		
Malvern	570		
Marlborough	750		
Oundle	584		
Radley	336		
Repton	425		
Rossall	500		
Sedbergh	425		
Sherborne	410		
Uppingham	500		
Wellington	600		
Bradfield	450		
Total	8,009	13.0	3.0
Total all well-known schools	13,891	23.1	5.6
Total other HMC schools[a]	37,532	62.5	15.6
Total all HMC schools	60,012	—	24.3

Source: Whittaker's Almanac 1930: Board of Education, *Annual Report,* 1931.
Note: Full-time pupils in secondary schools on the grant and efficient list, March 31, 1930 (boys only, England and Wales only): 240,388.
a. Scottish schools in HMC not included.

of the pupils in Headmasters' Conference schools but only 2.3 percent of the total enrollment for boys in secondary schools recognized by the Board of Education in England and Wales. The Headmasters' Conference as a whole educated a quarter of the boys attending English and Welsh secondary schools in 1930.

Weighing the significance of these figures poses two serious difficulties. First, the figures do not include the unrecorded enrollments of some unknown number of schools. Secondary schools were not required to register with the government until after the Second World War, although the number of schools that voluntarily requested inspection and certification increased rapidly during the prewar period.[12] Knowing these enrollments would reduce the proportions of secondary school students assigned to Headmasters' Conference schools in table 1. Second, the validity of projecting these figures backward in time poses another major difficulty. Civil servants in the midst of their careers during the interwar period were schoolboys before the First World War. Both the enrollments and the status of individual schools as well as the membership of the Headmasters' Conference would have changed during the intervening decades.

The passage of time and the vagaries of public esteem must undermine the credibility of any "long" list of "well-known" schools.[13] The Clarendon schools, however, have retained the éclat they gained from their recognition by the Clarendon Commission. In all probability, the Clarendon schools at the turn of the century accounted for the same proportion (between 5 and 10 percent) of total enrollment in Headmasters' Conference schools as they did in 1930. The Headmasters' Conference was much smaller at the earlier date, but then so were enrollments—although the Clarendon schools had relatively large enrollments from the latter part of the nineteenth century. Headmasters' Conference schools together, however, could have represented as much as 40 percent of those boys attending grammar and proprietary schools and pursuing an academic secondary education in preparation for entering university around 1900.[14]

These figures provide approximate benchmarks for the evaluation of the educational experience of any elite group in the early twentieth century. The structure of secondary education in England would produce a group with about 5 percent from the Clarendon schools and less than half from Headmasters' Conference schools. Proportions greater than these, however, would suggest the presence of some additional factor in shaping the character of the group.

Education and the Home Civil Service

The significance of the educational experience of the officials who staffed the social service ministries rests not only on how it compares with the educational experience of the population at large, but also on how it compares with that of the home civil service taken as a whole. Another classic work, R. K. Kelsall's 1955 study of the civil service, provides the basis for making such a comparison. Kelsall's analysis underlines the importance of an Oxford or Cambridge education for a civil service career.[15] The type of university education that Kelsall found characteristic of the higher civil service does not at all correspond to the distribution of students among British universities. The dominance of Oxford graduates stands out as especially striking. Oxford graduates outnumbered Cambridge graduates by a factor of two, although Cambridge had a larger student body and produced more first degrees. Indeed, the number of Oxford graduates alone exceeded the combined number of Oxford and Cambridge graduates we might expect, given the student population of these two universities.

Kelsall, when he considered secondary education, found that the Clarendon schools had produced 22.6 percent of high-ranking civil servants in 1929. These nine schools still accounted for the secondary education of 16.5 percent of these civil servants in 1939.[16] Kelsall did not distinguish Headmasters' Conference schools as such in his analysis; but combining his categories of day schools belonging to the Headmasters' Conference with his list of twenty best-known schools (even though this does not include all the schools that belonged to the Headmasters' Conference) gives some measure of their importance.[17] Of the civil servants studied by Kelsall, 63.6 percent in 1929 and 58.1 percent in 1939 came from one of these schools. In contrast, only 14 percent of the 1929 civil servants came from a secondary school administered by a local education authority, and only 15.6 percent of the 1939 group had attended such schools.

When Kelsall examined the educational experience of all those who entered the civil service by open competition between 1909 and 1939, he found that 59 percent had been to one of the schools he regarded as best known, or to a day school in the Headmasters' Conference. In the period before the First World War, 66.1 percent of the open competition entrants had been to one or other of these types of schools in the Headmasters' Conference. Only 15.3 percent of the open competition entrants between 1909 and 1939 had been to a school administered by a local education authority; in the period before the First World War, only 5.9 percent had been to such a school.[18]

These figures display the social and academic bias of the English educational system; they also imply some bias on the part of the civil service in favor of Headmasters' Conference schools. The proportions of those who attended such schools exceed what we might expect by between 10 and 20 percent. The proportion of those who had attended a Clarendon school, however, is three or four times what we would expect to see. The secondary education of top civil servants, like their university education, not only indicates social origin but also manifests an active process that recruited selectively from among those equipped with the essential educational credentials. The preference for Clarendon-Oxford old boys operated to form an elite within an elite, which was even narrower than the public school-Oxbridge nexus popularly imputed to the civil service.

The Social Service Ministries

The educational experience of the officials of the Board of Education and the Ministries of Health, Labour, and Agriculture takes on a more complex significance against the backdrop of the structure of the English educational system and a profile of the entire home civil service. The social service ministries not only differed one from another, they exhibited a pattern of educational experience rather different from the civil service taken as a whole.

A comparison of Kelsall's figures on university attendance with the figures in table 2 reveals that the proportion of officials in the social service ministries under study here who attended Oxford was substantially smaller than the proportion of officials that Kelsall included in his study of the whole civil service.[19] According to Kelsall, of those who held high rank throughout the civil service in 1929, 51.2 percent had attended Oxford and 18.7 percent had attended Cambridge. Although 19.4 percent of all the civil servants at the Board of Education and the Ministries of Health, Labour, and Agriculture had been to Cambridge, only 29.7 percent had been to Oxford. However, the aggregate figures disguise some important differences among the departments. Of those officials at the Board of Education, 41.3 percent had attended Oxford. In contrast, only 27.8 percent of those at the Ministry of Health, 24.6 percent of those at the Ministry of Labour, and only 18.8 percent of those at the Ministry of Agriculture had done so.

Two different, but not mutually exclusive, explanations could account for this discrepancy. High proportions of Oxford-educated officials might have been concentrated in other departments—at the Treasury or the Home Office, for instance. Also, since Kelsall's figures reflect only the higher ranks whereas those in table 2 include all ranks, a larger proportion of the Oxford-educated might have been promoted from the lower to the higher ranks. The variation among the four social service ministries suggests the first possibility; and the following analysis of promotion patterns at these social service ministries establishes that such selectivity in promotion did in fact occur.

An examination of the secondary education of the officials who served in the social service ministries reveals the same pattern of variation. More of the officials of the Board of Education had attended one of the high-prestige Clarendon schools than the officials in the civil service as a whole (see table 3). Kelsall's study shows that of those civil servants who had enjoyed promo-

TABLE 2. *University Education of English Civil Servants, 1919–1939*

	Board of Education		*Ministry of Health*		*Ministry of Labour*		*Ministry of Agriculture*		*Total*	
	N	%	N	%	N	%	N	%	N	%
Oxford	74	41.3	42	27.8	41	24.6	16	18.8	173	29.7
Cambridge	41	22.9	33	21.9	23	13.8	16	18.8	113	19.4
London	6	3.4	6	4.0	14	8.4	12	14.1	38	6.5
Other English universities	4	2.2	1	0.7	1	0.6	1	1.2	7	1.2
Scottish universities	1	0.6	—	—	12	7.2	1	1.2	14	2.4
Other institutions	3	1.7	4	2.6	3	1.8	1	1.2	11	1.9
No university education	3	1.7	1	0.7	3	1.8	2	2.4	9	1.5
Missing	47	26.3	64	42.4	70	41.9	36	42.4	217	37.3
Total	179	100.0	151	100.0	167	100.0	85	100.0	582	100.0

Source: Calculations based on data compiled from *Civil Service Commission Annual Reports*, biographical dictionaries, and university directories.

tion to high rank in 1929, 22.6 percent had attended a Clarendon school. Of all the officials at the Board of Education between 1919 and 1939, 27.4 percent had attended a Clarendon school—more than twice the proportion of the Clarendon alumni at either the Ministry of Health or the Ministry of Labour and more than triple the proportion of Clarendon School graduates at the Ministry of Agriculture. Only at the Board of Education had more than half of the officials been to a secondary school in the Headmasters' Conference. In contrast, approximately a third of the officials at the Ministries of Health, Labour, and Agriculture had attended such a school. This lower figure approximates the proportion of secondary school pupils attending Headmasters' Conference schools immediately prior to the First World War.

These proportions are large (although, except for the Board of Education, not far from what we might expect), but an even larger proportion of the higher-ranking civil servants studied by Kelsall had been to a Headmasters' Conference school. Of those officials in the home civil service who had attained a rank above assistant secretary in 1929, somewhat more than 60 percent had attended a school in the Headmasters' Conference. By 1939 the figure had dropped to slightly less than 60 percent. This is the same kind of discrepancy that appeared in the analysis of university attendance, and the same possible explanations apply. Either even larger concentrations of officials educated at Headmasters' Conference schools existed in other ministries or officials with such an educational background had a greater likelihood of being promoted to the top ranks of the civil service.

Of the four ministries under study here, the Board of Education had the largest proportion of officials educated at prestigious institutions. The Clarendon schools produced more than a quarter of the Board's officials. Oxford and Cambridge graduates made up more than 65 percent of the Board's administrative staff, but Oxford graduates alone accounted for 41.3 percent of the Board's officials. A "particular" and very special type of education thus characterized the ministry that dealt with education policy.

The contrast between the Board of Education and the other three social service ministries shows that the educational background of civil servants could vary considerably from ministry to ministry. Such a pattern suggests that discrete educational paths led to different ministries. Differences among the ministries, defined and sustained by the ministries themselves, call into question the view that higher-level civil servants formed one undifferentiated, homogeneous group. Departments did not just passively reflect the social structure and educational system but rather—like the civil service as a whole—intervened to identify and to recruit those who might best serve departmental needs.

TABLE 3. *Secondary School Education of English Civil Servants, 1919–1939*

	Board of Education		*Ministry of Health*		*Ministry of Labour*		*Ministry of Agriculture*		*Total*	
	N	%	N	%	N	%	N	%	N	%
Clarendon Schools										
Eton	5	2.8	1	.7	4	2.4	1	1.2	11	1.9
Charterhouse	5	2.8	1	.7	2	1.2	—	—	8	1.4
Harrow	8	4.5	1	.7	4	2.4	—	—	13	2.2
Merchant Taylors’	2	1.1	1	.7	2	1.2	—	—	5	.9
Rugby	6	3.4	1	.7	1	.6	1	1.2	9	1.5
St. Paul’s	4	2.2	4	2.6	1	.6	1	1.2	10	1.7
Shrewsbury	3	1.7	2	1.3	1	.6	1	1.2	7	1.2
Westminster	5	2.8	7	4.6	2	1.2	1	1.2	15	2.6
Winchester	11	6.1	3	2.0	2	1.2	1	1.2	17	2.9
Total Clarendon Schools	49	27.4	21	14.0	19	11.4	6	7.2	95	16.3
Other well-known schools	19	10.8	12	8.2	19	11.4	8	9.6	58	10.0
Total well-known schools	68	38.2	33	22.2	38	22.8	14	16.8	153	26.3
Total HMC	102	54.2	58	38.7	57	34.2	29	34.4	246	42.3
Other private institutions	16	8.9	23	15.2	36	21.6	18	21.2	93	16.0
LEA	7	3.9	4	2.6	6	3.6	2	2.4	9	3.3
Missing	54	30.2	66	43.7	64	38.3	36	42.4	224	38.6
Total	179	100.0	151	100.0	167	100.0	85	100.0	582	100.0

Source: Calculations based on data compiled from *Civil Service Commission Annual Reports,* biographical dictionaries, and school directories.

The Political Significance of a "Particular" Education

In the English case, the association between an individual's social identity and that person's opportunity to obtain a higher education is so close that having attended a secondary school can serve as a rough and ready indication of social origin—at least by marking the disjuncture between the middle class and the working class. But the education of public officials is important not only for what it can tell us of their social origin, but also for what it can tell us about the formation of their opinions and attitudes. Schools, after all, do more than certify the social background of their graduates for the convenience of subsequent investigators. They also endeavor to form the characters and train the minds of their pupils. Indeed, the suspicion with which many regard a civil service dominated by the products of a few elite institutions stems in part from the commonsense notion that a child's formative experiences must shape adult behavior. The straightforward simplicity and appeal of this intuition, however, belie the difficulties inherent in demonstrating such a process at work in particular instances. A survey of the well-known features of the public school ethos will weigh how such an influence might manifest itself in the work of the civil service.

The cultural environment of public schools underwent an important change during the nineteenth century.[20] The middle and the upper classes each made a unique contribution to this evolution of the public school ethos. Middle-class parents demanded that the schools should maintain a high moral tone and a seriousness of purpose quite foreign to the older aristocratic tradition. Thomas Hughes used Flashman, the rakish villain of *Tom Brown's School Days* who is expelled from Rugby for drunkenness, to portray the aristocratic side of this cultural conflict. In real life, as late as 1872, the headmaster of Wellington, E. W. Benson, found himself at odds with his board of governors after expelling three boys for "misbehaving" with a servant girl. The more aristocratic board of governors did not see the boys' offense in the same light as Benson did. Where Benson, who had served as a master at Rugby under Thomas Arnold, saw a heinous moral crime, the board of governors saw only a mildly amusing peccadillo. The standards set by the middle class, and enforced by enthusiastic headmasters, eventually percolated up to the ranks of the aristocracy, teaching the value of discretion if not actually changing behavior. At the same time, however, the middle class gradually took upon itself the traditionally aristocratic burdens of public service.[21]

By insisting upon the subordination of individual desires to group needs, the public schools transformed the "fierce individualistic striving" of the potential capitalist and entrepreneur into the unshakable dedication of the public servant. Profit making became "unfashionable, a vulgar and slightly selfish pursuit." A career in the church, politics, the military, or the civil service not only marked one as a gentleman, but also allowed one to serve some end larger than self. Sir Stephen Tallents, for example, recalled his career as a public servant as one that had "yielded the satisfaction . . . of work done for the public advantage rather than for private profit." Tallents, a graduate of Harrow and Balliol College, Oxford, had served as an official in a variety of ministries and government departments including the Board of Trade, the Empire Marketing Board, the Post Office, the BBC, and the Ministry of Town and Country Planning.[22]

Public school education thus helped forge a distinctive culture of class that bound the sons of the wealthy and the aristocratic to the sons of the aspiring middle class. In this process, public service became imbued with an aura that combined moral approval and social esteem. But such a diffuse ambience could not by itself leave an imprint on the actual day-to-day formulation of government policy. Tracing the culture of class as transmitted by a public school education depends upon the presence of some more concrete and readily identifiable mark of such an education—if not a smoking gun, at least a smudged fingerprint. Two possibilities exist. The curriculum of public schools could embody a particular view of a subject likely to become the focus of government policy. In addition, schools sought to shape the character of their students as well as to impart a body of knowledge. Consequently, those who managed to conform to the ideal type might approach their work in recognizable ways.

The course of study traditionally offered by public schools was narrow. The public school curriculum consisted of an academic education with an emphasis on the Greek and Roman classics. Although modern history and modern languages became a part of the curriculum during the nineteenth century, the natural and applied sciences never found a congenial home in the public schools. T. H. Huxley once commented in disgust that if you asked a public school boy about science, "The only idea the word would suggest to his mind would be dexterity in boxing." Critics of the public schools cited this gap in the curriculum as a factor in the failure of British industry to keep pace with German and American industry in the development of technology in the late nineteenth and early twentieth century.[23]

Defenders of the classical curriculum made great claims for its efficacy in the training of future leaders. A study of the humanities formed a mind at once open and vigorous, and developed a flexible outlook. A leader needed versatility more than technical expertise. Thomas Macaulay, himself a poet, essayist, and historian as well as an Indian administrator and MP, opposed the inclusion of technical subjects on the grounds that a general education provided a better preparation for officials.[24] This glorification of the amateur inhibited the inclusion of "practical" subjects into the public school curriculum. Science and technology smacked of vocational education, and this attitude in turn reflected certain class-based notions of the function of education. A gentleman, after all, did not have to earn a living. Consequently, he had no need to study anything practical.[25] A gentleman was, first and foremost, a leader. Public schools taught boys to be gentlemen (and leaders) but did not teach them how to do anything in particular.

In the nineteenth century, public schools had come to represent much more than merely a particular type of secondary education. The idiosyncracies of public school education took on moral and class connotations that made alternative forms of secondary education not just different but less worthy. Coeducation, for instance, instead of being one way to include girls in an already functioning secondary school system, remained a "radical" idea into the twentieth century.[26] Science and technology were not just subjects that one had not been taught, but fields that no gentleman took an interest in. This point of view effectively shaped the educational philosophy of civil servants at the Board of Education, affecting in important ways their administration of the state-supported school system.

The intellectual justifications advanced to defend the traditional public school curriculum also decidedly influenced the recruitment of civil servants. The open competition examination embodied the preference for versatility over expert knowledge—a preference that formed a fundamental principle of recruitment to the highest levels of the civil service during the first half of the twentieth century. As we shall see, the tide favoring this vision became irresistible after the First World War, forcing both the reluctant Board of Education and the Ministry of Agriculture into the mainstream. At the Ministry of Health, the department that came closest to putting this approach into practice, this philosophy of recruitment would have a significant influence on the formulation of policy.

Thomas Arnold had justified the classical curriculum on the grounds that the primary object of the school was the building of moral character. He saw the study of science, for instance, as antithetical to this goal. Arnold's aims were "first, to instill religious and moral principles; secondly, to set standards of gentlemanly conduct; and, thirdly, to encourage intellectual ability." Arnold wanted to make the public school into an institution to transform adolescent boys into Christian gentlemen. Later in the nineteenth century manliness replaced piety as the most desirable moral attribute for an English gentleman, but the building of character remained the most important function of the public school.[27]

If building character formed the essential mission of the public school, what was the ideal character? English men of the late nineteenth and early twentieth century had no difficulty identifying its key elements. In *Tom Brown's School Days,* that quintessential public school novel written by Thomas Hughes in 1858, Squire Brown knew exactly why he was sending his son Tom to Rugby—not just to learn, but to become a "brave, helpful, truth-telling Englishman, and a Christian."[28]

Later in the century Matthew Arnold, Thomas Arnold's son, eulogized a young army officer who died at the age of twenty-two while on active duty in South Africa, providing a more elegant and more complete definition of the ideal. Arnold concluded his essay on this fallen hero by asserting that the young man's diary and letters revealed:

> a nature fresh, wholesome, gay; an English boy . . . with a keen love of sport, with a genuine love for the country . . . Greek in his simplicity and truth of feeling, Greek in his simplicity and truth of touch. We see him full of natural affection, and not ashamed of manifesting it; bred in habits of religion and not ashamed of retaining them; without a speck of affectation, without a shadow of pretension, unsullied, brave, true, kind, respectful, grateful, in-censorious, uncomplaining; in the time to act, cheerfully acting; in the time to suffer, cheerfully enduring.

Arnold gave a good part of the credit for this young man's noble character to his school, Eton. Although a bitter critic of the abuses of the public schools, Arnold thought that despite their failings they "bred great and precious virtues."[29]

A simpler and more vulgar version of this ideal appears in the popular adventure stories for boys written by G. A. Henty. These novels, which helped to preserve the public school ideal, retained their popularity well into the twentieth century. Sir Stephen Tallents recalled receiving a new Henty novel every Christmas, and he was only one of the many similarly favored.[30] Henty's heroes—athletic, cheerful, brave, determined, sharp or clever but not intellectual—never tell a lie, no matter what the circumstances. All three of these authors, as well as their respective audiences, shared a remarkably consistent vision of the ideal character, and all looked to the public schools to form young boys into this mold.

As the religious fervor of the early nineteenth century subsided, a simple and straightforward faith in the fundamentals of Christianity, "muscular" Christianity, replaced the almost obsessive concern with the doctrinal and moral niceties exhibited by both Evangelicals and Tractarians. The increasing emphasis on the virtues of manliness led to the glorification of playing games as a means to develop moral character. Participation in games became compulsory, and the most skilled athletes (known as "bloods") became the most respected and honored boys in the schools. The cult of games remained a fixture of public school life into the twentieth century. Spencer Leeson, a former official of the Board of Education who had been headmaster at Merchant Taylors' as well as at Winchester, could still write in 1947 that "the moral and physical value of team games is beyond argument." Team sports helped to inculcate many of the values held so dear by the public school community. Competition between houses within the schools and between schools encouraged the identification of the individual with the group. The relationship of the team to the captain reinforced the hierarchical arrangement of the schools themselves. Games, like bureaucracies, depend upon the players' adherence to arbitrary rules.[31]

By building character, public school education might mold particular personality types that reacted to certain situations in predictable ways. Analysts of British society have often made such claims for a public school education, although they disagree about whether this constitutes a benefit to the nation. J. Donald Kingsley, in an analysis of the British civil service, asserted that a British secondary school education fostered conformity, snobbishness, paternalism, a thirst for power, and an "aristocratic contempt for useful knowledge." Rupert Wilkinson, in his study of the public school tradition, argued that the generalist and humanistic bias of the public school curriculum put a premium on flexibility of mind; that the emphasis on games taught group loyalty, the value of cooperation, and a respect for rules; while the prefects system brought home the connection between social privilege and social responsibility. Although Wilkinson and Kingsley clearly differ on both the nature and the value of the influence they attribute to a public school education, they share the widespread assumption that such an influence exists.[32]

Other, more sociological studies of contemporary public schools have also dealt with this issue. John Wakeford, in a study of one unidentified public school, found that boys usually adjusted to the boarding school environment by outwardly conforming to authority but inwardly retaining reservations about that authority. Boys stayed out of trouble as best they could but frequently ridiculed the rules and traditions for their school. Wakeford noted, for instance, that some senior boys held "a meeting identical to that used to confer sports colours" in order to award colors for tiddlywinks. He found that the rugger teams often arranged in advance the outcome of the matches constituting their daily compulsory sport. He commented:

> The superficial impression at many of these matches was one of great effort, with appropriate groans in the scrums, displays of speed by the wingers, a chorus of cheers for points scored, and pointed concern over "injuries" sustained, while in reality the participants were putting on an act for the benefit of the referee and spectators.[33]

This finding must qualify an earlier investigation of public school education, which concluded that "the most general mode of adaptation is that the boy accepts the institution's view of him and conforms to its demands."[34] The investigators who conducted these studies differ on the extent to which the pupils of public schools internalize public school values, but public schools emerge in both studies as organizations that were extremely efficient at controlling the behavior of their members.

In general, the continuity and coherence of the agreement about the thrust of a public school education (despite disagreement about its merits) argues for the power of the public school experience. The difficulty lies in discerning such generalized traits and styles of character in particular cases and, at the same time, avoiding the frequent but reductionist assumption that public schools stamped out old boys who obediently acted out public school values for the rest of their lives. The social service ministries themselves offer a solution to these analytical problems.

Conclusion

The personnel policies of the different departments display sensitivity to both the social and intellectual import of different kinds of educational experience. Ministries utilized recruitment and promotion as tools to select from among those who pursued a career in government service and to reward those who conformed to departmental expectations. The variation in the educational attributes of the officials who staffed the social service ministries indicates not only that the criteria for such judgments differed from department to department but also that they had some relation to the educational credentials individuals brought to a civil service career.

In the Ministry of Agriculture and the Ministry of Labour, a respect for technical expertise led these departments to seek a broader range of recruits and to employ a broader range of recruiting methods than other government departments. This in turn sustained a proclivity for a more activist and innovative approach to policy making in both departments, although only Agriculture officials enjoyed a position that favored their efforts to shape policy. Conversely, the adherence of the Ministry of Health to the generalist tradition—the idea that an expert in nothing had the flexibility to become a leader in anything—led that department to welcome the recruits provided by the system of open competition. This not only shaped its social identity but had important implications for the development of departmental policy. With no independent stake in the policies at issue, officials tended to identify the state as their constituency, and administrative efficiency as their chief goal. The Board of Education, by virtue of its area of responsibility, could equate the credentials of a Clarendon-Oxford education with expertise—a link that had enormous implications for education policy.

The civil service and the educational system thus exhibited a relationship at once dynamic and interactive. Civil servants, prompted by a particular departmental vision of what constituted expertise, sought candidates with the requisites for that expertise, thereby generating the various departmental profiles. The recruitment and promotion practices officials employed had a social significance because of the close relationship between class structure and educational opportunity and had a political significance because they formed a context within which departments responded to questions of policy as they arose.

The next stage of my analysis examines the career patterns of the officials who staffed the four social service ministries. I will show in detail how recruitment and promotion interacted with the pool of aspiring government servants to define the character of each ministry. That character in turn became the backdrop for the work of ministry officials as they formulated policy. The analysis of the civil servants' view of policy that occupies the core of this study delineates the extent to which departmental values—revealed by personnel practices—are also revealed in the ways officials carried out their duties.

2 Recruitment and Promotion in the Social Service Ministries

■ *The cohesion of British administration is much promoted, to say the least, by the simple fact that most of the men holding positions of authority in the great departments of state, received the same kind of education, were at the same universities and colleges, and entered the service by the same path and at the same time.*

—H. E. Dale

The social service ministries exercised considerable control over their own personnel policies prior to the First World War. Even after the recommendations of the 1912 Royal Commission on the Civil Service (known as the MacDonnell Commission) were implemented in 1919, imposing a certain measure of uniformity on recruitment throughout the civil service, differences in promotion practices continued to persist.[1] Departments deliberately utilized recruitment and promotion to define a departmental point of view.

To the extent that government departments determined their own character, they worked counter to the generalist spirit of a neutral, meritocratic government service recruited by open competition examination. The replacement of patronage appointment by competitive examination as the mechanism to appoint government officials stands as one of the landmarks in England's transition to a modern state.[2] By 1919 the 1870 Order in Council that mandated this recruitment method for the upper levels of the English civil service was almost fifty years old. On the grounds that a liberal education constituted the best preparation for an administrative career, the examination consisted of a series of essays to test a candidate's grasp of the range of subjects encompassed by the contemporary university curriculum. The number of subject areas increased over time, but they never included technical or applied topics.[3]

In their *Fourth Report,* the MacDonnell Commission observed with approval that open competition had become the "normal method" by which candidates entered the civil service and that it governed the staffing of one-third of all civil service positions.[4] The MacDonnell Commission's view, reiterated more than two decades later by H. E. Dale, became a commonplace truism about the civil service. This assessment, however, neglects the nuance and range of departmental experience. A variety of recruiting practices continued in operation alongside the more modern system, and open competition actually remained the exception rather than the rule for recruitment to the social service ministries prior to the First World War.

Neither the Board of Education nor the Board of Agriculture took advantage of open competition to recruit their staff. This distinction would lead the MacDonnell Commission to focus special attention on recruitment procedures in these two ministries. The Board of Trade's Labour Department, which formed the nucleus of the Ministry of Labour created in 1917, had expanded rapidly in 1909 with the addition of labour exchanges to its responsibilities. As a consequence, large numbers of men entered the Labour Department by appointment rather than by competitive examination. Only the Local Government Board (LGB)—in 1920 transformed into the Ministry of Health along with the National Health Insurance Commission (NHIC)—routinely recruited its higher administrative staff through the "normal" procedure of competitive examination. Even so, the creation of the NHIC in 1911 necessitated the addition of a number of new positions, and some of these were filled by unorthodox methods.

This chapter sets out in detail the way each of these departments used recruitment and promotion to build up its staff. An examination of the composition of the candidate pool and an evaluation of the impact of departmental practice on the character of the social service ministries delimit the degree to which these departments could define their own identities. Education and Agriculture in particular managed to maintain a departmental distinctiveness, even though their efforts to defend their autonomy to the MacDonnell Commission proved unsuccessful. Testimony presented to the MacDonnell Commission during its evaluation of the internal workings of the civil service reveals how various interested parties viewed the issues at stake. Placing the disagreements over recruitment in the context of actual practice shows that these issues, although ostensibly administrative, had a social significance not necessarily clear to (or admitted by) the combatants.

Open Competition and the Competitors

The university-educated population constituted the pool of potential candidates for the higher civil service. However, the civil service could recruit only those who actively sought a career in government. What sort of individual chose to pursue this professional avenue? And to what extent did such self-selection define the educational profile of the civil service? The absence of systematic information on the educational careers of candidates who proved unsuccessful at the open competition examination during the pre–First World War years prohibits a full investigation of these questions. Concern about whether the civil service was attracting the best-qualified candidates, however, led the Civil Service Commission to analyze the secondary education of the entire candidate pool in 1936 and 1937, and the 1938 candidates' university education.[5] Although an examination of only three years cannot provide a safe basis for generalization about the entire period, the results of these inquiries do suggest that self-selection had a significant impact on the nature of the civil service's candidate pool.

The investigation of the university education of 1938 candidates showed that more Oxford graduates (160) than Cambridge graduates (141) took the examination that year. Oxford and Cambridge graduates together greatly outnumbered those (91) who had attended other universities. Oxbridge graduates were even more overrepresented among those who passed the examination: Oxford graduates made up 40.8 percent of all those who took the examination and 46.1 percent of successful candidates; Cambridge graduates made up 35.19 and 44.7 percent, respectively. Such a result indicates that Oxbridge graduates enjoyed at least a modest advantage over other candidates. Graduates of Scottish universities did not conform to this pattern, however. Very few (ten) Scottish graduates took the examination (3.31 percent of all candidates) in 1938, but they secured the highest success rate of all (23.07 percent).[6]

The results of only one competition so late in the period under study cannot be more than a clue to an earlier period. However, these figures do tend to support the explanations for the predominance of Oxford graduates among successful candidates to the civil service that had been put forward by the educational authorities questioned by the MacDonnell Commission almost thirty years previously. The presence of so many Oxbridge graduates, especially Oxford graduates, in the higher levels of the civil service troubled the MacDonnell Commission because of the possibility that bias in the examination itself produced this result. Such bias would be incompatible with the meritocratic ideal embodied by the examination system. They therefore turned to the university community to evaluate how well the system worked in selecting the best-qualified candidates from among the university-educated.

Representatives of the newer English universities agreed that the examination tended to favor Oxbridge graduates and to reward the study of the classics over more modern courses of study. C. E. Vaughn, appearing on behalf of the University of Leeds, declared that only the Oxford Greats adequately prepared a man to take the open competition examination without special tuition in addition to his regular course of study at university.[7] Sir Stanley Leathes, first commissioner of the Civil Service Commission, conceded as much in his testimony. (Leathes, however, probably thought the advantage enjoyed by those who had studied the Oxford Greats all to the good because he believed that course of study produced the ideal civil servant.)[8]

The representatives of the Scottish universities did not regard their students similarly handicapped, however. Professor Dudley J. Medley of the University of Glasgow conceded that the examination slightly favored Oxbridge graduates, but the representative from Edinburgh, Professor Richard Lodge, argued that the successful performances of their graduates on the examination did not bear out this widespread perception of favoritism. Professor John Burnet of the University of St. Andrews put the case even more strongly, declaring that there was "no case at all of anyone who gets first class honours with us ever failing to get into the civil service if he wished to do so," and that the examination "suits us exactly."[9]

Testimony by members of the British academic community suggest an alternative explanation for the large number of Oxbridge graduates among those who succeeded in the open competition examination. They pointed out that far more students from Oxford and Cambridge attempted the examinations than students from other universities. Those from other universities who tried their luck, however, did well. This view accords exactly with the results of the 1938 examination. Witnesses proffered several different explanations for this pattern. Professor Lodge of Edinburgh and Professor Burnet of St. Andrews noted the absence of a strong tradition of government service as a profession among students attending their institutions. Consequently, few of those students who would be expected to do well presented themselves for the examination. The perception that the examination favored the older universities also discouraged able students from making the attempt. In addition, Sir Harry R. Reichel believed that Welsh students felt at a disadvantage because their comparatively meager means precluded their utilizing specialized tuition to prepare themselves for the examination.[10]

Recruitment procedures did not remain static during the first half of the twentieth century. After the First World War, recruitment became increasingly restricted to those who submitted to open competitive examination. The addition of a personal interview to the process tended, if anything, to accentuate the advantage Oxbridge graduates already enjoyed.[11] Indeed, a comparison of the university education of prewar and postwar open competition recruits shows a dramatic increase in the proportion of both Oxford and Cambridge graduates. Of 862 men who entered the civil service by open competition between 1906 and 1910, 247 (or 28.65 percent) had Oxford degrees and 142 (or 16.47 percent) had Cambridge degrees. The remaining 473 individuals (54.87 percent) had some other kind of postsecondary education. In contrast, of the 489 junior officials who succeeded in open competitions held from 1925 through 1938, 203 (or 41.5 percent) had attended Oxford, 223 (or 45.6 percent) had attended Cambridge, and only 63 (or 12.8 percent) had not had the advantage of an Oxbridge education.[12] This increase occurred at a time when Oxford and Cambridge produced a decreasing share of the total university-educated population.

During the interwar period, officials who believed that Oxford and Cambridge furnished the best candidates for the civil service could view this result with satisfaction.[13] However, the outbreak of the Second World War brought an end to competitive examination for the duration. The war effort required a great expansion of the state apparatus at the same time as the armed services put enormous demands on the population of able-bodied men. As a wartime expedient, the Civil Service Commission set up a central interviewing board to screen recruits to the civil service. A concern that this departure from standard procedure would lead to a dilution of the quality of officials entering the civil service motivated a comparison between the university educations of those recruited during the autumn of 1941 and those who entered the civil service by open competition during the interwar years.

This exercise revealed that a profound change in the candidate pool had taken place. Of the 242 interviewees assessed toward the end of 1941, the largest group of 87 (or 35.95 percent) had attended London University (see table 4). The educational profile of these candidates was much closer to that of the university-educated population as a whole, although both the entire

TABLE 4
University Education and Method of Recruitment for the Civil Service

	Open Competition 1925–1939		*Selection Board Recruitment: All Candidates (fall 1941)*		*Selection Board Recruitment: Superior Candidates (fall 1941)*	
	N	%	N	%	N	%
Oxford University	203	41.50	61	25.20	8	25.00
Cambridge University	223	45.60	32	13.20	5	15.60
London University	27	5.50	87	35.95	12	37.50
Scottish universities	27	5.50	29	11.98	3	10.30
Other universities	9	1.80	33	13.60	4	12.10
Total	489	100.00	242	100.00	32	100.00

Source: Note B by the First Civil Service Commissioner for the Vice-Chancellor's Subcommittee on Postwar Recruitment to the Civil Service. A.P.W., October 30, 1941 (PRO ED 136/327).

candidate pool and those rated as superior still included twice as many Oxford graduates as Cambridge graduates. Also, the system employed in 1941 did not produce a select group with an educational profile that was different from the larger candidate pool.

The decline in the number of candidates from the ancient universities gave the Civil Service Commission some grounds for concern, given their assumption that Oxford and Cambridge produced the best recruits to government service. The results of the selection board's assessment of these candidates allayed these worries somewhat. Among those rated as superior by the selection board, Oxbridge graduates did not exhibit any advantage over the graduates of other universities. Indeed, London University graduates predominated in the superior group. Of these individuals (a good many of them women), only eight (or 25 percent) had attended Oxford, and only five (or 15.62 percent) had attended Cambridge. On the basis of these results, the Civil Service Commission concluded: "A much larger proportion of first class candidates (judged mainly by personality) is available from the younger universities than has actually been forthcoming under pre-war conditions."[14] The impact of wartime conditions on the candidate pool underlines the extent to which self-selection had effected a bias toward Oxbridge graduates in the prewar candidate pool.

The civil service commissioners did not consider the secondary education of this group. But immediately prior to the war, the Treasury had requested from them an assessment of the relationship between secondary education and recruitment by competitive examination. The commissioners had consequently conducted an evaluation of the relationship between the secondary education and the performance of those who entered the 1936 and 1937 competitions. This inquiry revealed a pattern similar to that shown by the analysis of the university education of 1938 candidates.

A comparison between the secondary educations of the successful candidates and of the entire pool of candidates in 1936 and 1937 shows that graduates of the Clarendon schools enjoyed a small advantage in both groups, but the comparison does not show that the examination itself favored them. In 1937 the success rate of the Clarendon school graduates (27.02 percent) exceeded the overall success rate (14.57 percent). However, their performance (16.2 percent) fell below the average (21.27 percent) in 1936, a year when not one of the six Etonians who took the examination secured a place in the civil service. Indeed, of those who attained the top twenty places that year only one had attended a Clarendon school.[15]

The school whose graduates fared best in these two years was Manchester Grammar School, not a Clarendon school at all. As a group, grammar school graduates exhibited the most consistency, with a success rate well above average in both years (24.00 and 28.12 percent, respectively). Of the fourteen candidates educated at Manchester Grammar School, six won places in 1936 and another secured a civil service position in 1937. Only Rugby came close to rivaling this achievement, offering eighteen candidates in all, of whom two won places in 1936 and three won places in 1937.[16]

The predominance among civil servants enjoyed by the graduates of the Clarendon schools and other major public schools stems in large measure from their overrepresentation in the candidate pool.[17] A small group of schools—those identified by the Civil Service Commission as the most important public schools—thus accounted for approximately 45 percent of the candidates in each of these two years. Consequently, even if they did not perform particularly well on the examination (as in 1936), they still constituted over 40 percent of new entrants. The analysis of two years only cannot support anything but the most tentative of conclusions. Nevertheless, that these schools—which in 1930 had a combined enrollment of 20,961 boys, representing only 8.7 percent of the total enrollment of boys in recognized secondary schools that year—produced such a high proportion of candidates implies a very close relationship between educational experience and career choice.

The group that succeeded in passing the open competition examination did not represent the university-educated population, but then neither did the group that took the examination. Oxford graduates in particular were greatly overrepresented in both groups. By the 1930s, the explanation for this lay much more in the greater inclination of the graduates of Oxford and some of the major public schools to pursue a civil service career than in the undoubted bias of the examination itself, although the widespread reputation of the examination's bias probably tended to transform any bias into a self-fulfilling prophecy. The inclusion of a personal interview in the competition process after the First World War allowed some scope for the expression of the preference for the graduates of public schools and Oxford and Cambridge. This, however, served to accentuate further the characteristics of a group already decisively shaped by self-selection.

Recruitment

The Board of Education and the Board of Agriculture

Before 1919, both the Board of Education and the Board of Agriculture virtually controlled their own recruiting. Neither department drew upon the open competition examination for new officers; instead they used procedures that appeared anomalous to the MacDonnell Commission, who therefore scrutinized them closely. Sir Lewis Amherst Selby-Bigge (see appendix), permanent secretary of the Board of Education, sought to defend departmental practice in his testimony before the MacDonnell Commission. Because of the "extraordinarily controversial" nature of the Board of Education's work, explained Selby-Bigge, it was "particularly important to recruit the office with men of rather greater age than ordinarily enter the Civil Service and of rather more varied experience and character." Selby-Bigge argued that the Board of Education using their own selection process had collected together a staff of very high standard, including many who had experience in teaching. He summed up the criteria the Board used to evaluate prospective officers by saying: "We like men with a taste for education as well as a taste for administration."[18]

As a consequence of this approach to recruiting, between 1900 and 1912, the educational experience of seventy-nine entrants to the Board of Education differed markedly from the educational experience of those who succeeded at the open competition examination during approximately the same period. The educational profile of the recruit preferred by the Board of Education undercut the force of Selby-Bigge's arguments. Almost 45 percent of those who succeeded at the open competition examination between 1906 and 1910—but over 80 percent of those appointed to the Board of Education between 1900 and 1912—were Oxbridge graduates. The predominance of Oxford over any other university is striking among the successful products of the open competition examination, but this predominance became overwhelming among Board of Education examiners, half of whom had attended Oxford.[19]

A profile of the secondary schools attended by appointees to the Board of Education underlines how much the Board's recruitment practices exaggerated the patterns of bias generated by the system of open competition examination. The Clarendon schools graduated over one-fifth of the successful open competition candidates between 1896 and 1911, but they produced 47 percent of those who were appointed to positions as examiners in the Board of Education from 1900 to 1912. Almost 80 percent of the examiners had attended public school. In contrast, 53.69 percent of the open competition candidates had attended one of these schools. Conversely, only 14 (17.72 percent) of the 79 examiners appointed had not attended a public school, whereas 412, more than one-quarter (27.16 percent), of the 1,557 successful open competition candidates lacked that advantage.[20]

The Board of Education secured its officials from among those who had attended the most prestigious educational institutions in Britain. The narrow range of educational experience that characterized the staff of the Board of Education belied Selby-Bigge's arguments that the Board's power to select its officers allowed them to recruit those of more "varied" experience. In the case of the Board of Education, the freedom to manage its own recruitment resulted in an exaggeration of the elitist tendencies of the English civil service almost to the point of caricature.

Selby-Bigge's explanation of the methods employed by the Board of Education to recruit new staff does not fully account for the extraordinary consistency of the type of individual who served the Board. According to Selby-Bigge, the Board did not advertise vacancies but merely drew upon a list of prospective candidates compiled from applications made directly to the Board. In Selby-Bigge's view, the length of the list on file at the Board (202 candidates for the position of examiner and 670 candidates for the position of inspector in 1912) indicated that this procedure informed a sufficiently wide range of the public about the prospects for employment by the Board to obviate the need for more aggressive advertisement.[21]

The MacDonnell Commission remained unsatisfied with this explanation. They pressed Edmund Phipps, principal assistant secretary of the Board's Elementary Education Branch, to explain the presence of so many Winchester–New College men on the Board's staff. (In 1919 three of the Board's most senior officials, including Phipps himself and the president of the Board, had attended Winchester and New College.) Phipps could think of no better reply than to say that the individuals involved had entered the Board's service at different times, that they had been previously unacquainted, and that their service together was nothing more than "a curious coincidence."[22] That such consistency could be merely coincidental strained the credulity of the members of the Royal Commission.

The testimony of N. Waterfield, secretary of the Oxford Appointments Committee, illuminates the role of coincidence in the Board of Education's recruiting methods. He told the MacDonnell Commission that the Board of Education, as well as other government departments, would ask the appointments committee to send forward suitable candidates; and that he personally had been responsible for recommending several successful candidates to the Board of Education.[23] Such an informal process would explain both the homogeneity of the Board of Education staff and the overrepresentation of the Oxford-educated as opposed to the Cambridge-educated on the Board of Education's staff. The Cambridge Appointments Board apparently did not have a similarly close relationship with government departments, and Cambridge graduates sought out a wider variety of careers through their appointments board.[24]

The active interest that all the universities, especially Oxford and Cambridge, took in placing their graduates in suitable professions formed a network of influence that depended less upon personal acquaintance than on the possession of certain intellectual and social attributes endowed by a common educational experience. Waterfield, for example, explained that when selecting a man to recommend to a prospective employer he looked for athletic ability, leadership in student affairs, and good moral character, in addition to a good academic record. Waterfield summed up these qualities with the phrase "vigour of mind and vigour of body"—a phrase that also epitomized the Edwardian male ideal type. The application of such criteria, at once subjective and vague, would allow the free play of social bias even in a system relatively untainted by personal patronage (although that too undoubtedly intruded on the recruitment process).[25]

The MacDonnell Commission probed for evidence of such personal influence at work, questioning Board of Education officials closely about several appointments that appeared to be the result of personal influence. The stepson of a president of the Board of Education, the son-in-law of a Cabinet minister, and two sons of upper-level Board officials had all received appointments as examiners or inspectors. Board officials strenuously resisted the suggestion that anything resembling patronage played a role in the selection process, but Selby-Bigge could not dispel the suspicion that the Board's hiring practices made the Board vulnerable to pressure to make such appointments.[26]

In terms of their educational experience, civil servants at the Board of Education formed the pinnacle of an elite. Exemption from the rigors of competitive examination enabled the Board to assemble an extraordinarily homogeneous staff drawn from a narrow range of educational institutions. On the other hand, the Board of Agriculture, which enjoyed a similar privilege, recruited its officers from much less eminent schools. Of the forty-seven men on the administrative staff of the Ministry of Agriculture during the interwar years who had entered that office prior to 1919, only three had attended one of the Clarendon schools. Of those in this group whose university education is recorded, twice as many had attended the University of London (ten) than had attended Oxford (five). This pattern differs markedly not only from that characteristic of the Board of Education but also from that produced by the system of open competition examination.

Sir Thomas H. Elliott, who had become permanent secretary of the Board of Agriculture in 1892, defended the Board's recruiting practices to the 1912 Royal Commission. Elliott, like Selby-Bigge, couched his defense in terms of the special needs of his department. Elliott, in contrast to Selby-Bigge, also criticized the structure of the open competition examination itself. In the evidence he presented to the Royal Commission, Elliott first detailed the special examinations the Board of Agriculture used instead.

Lord MacDonnell had noted with some surprise that the Board of Agriculture utilized no fewer than twenty-two special examinations, each unique to that department. Elliott, by way of explanation, commented that "the duties of the Board of Agriculture and Fisheries are of an extremely miscellaneous nature" and that

> the Board have proceeded on the assumption that, for the purposes of the higher indoor establishment, it is essential that they should have men pos-

> sessing special knowledge in particular directions, and the schemes of examinations are designed to attract to our service men especially competent to deal with the very miscellaneous duties which we have to discharge.[27]

This view ran directly counter the theory favored by the MacDonnell Commission, that a general education constituted the best preparation for a civil servant. In addition to these examinations, the president of the Board of Agriculture personally interviewed candidates for the outdoor branch. Elliott told the Royal Commission that officers in that branch

> must have good manners and address sufficiently to enable them to get the work of the Board done, very often under difficult circumstances, when stock-owners are unwilling to comply with our regulations; they must have a good general knowledge of country life, because in order to influence farmers, you must have men who are not, shall I say, too urban in character; they must be able to speak the farmer's language.

They then entered a two-year probationary period, during which they had to pass qualifying examinations in specialized subjects. The Board thus recruited its higher administrative staff by an arrangement that Elliott described as "open competition in special subjects" conducted through the Civil Service Commission. In addition, a few men obtained their appointments solely on the basis of their technical qualifications and did not have to submit themselves to any qualifying examination, a practice that MacDonnell himself called "pure patronage."[28]

An important aspect of Elliott's explanation of the recruiting practices of the Board of Agriculture took the form of a critique of the open competition examination. Elliott testified: "We are not satisfied to recruit those higher places from the ordinary Class I examinations because we think it of considerable importance that the actual requirements of each individual department should be taken into account." He went on to argue that the Class 1 examination had too general a nature and that more stress needed to be placed on English composition, law, economics, and modern languages. Elliott also pointed out that as the scale of pay at the Board of Agriculture was lower than those in other departments, the Board could not expect to get the best-qualified candidates that the examination produced.[29]

The origins of the sixteen assistants to the Board's departmental heads in 1912 best illustrate Elliott's attitude toward recruiting the higher levels of his administrative staff. Six had taken special qualifying examinations and nine had been promoted from the Second Division (one had been on the old establishment taken over by the Board upon its constitution).[30] The Board of Agriculture thus recruited its higher-level administrative staff by a variety of methods—special examination, special appointment, and promotion from the lower ranks—all under the direct control of the department.

Such a large number of promotees marked the Board of Agriculture as idiosyncratic among government departments. Promotion from the lower ranks of the civil service usually played only a relatively small role in filling higher-level positions. No one denied that the exceptionally able man should have the opportunity to advance, but the consensus suggested that such occasions would not arise often. In recommending that the administrative class be recruited almost exclusively by competitive examination, the MacDonnell Commission's *Majority Report* cited evidence presented by Sir Laurence Guillemard, the chairman of the Board of Customs and Excise. That department had deliberately adopted a policy of promotion from the Second Division for a number of years but had not been satisfied with the results. Guillemard testified: "While classes of the Second Division . . . do undoubtedly contain individuals capable of filling the higher posts, these men are the rare exceptions."[31]

This view continued to dominate the civil service during the interwar period. The 532 recruits to the administrative class between 1925 and 1939 included only 106 (19.92 percent) promotees.[32] Among the ministries under study here, Agriculture alone routinely promoted men from the Second Division to fill its higher-level positions. A 1928 survey taken by the Treasury on the origins of those holding the rank of assistant principal underlined the uniqueness of the Ministry of Agriculture. Promotions produced about one-fifth (eleven out of fifty-one) of the assistant principals in the other social service departments, a figure that reflected the overall proportion of promotees in the civil service as a whole, but over half (seven out of eleven) of the Ministry of Agriculture's assistant principals.[33] The emphasis placed on expertise in special subjects rather than on general ability gave that department's Second Division much more opportunity for advancement than they could have found in other ministries.

Elliott, like Selby-Bigge, also had to explain particular appointments that aroused the suspicions of the Royal Commission. One individual appointed as Fisheries inspector had a brother already in the office, one was the son of a high official in the Board of Education, and a third was the son of a high official in the Board of Agriculture. Elliott asserted that the qualifications of all these men admirably fitted them for their appointments and that no process could eliminate the suspicion with which many persisted in regarding civil service appointments.[34] The MacDonnell Commission unequivocally rejected Elliott's arguments. The *Majority Report* stated firmly:

> the appointment of high-placed officials by patronage or through specialized examination is contrary to the principles which we have recommended, and which, indeed, are generally accepted. . . . We are convinced that it would be far better to recruit for the administrative staff of the Department in the

> usual way, and trust to the officials learning by experience and study in this, as they do in other departments, the specialized subjects of use to them in their daily work.[35]

Selby-Bigge's defense of the recruitment practices of the Board of Education fared no better with the MacDonnell Commission. On this issue the *Majority Report* concluded:

> After listening carefully to the arguments which were submitted to us in favour of this exceptional method of recruitment, we are unanimously of the opinion that its continuance cannot be justified; and that the method of filling the administrative appointments in this department should be assimilated to that which has been adopted in all the other important departments of State.[36]

Both the Board of Education and the Board of Agriculture thus had to abandon departmental recruiting practices so that the administrative class of the home civil service could become the unified, homogeneous body envisioned by the Royal Commission.

The outbreak of the First World War intervened to delay the implementation of the recommendations of the MacDonnell Commission, however, and the Board of Education and the Board of Agriculture—reconstituted as a ministry after the war—did not begin to recruit their higher administrative staff through open competition examination until 1919. This change had a profound effect on the sort of person who took up duties in the two departments, but it did not entirely eradicate the differences between them. The proportion of those who had attended one of the Clarendon schools dropped sharply in the Board of Education (from 51.4 to 23.9 percent). Conversely, at the Ministry of Agriculture, the proportion of those who had attended a Headmasters' Conference school increased (from 35 to 55.6 percent).

The change in recruitment did not have so dramatic an impact on the university affiliation of the new entrants to the Board of Education, although the number of those who had attended a university other than Oxford or Cambridge did increase from two (before 1919) to seven (in 1919 or after). The proportion of non-Oxbridge graduates among new recruits to Education remained under 20 percent, although this group grew by a factor of three, from 5.7 to 15.2 percent of the total. In contrast to this modest adjustment, at the Ministry of Agriculture the proportion with an Oxbridge university education more than doubled, increasing from 40 to 84.4 percent of new entrants.

These changes brought greater homogeneity to the civil service and show the efficacy of recruitment in producing such change. Such innovation did not, however, erase the differences between the Board of Education and the

Ministry of Agriculture. Even though both departments drew upon the same pool of candidates after 1919, more Clarendon school alumni began their careers at Education, where they formed 23.9 percent of junior officials, than at Agriculture, where only 11.1 percent of new entrants possessed this prestigious credential. In addition, Cambridge graduates continued to have a stronger presence at Agriculture, where they accounted for 44.4 percent of postwar recruits, than at Education, where they constituted 28.3 percent of new entrants.

The Ministry of Labour and the Ministry of Health

Neither the Labour nor the Health Ministries had independent standing as a department of state prior to the First World War, but each was greatly influenced by its administrative precursors. The Ministry of Labour became a separate department in 1917. Created by hiving off the Board of Trade's Labour Department, the new ministry drew upon that department for its staff. The Labour Department had originally been formed in 1893 under the leadership of Hubert Llewellyn Smith, who later became permanent secretary of the Board of Trade.[37] The Labour Department rapidly expanded as it absorbed new duties and functions, particularly after passage of the 1909 legislation that established labour exchanges and the 1911 legislation that established unemployment insurance.

W. H. Beveridge, at the beginning of his long and influential career in public service, entered the Board of Trade especially to set up the machinery for labour exchanges. The addition of these duties naturally required a commensurate expansion in staff, but the Board of Trade did not turn to open competition examination to select prospective candidates. Instead, Beveridge and Llewellyn Smith chose their candidates by sifting through written applications and by personally interviewing the most likely individuals. Although no formal advertisement had been published (as Beveridge informed the MacDonnell Commission), the Board of Trade received some thirteen thousand applications following a statement made in Parliament about the availability of new posts. Beveridge explained that in considering these men, he looked for "general administrative capacity" rather than for "any particular kind of experience or industrial knowledge."[38]

The new men did indeed have a wide variety of experience: one, J. S. Adams (see appendix), had demonstrated his administrative capacity by acting as second-in-command on the British expedition to Antarctica. Beveridge, like Selby-Bigge and Elliott, found himself examined closely about those individuals hired who had close relatives in the civil service. One man had a brother in the Treasury, and another was the son of a Board of Trade official. Beveridge insisted to a skeptical audience that merit rather than influence determined which individuals secured positions.[39]

As a consequence of this rapid expansion, men who had entered the Board of Trade by appointment dominated its Labour Department and subsequently dominated the new Ministry of Labour. The MacDonnell Commission noted that in 1912 only three of the eight principal officers of the Board of Trade had entered the civil service by open competition examination.[40] In 1919, only ten of the Ministry of Labour's administrative class staff (still bloated by its wartime responsibilities and wartime appointments) had originally entered the civil service by open competition examination. In contrast, between 1909 and 1912, twenty-one had entered the Board of Trade by appointment (thirteen of these in 1912 alone). These appointments had not necessarily been to administrative-level posts originally, but throughout the interwar period individuals who, like Adams, had entered the civil service by appointment continued to filter into the administrative class by promotion.

After 1919, however, new appointments went exclusively to those candidates who succeeded at the open competition examination. Sixteen new officers joined the Ministry of Labour after taking the special Reconstruction competition held in 1920.[41] By 1937, the overwhelming majority of the Ministry of Labour's administrative staff had entered the civil service by competitive examination. In that year, that route had been used by forty-one of the forty-seven administrative class staff whose method of entrance is known. The remainder can be definitely identified as the remnants of the prewar appointees.

The change in the method of selection produced a corresponding change in the educational credentials of those who staffed the Ministry of Labour. A comparison of those who entered the Ministry of Labour before 1919 and those who entered it in 1919 or after shows a strong relationship between university education and entrance year; the overwhelming majority of Oxbridge graduates entered after the First World War. Of the twenty officers who began their career at the Ministry of Labour prior to 1919, only seven had attended Oxford or Cambridge. In contrast, thirty of the forty-two postwar recruits had an Oxbridge degree. A comparison of the university education of those whose method of entrance is definitely known substantiates this finding. Almost three-quarters (45 of 62) of those who had taken the competitive examination had attended either Oxford or Cambridge. Among the appointees, however, only one in five had an Oxbridge degree.

Unlike the Board of Agriculture and the Board of Education, the Board of Trade ostensibly recruited its staff through competitive examination. The large numbers of appointments made between 1909 and 1911 could be regarded as an emergency measure necessitated by the legislation that so rapidly expanded the duties and the responsibilities of the Board of Trade. Emergency or not, the recruiting done in those years—largely the responsibility of W. H. Beveridge—left a long-lasting mark on the Ministry of Labour, which drew heavily on this group of men during its early years.

The Ministry of Labour, like both the Board of Education and the newly designated Ministry of Agriculture and Fisheries, had a staff whose nature (at least in the first decade of the interwar period) was shaped by recruiting practices in the hands of ministry officials. Like the prewar Board of Agriculture but in contrast to the Board of Education, the Board of Trade had recruited more broadly among those qualified to enter the civil service than did the Civil Service Commission through the open competition examination. At the Ministry of Labour too, like the Board of Education and the Ministry of Agriculture and Fisheries, recruitment by open competition examination as a "normal" procedure did not begin until after the First World War, then making a definite impact on the sort of educational credentials that characterized new entrants to the department.

Among these four ministries, only the Ministry of Health began the interwar decades with a staff drawn largely from the open competition examination. Of the seventy-one administrative class officers at the new Ministry of Health in 1920, forty-five had entered the civil service by competitive examination. This pattern reflected the recruitment policies of its primary administrative parent, the Local Government Board (LGB). The Ministry of Health, upon its creation, absorbed the staff of the LGB along with that of the much smaller National Health Insurance Commission (NHIC).

Previous departmental affiliation rather than route of entry thus divided the staff of the new Ministry of Health. This distinction had an important bearing on the ministry's efficacy in carrying out its mission. Its creation has been portrayed as an administrative reform, of which at least one aim was to dismantle the Poor Law.[42] The reform of the Poor Law—so closely associated with the LGB—seemed to require first the elimination of the LGB. The NHIC, a far more dynamic government body, had been created in part because of a widespread feeling that the LGB could not be entrusted with forward-looking social legislation. Dismantling both governmental bodies and combining their staffs in a new ministry did not, however, uproot the LGB point of view.

In the new Ministry of Health, the LGB's staff overwhelmed that of the NHIC. Of those men whose origins are known, thirty-three (virtually one-half of the staff) had been with the LGB, whereas only fifteen had come from the NHIC. In addition, the 1920 Reconstruction examination produced seven new appointments, and at least two other men transferred to the new ministry from other departments. The most important of these was Arthur Robinson (see appendix), who became permanent secretary upon the sudden death of Sir Robert Morant in 1920. Morant had made a name for himself as a dynamic and forceful administrator first at the Board of Education and then at the NHIC. His successor enjoyed an equally successful but more orthodox career. Robinson entered the civil service by competitive examination in 1897. After beginning his career in the Colonial Office, he rose very rapidly to the position of permanent secretary of the Admiralty before his appointment to the Ministry of Health.

Officials who had served at the NHIC held several of the highest positions in the new Ministry of Health. The solicitor, the accountant-general, the director of Establishments, and three of the assistant secretaries came from the NHIC. But the remainder of the eleven assistant secretaries had held posts in the LGB, and the second secretary had been in the LGB since 1898. In addition, the new permanent secretary had no particular expertise in social policy as such. In his account of the campaign for a Ministry of Health, Frank Honigsbaum concluded: "All the key posts in the new Department went to N.H.I. figures."[43] But this observation referred only to the brief period before Robert Morant's death and Arthur Robinson's appointment as permanent secretary; it does not take account of the origins of the new ministry's staff below the very highest levels.

The staff of the NHIC, like that of the Board of Trade's Labour Department, had been drawn from more diverse backgrounds than was typical for open competition recruits. Of the fifteen men who had come to the Ministry of Health from the NHIC, eight had entered the home civil service by open competition examination—two of these had originally been officers at the LGB. The other seven had been appointed in 1912. In contrast, only three of the LGB officials had entered the civil service by appointment. The LGB had also occasionally promoted men from the Second Division. (According to Sir Horace Munro's testimony before the MacDonnell Commission, eight such promotions had taken place during the early years of the twentieth century.)[44] Despite these exceptions, the open competition examination shaped the character of the LGB's staff—and consequently the staff of the Ministry of Health—in a much more substantial way than it did the other social service ministries.

The creation of the new ministry in 1920 thus did not involve a break in continuity in the style of recruiting. Unlike the other ministries, the educational credentials of men who entered the Ministry of Health after the First World War did not differ markedly from those who entered the service before the war. Those men who came from the NHIC stand as a partial exception to this generalization, but they formed such a small group that only extremely forceful individuals could have altered the atmosphere of the office. During the interwar decades those whose careers began in the LGB dominated the councils of the Ministry of Health.[45]

Recruiting by Competitive Examination

Recruitment by competitive examination gained widespread acceptance during the early years of the twentieth century both inside and outside the civil service. Resistance to the application of this method to individual departments stemmed from the desire to attract men with a particular expertise or with a more varied experience than those ordinarily produced by the open competition examination. These overt concerns collided with a more basic issue of political power. Who should, after all, control hiring to government positions? Departments naturally wished to retain this authority, arguing that they knew their own needs best and could therefore best judge the qualifications of prospective officers.

The case for recruiting through a centralized agency independent of the departments, by means of a competitive examination, rested on two different types of assumptions. First, such a procedure seemed less liable to the abuses of patronage, nepotism, and special influence. The MacDonnell Commission repeatedly questioned departmental witnesses about suspicious appointments. Recruiting carried out directly by particular departments generated such suspicions, irrespective of their substance. Only taking this power out of departmental hands could dispel them. Second, the argument for recruiting by examination also had a more positive component. According to this view, the government would be better served by a civil service that formed a unified body of men of high academic qualifications who developed an expertise in particular fields as they worked at their jobs. Men with a good general education and of outstanding intelligence could, the argument ran, undertake with facility a variety of assignments, thus allowing a freer interchange of officers among departments. Recruitment by an independent body through competitive examination thus represented not only a system both fair and above reproach, but also one that would produce a more effective, responsive, and efficient civil service.

Many departments, such as the LGB and the Board of Customs and Excise, found little to object to as this system matured. The Board of Education and the Board of Agriculture, however, had each built up its own system for the recruitment of new officers, systems that officials unsuccessfully sought to preserve. While recruitment remained in the hands of these departments, officials used this power to select individuals who they believed were especially qualified to carry out the responsibilities of their departments. In the case of the Board of Education this meant, in practice, such an emphasis on academic attainments in the traditional sense that the Board drew its staff from the most prestigious educational institutions in the nation. The change to competitive examination in 1919 probably diluted the high intellectual calibre of the Board's staff, but it also broadened its educational base somewhat.[46] In contrast, the Board of Agriculture sought a different type of expert, so they tested for special rather than general knowledge. Valuing the expertise grounded in experience, Agriculture promoted more freely than other departments, and consequently, their staff became one of the most varied in the civil service. The change to competitive examination actually narrowed the educational base from which the postwar Ministry of Agriculture drew its staff.

The Board of Trade, although one of the major departments that recruited its staff through the open competition examination, often resorted to special appointments. Unlike the permanent secretaries of the Board of Education and the Board of Agriculture, Board of Trade officials defended their departures from normal recruiting procedures on the grounds of expediency rather than principle. Even so, Llewellyn Smith and Beveridge seized what opportunities they could to secure the services of men of more varied experience than those usually produced by the open competition examination. After the period of rapid expansion occasioned by the legislation of 1909 and 1911 and the upheavals associated with wartime conditions, the Ministry of Labour settled without protest into the routine recruitment of new officers by examination. The educational base of its staff underwent a narrowing similar to that experienced at the Ministry of Agriculture. The higher-level staff of the Ministry of Health did not exhibit a comparable change in composition. The departments that combined to form the new ministry, especially the LGB, had always relied on the open competition examination for its new officers. The creation of the new ministry thus overlay a continuity of staffing policies.

Promotion

The measures that created an increasingly homogeneous and unified civil service necessarily involved a certain loss of autonomy by individual departments over the recruiting process. Promotions within the administrative class, however, remained for all practical purposes under the departmental purview, with the exception of special appointments of outsiders to civil service positions, promotions from the lower ranks of the civil service to the administrative class, and promotions to the very highest rank (such as permanent secretary, second secretary), all of which required Treasury approval. (The Treasury did not give this approval perfunctorily; departmental requests for such appointments and promotions could be rejected.) By selecting the officers that could advance from rank to rank, officials in practice formulated and applied departmental criteria of excellence.

A department-by-department analysis of the promotions granted in these four social service ministries during the interwar period shows that the same values that shaped each department's recruiting practices informed the promotion process as well.[47] In three of the four departments under study here (Education, Health, and Agriculture), the criteria used to grant promotions also bore some relationship to the candidates' educational experience. Only in the Ministry of Labour does career success appear to have been unrelated to an individual's educational credentials.

A new entrant to the administrative class held the rank of assistant principal. An individual could expect to hold that rank for at least six or seven years before being promoted to principal.[48] Promotion did not come automatically, but approximately one-half of assistant principals could expect to advance to the rank of principal.[49] Promotion from principal to assistant secretary was more competitive, and this step represented a crucial point in a civil servant's career. Assistant secretaries held positions of real authority. They headed the various departments that carried on the different aspects of each ministry's work, and they could play an active role in formulating policy. Promotion to the rank of assistant secretary could culminate a modestly successful career in the civil service, even if a man advanced no further up the hierarchy. Approximately one-third of principals attained this mark of success. Again, almost one-third of assistant secretaries received further advancement to the rank of principal assistant secretary. Those who reached this rank concerned themselves with setting policy and formed the pool from which the permanent heads of ministries were ultimately drawn.

Different ministries offered different prospects for advancement. The Ministry of Agriculture, although the smallest of the social service ministries, provided the greatest opportunities for promotion. On average, however, a new entrant had approximately a 16.5 percent chance of advancing to the rank of assistant secretary, but only a 4.9 percent chance of becoming a principal assistant secretary. On this bureaucratic ladder, an individual's educational background could influence his prospects for advancement. The pattern of that influence varied from department to department, and the analysis below details that variation.

The Board of Education and the Ministry of Health

At first glance, the relationship between educational experience and promotion prospects in the Board of Education does not appear to be very strong. At the Board of Education, 48.7 percent of officials experienced at least one promotion during the interwar decades. Disaggregating this group according to various educational subcategories reveals a small range of variation—from a 57.5 percent promotion rate for those who had attended a Headmasters' Conference school, to 46.2 percent for Clarendon school old boys, to 45.5 percent for all others. An analysis of university education shows an even narrower range of variation—with 53.2 percent of Oxford graduates and 53.1 percent of Cambridge graduates winning promotions, as opposed to all others, who were promoted at a rate of 41.9 percent, a figure that fell somewhat below the overall average of 48.7. The relationship between an individual's education and whether he received any promotion at all is so weak as to be negligible. Indeed, promotion from assistant principal to principal is not related to educational experience at all. Neither Headmasters' Conference schools alumni nor Oxford and Cambridge alumni advanced to the rank of principal in greater numbers than one might expect, although these groups did form a higher proportion of junior officers at the Board of Education than at other departments.[50]

Promotions to the next level, however, exhibit a distinctly different pattern. Having attended one of the Clarendon schools and then Oxford definitely enhanced an individual's chances for promotion to assistant secretary (see figure 1). Approximately one-third of all the Board of Education's principals advanced to that rank, but nearly half of the Oxford-educated and almost 60 percent of those who had attended a Clarendon school received such a promotion. In contrast, neither a Cambridge education nor an education at one of the Headmasters' Conference schools similarly aided an individual's career. This pattern repeats itself at the next level of promotions,

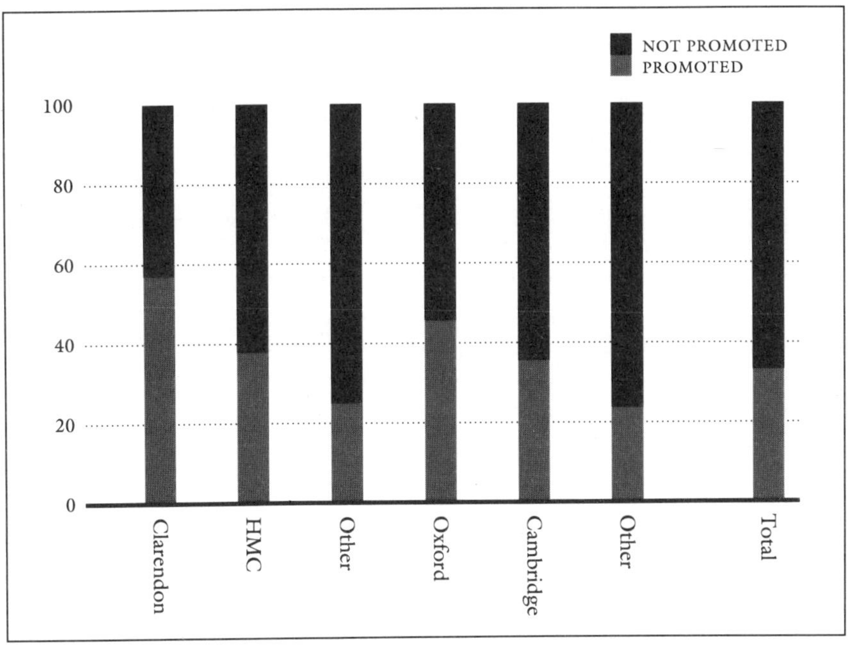

Figure 1. *Promotion and Education at the Board of Education: Principal to Assistant Secretary*

although the strength of the relationship diminished (see figure 2). The effect of recruitment and promotion practices together created a pool of candidates so similar that conscious preference need not have played a role in the selection of principal assistant secretaries.

The upper levels of the Board of Education thus constituted a group of men characterized by an extremely narrow and homogeneous educational experience (see table 5). In 1920, Oxford graduates held all the higher-level positions at the Board of Education except that of permanent secretary of the Welsh Department. Of these seven men, three had been at the same college, Balliol. Their secondary education reinforced this homogeneity. Three had attended Winchester, two had been at Harrow, and one had been at Eton. The only man not a product of one of the Clarendon schools had attended Manchester Grammar School. By 1938 the picture had altered somewhat. Including the Welsh secretary, three Cambridge men had managed to attain this rank, but there were still three Balliol men. No two men came from the same secondary school, but the secondary schools were all quite prestigious, including two Clarendon schools (Shrewsbury, Winchester), two exclusive public schools (Wellington, Clifton), and three less-well-known Headmas-

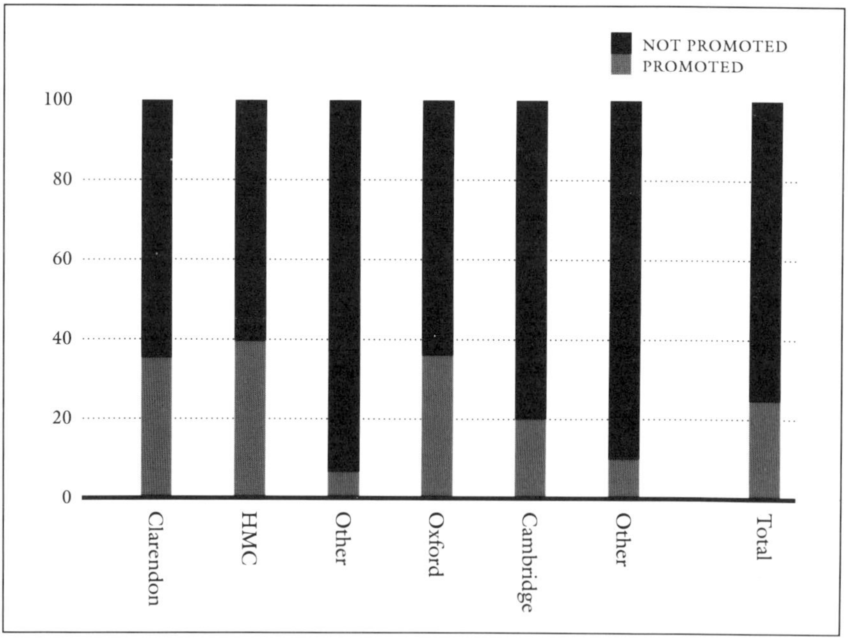

Figure 2. *Promotion and Education at the Board of Education: Assistant Secretary to Principal Assistant Secretary*

TABLE 5. *Ministers and Top-Ranked Civil Servants at the Board of Education, 1919–1939*

Year	*Minister*	*Permanent Secretary*	*Second Secretary*	*Permanent Secretary, Welsh Department*	*Accountant-General*
1919	H.A.L. Fisher Winchester New College, Oxford	L. A. Selby-Bigge Winchester Christ Church, Oxford		A. T. Davies Waterloo High School (near Liverpool) University College of Wales, Abyrswyth	H. W. Orange Winchester New College, Oxford
1920			W. N. Bruce Harrow Balliol College, Oxford		
1922	Halifax Eton Christ Church, Oxford		E. K. Chambers Marlborough Corpus Christi College, Oxford		
1924	C. P. Trevelyan Harrow Trinity College, Cambridge				
1925	Eustace Percy Eton Oxford				
1926		Aubrey Symonds Bedford School University College, Oxford	E. B. Phipps	Percy E. Watkins Oswestry High School	
1929	C. P. Trevelyan		E. H. Pelham		E. G. Howorth Shrewsbury Trinity College, Oxford
1930					
1931	R. E. Lees-Smith Aldenham School Queen's College, Oxford	E. H. Pelham			
1932	Sir David MacLean		M. G. Holmes		
1933	Halifax				
1934				W. P. Wheldon Oswestry High School University College of Wales, Bangor St. John's College, Cambridge	
1935	Oliver Stanley Eton, Oxford				
1936					
1937	Lord Stanhope Eton Magdalen College, Oxford	M.G. Holmes	E.G. Howorth		D. du B. Davidson Winchester Balliol College, Oxford
1939	Earl de la Warr Eton				

Table 5. *Continued*

Year	*Principal Assistant Secretary*	*Principal Assistant Secretary*	*Principal Assistant Secretary*	*Principal Assistant Secretary*
1919	G.G.A. Murry	E. B. Phipps Winchester New College, Oxford	W. R. Barber Marlborough Westminster College, Oxford	W. N. Bruce Harrow Balliol College, Oxford
1920	W. R. Davies Manchester Grammar School Balliol College, Oxford		E. H. Pelham Harrow Balliol College, Oxford	R.J.G. Mayer Eton King's College, Cambridge
1922				
1924				
1925				
1926		M. G. Holmes Wellington Balliol College, Oxford		
1929			A. P. Oppé Charterhouse New College, Oxford	
1930	W. C. Eaton Winchester New College, Oxford			Between 1926 and 1935 there were only three principal assistant secretaries
1931				
1932		A. R. Ainsworth Ipswich Grammar School King's College, Cambridge		
1933				
1934				
1935				
1936	C.W. Maudsley Clifton College Exeter College, Oxford			R. S. Wood City of London School Jesus College, Cambridge
1937				
1939		S. H. Wood University College, London	R.W. Wallis King Edward VI School, Birmingham Balliol College, Oxford	

ters' Conference schools (City of London School, King Edward VI School, Birmingham, and Ipswich Grammar School).

To what extent was this homogeneity at the upper rank simply a function of the homogeneous background of those who entered the Board? The composition of the candidate pool could easily have determined the educational attributes of those selected for promotion. For example, the position of second secretary was filled three times during the interwar period, in 1926, 1930, and 1932. In every case an Oxford graduate won the position, but at no time was a man from any other university ever in contention.

Close examination of the chains of promotions that took place in 1926, 1930, 1931, and 1932 reveals that out of the twenty-five promotions that occurred in those years, thirteen went to Oxford men, only four went to Cambridge graduates, and six went to graduates of some other university. Two of the Oxford men each received two promotions. Analysis of individual promotions reveals that the preference for the Oxford-educated frequently reflected consequences of recruitment rather than the independent judgment of those responsible for promotion decisions.

A vacancy at the principal assistant secretary level appeared in all four of these years. Although three of the four men promoted to this rank were Oxford graduates, the number of assistant secretaries might suggest a less homogeneous selection pool than actually existed. In 1925 eight out of the ten possible candidates were Oxford graduates, and in 1929 four of the six candidates had an Oxford education. In the first year there was only one Cambridge graduate in the selection pool, and in the second there were no Cambridge graduates. The least homogeneous group of assistant secretaries turned up in 1930. Of the five candidates, one was an Oxford graduate, two were Cambridge graduates, and two had been to some other university. Out of this group the sole Oxford graduate was promoted. The only promotion of a Cambridge man at this level took place the following year. The selection pool again consisted of five men (three from Oxford and two from Cambridge), but this time the Cambridge man, for reasons of age and seniority, was the most appropriate choice. This man was also one of the few men promoted to principal assistant secretary who had attended a secondary school of only moderate prestige. Thus, only two of these seven promotions came out of a heterogeneous selection pool.

In these four years, seven promotions to assistant secretary or an equivalent rank took place. In every case, the selection pool was not only much larger than that for principal assistant secretary but was much more varied. In each year the number of Oxford and Cambridge men was approximately equal, whereas the number of men from other universities always exceeded the number in either of the first two categories. Only here does any bias toward an Oxbridge education emerge in the promotion process. Only two of those promoted had not been to Oxford or Cambridge, although that category constituted the largest of the three groups in each selection pool. Most striking are the 1931 promotions to assistant secretary when, out of fifteen possible candidates, the two chosen were both graduates of Balliol College, Oxford. Four of the seven men promoted had attended Clarendon schools although the secondary school background of those who composed the selection pool was at least as heterogeneous as their university background.

In contrast to the principals eligible for promotion to assistant secretary, the assistant principals being considered for principal either were Oxford men or came from some university besides Cambridge. The university education of those promoted from assistant principal to principal almost exactly reflected the proportions of each category of university education represented in the selection pool. Only one of those promoted to principal had been to a Clarendon school.

The evidence provided by these series of promotions sustains the conclusions suggested by the quantitative analysis of promotion. If those responsible for selecting people for promotion did have a conscious bias toward the Oxford-educated and those who had been to the prestigious public schools, they could have acted upon such a bias at only one point on the promotion ladder. The movement from principal to assistant secretary appears to have been a pivotal gatepost of a civil service career. The aggregate evidence and the evidence of the promotions from assistant principal to principal in these four years show no signs of any such bias at work at the lower level. The Oxford-educated so dominated the selection pools for the ranks above assistant secretary that it predetermined the educational homogeneity of those promoted.

Both age and seniority played a role in determining suitable candidates for promotion, but neither the Board of Education nor other ministries adhered strictly to seniority in its promotions. For example, of the seventy-seven promotions to principal, assistant secretary, and principal assistant secretary in the Ministry of Health between 1930 and 1939, twenty-seven (35.06 percent) were made in advance of seniority order.[51] This flexibility allowed the encouragement of promising men; others, passed over, left the service. When the time came to select future assistant secretaries at the Board of Education, the educational background of the candidates influenced their chances for promotion. Those who helped prepare England's educational policy preferred colleagues who were educated first at a public school and then at Oxford. Such preference manifested itself actively in the promotion process only at the step up from principal to assistant secretary, but this had a critical impact on both the individual career and the department.

A civil servant who achieved the rank of assistant secretary also achieved some measure of career success, even if no further promotions came his way. The promotions to assistant secretary were also important for the Board of Education, because an assistant secretary could begin to deal with policy as such, rather than just routine administrative matters. The assistant secretaries also composed the basic selection pool for all the higher ranks.

Promotions at the Ministry of Health display a pattern similar to those at the Board of Education. The association between educational experience and promotion exhibits a stronger relationship in aggregate at the Ministry of Health than at the Board of Education; overall, 53 percent of Health officials obtained at least one promotion during the interwar decades, but 70.6 percent of the graduates of Clarendon schools and 63.6 percent of Oxford graduates secured a promotion. In contrast, the promotion records of those who did not attend a Headmasters' Conference school or did not have an Oxbridge degree fell well below average, at 44.1 and 45.9 percent, respectively. The preference for the Clarendon schools and Oxford comes through again in the first round of promotions: 48.5 percent of assistant principals advanced to the rank of principal, but 80 percent of those educated at one of the Clarendon schools and 62.5 percent of the Oxford-educated achieved this modicum of career success. The next level of promotion, from principal to assistant secretary, displays a strong and definite preference for alumni of Headmasters' Conference schools and of Oxford and Cambridge (see figure 3).

As at the Board of Education, the Clarendon school alumni achieved a far higher rate of success than those from other Headmasters' Conference schools. Oxford graduates also enjoyed an advantage over Cambridge graduates at the Ministry of Health. The relationship between educational experience, although still present, weakens at the next level of promotions. Cambridge alumni proved dramatically successful at this level. Nevertheless, the upper reaches of the Ministry of Health, like those of the Board of Education, remained largely the province of the Oxford-educated (see table 6). In both departments promotion enhanced a homogeneity that was first established by recruitment.

The Ministry of Labour and the Ministry of Agriculture

Of the social service ministries, only in the Ministry of Labour does promotion appear to be totally unrelated to the educational experience of its officers. An aggregation of all the interwar promotions shows a weak but statistically significant relationship between promotion and education, but this pattern disappears when the promotions are disaggregated by rank. At no rank level does either secondary or university education serve to predict an individual's promotion prospects in the Ministry of Labour. Partly as a consequence of this and partly as a consequence of the variety of recruits brought into the department prior to the First World War, Oxbridge gradu-

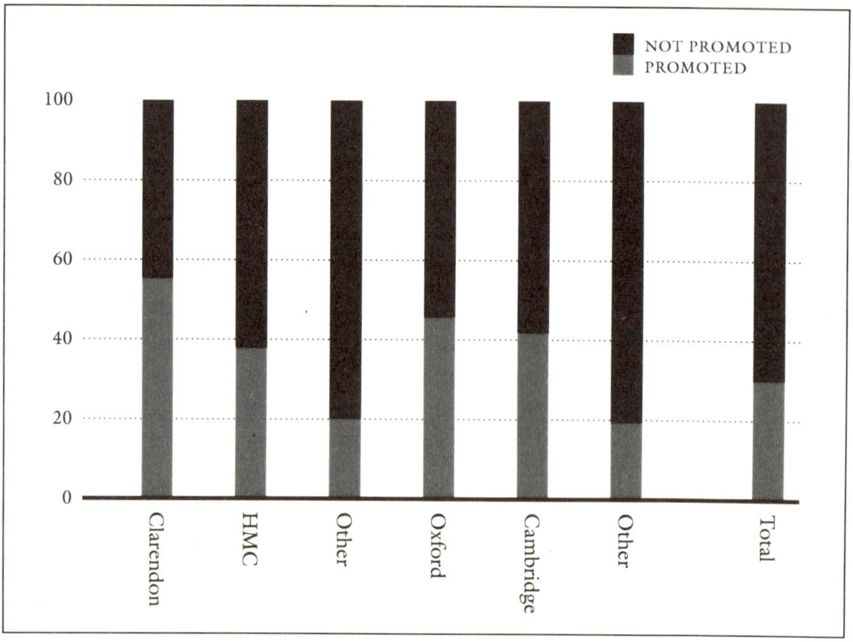

Figure 3. *Promotion and Education at the Ministry of Health: Principal to Assistant Secretary*

ates did not dominate the highest levels of the Ministry of Labour to quite the same extent as in other ministries (see table 7). In concrete terms, this simply means that London University graduates formed the second largest group (six) at the ministry's highest ranks, behind Oxford graduates (eight), but ahead of Cambridge graduates (three). It is an index of the restrictive nature of the English educational ladder that the presence of the alumni of three, rather than just two, universities at these ranks indicates a significant increase in variation.

At first glance, there also appears to be no relationship between the educational experience of the administrative class staff of the Ministry of Agriculture and their prospects for promotion. Neither selection for service in the ministry's private office (ordinarily a plum that placed a young man in a favorable position for subsequent promotion) nor whether a man was promoted at all appears to be a function of a man's educational experience. Breaking down promotions by rank reveals that aggregation disguises two contradictory tendencies, however. At the assistant principal level, promotion manifests a negative association with a Headmasters' Conference–Oxbridge education (see figure 4). This pattern stands as unique among the social ser-

TABLE 6. *Ministers and Top-Ranked Civil Servants at the Ministry of Health, 1919–1939*

Year	*Minister*	*Parliamentary Secretary*	*Permanent Secretary*	*Second Secretary*	*Principal Assistant Secretary*
1919					
1920	C. Addison Trinity College, Harrowgate St. Bart's Hospital	Viscount Astor Eton New College, Oxford	Arthur Robinson Appleby School Queen's College, Oxford	Aubrey V. Symonds[a] Bedford School University College, Oxford	Frederick J. Willis[a] Clifton
1921					
1922	Sir Alfred Mond Cheltenham College St. John's College, Cambridge	Earl of Onslow Eton New College, Oxford			E. R. Forber[b] Liverpool College Trinity College, Cambridge
1923	Sir Arthur Griffith-Boscawen Rugby Queen's College, Oxford				
1924	J. Wheatley Elementary School Lord Eustace Percy Eton, Oxford				
1925	Neville Chamberlain Rugby Birmingham University	H. Kingsley Wood Central Foundation Boy's School		E. R. Forber	
1926					I. G. Gibbon[a] High School, Oswestry LSE, London Univ.
1928					
1930	Arthur Greenwood Victoria University	Susan Lawrence Newham College, Cambridge		E. J. Strohmenger	
1932	Hilton Young Eton Trinity College, Cambridge	Ernest Brown Torquay			
1933		G. H. Shakespeare Highgate School Emmanuel College, Cambridge		Sir Arthur B. Lowry[a] Eton Trinity College, Oxford	
1934				E. J. Maude Rugby Exeter College, Oxford	
1935			Sir George Chrystal George Watson's College Edinburgh University Balliol College, Oxford		
1936	Sir Kingsley Wood Central Foundation's Boys School				R. B. Cross[b] Dulwich Corpus Christi College, Oxford
1937		R. S. Hudson Eton Magdalen College, Oxford			
1938		Robert Bernays Rossall Worcester College, Oxford			
1939	Walter Elliott Glasgow Academy Glasgow University				

a. Local Government Board

b. National Health Insurance Commission

Table 6. *Continued*

Year	*Principal Assistant Secretary Accountant-General*	*Principal Assistant Secretary Registrar-General*	*Principal Assistant Secretary*	*Principal Assistant Secretary*	*Principal Assistant Secretary*
1919					
1920	E. J. Strohmenger[b]				
1921		S. P. Vivian[b] St. Paul's School St. John's College, Oxford			
1922					
1923					
1924					
1925			L. G. Brock[b] Dulwich Corpus Christi College, Oxford		
1926					
1928			A. B. Maclachlan[a] Merchant Taylors' School St. John's College, Cambridge		
1930	S.H.G. Hughes[b] Allyn's School Dulwich University College, London			H.W.S. Francis Blumdell's School, Balliol College, Oxford	
1932					
1933					
1934					
1935					(Director of Housing, Town Planning)
1936					J. C. Wrigley[a] Bury Grammar School Lancashire Corpus Christi College, Cambridge
1937					
1938			H. A. de Montmorency[b] Winchester Brasenose College, Oxford	A. W. Neville[b] Westminster City School Jesus College, Cambridge	
1939					

TABLE 7. *Education of Ministers and Top-Ranked Civil Servants in the Ministry of Labour, 1919–1939*

Year	*Minister*	*Parliamentary Secretary*	*Permanent Secretary*	*Second Secretary*	*Chief Labour/Industrial Advisor*
1919	Sir Robert Horne George Watson's College University of Glasgow	G. J. Wardle Wesleyan Day School, Keighley Yorkshire	Sir David Shackleton Hadinton Elementary School		
1920	T. J. MacNamara St. Thomas School Exeter, Borough Road Training College for Teachers	Sir Montague Barlowe Repton School, King's College, Cambridge	David Shackleton Sir James Masterson-Smith Harrow Hertford College, Oxford	E. C. Cunningham Haileybury Trinity College, Cambridge	
1921					Sir David Shackleton
1922			H. J. Wilson		
1923	Sir Montague-Barlow	Maj. A. B. Boyd-Carpenter Harrow, Balliol College, Oxford			
1924	T. Shaw				
1925	Sir Arthur Steel-Maitland, Rugby Balliol College, Oxford	H. B. Betterton, Rugby, Christ College, Oxford		T. W. Phillips	
1926					
1930	Margaret Bondfiield	F. W. Hadden			
1931			F. Floud Cranleigh School King's College, London		H. J. Wilson
1932	H. B. Betterton	R. S. Hudson, Eton Magdalen College, Oxford			
1934					
1935	Oliver Stanley Eton Oxford		T. W. Phillips	J. F. G. Price	
1936	Ernest Brown Torquay	Lt. Col. A. J. Muirhead, Eton Magdalen College, Oxford			
1937					
1938				Hubert Wolfe	
1939		A. J. Lennox-Boyd Sherborne School Christ Church, Oxford			

a. Seconded to ILO, Humbert Wolfe acting

Table 7. *Continued*

Year	*Principal Assistant Secretary (Dr. of Estab.)*	*Principal Assistant Secretary*	*Principal Assistant Secretary*	*Principal Assistant Secretary*	*Principal Assistant Secretary*
1919			H. J. Wilson Kurnella School, Bournemouth LSE. London University	T. W. Phillips Machynlleth County School Jesus College, Oxford	
1920	A. W. Watson Cheltenham College, Uppingham School Magdalen College, Cambridge	H. B. Butler[a] Eton Balliol College, Oxford			
1921		Humbert Wolfe Bradford Grammar School Oxford			
1922			J. B. Adams Aberdeen Grammar School		
1923					
1924			J.A.N. Barlow Marlborough, Corpus Christi College, Oxford		
1925				J.F.G. Price Westminster City School	
1926	W. W. March Twyford Village School Kings College, London				
1930	Humbert Wolfe	C. Eady Clifton Jesus College, Cambridge			F. W. Leggett Strand School LSE, London
1931					
1932					
1934	J. A. Dale Cardiff High School Jesus College, Oxford	Humbert Wolfe			
1935				J. S. Nicolson Malvern Oriel College, Oxford	
1936					
1937			J. M. Glen Daniel Stewart's College, Edinburgh Edinburgh University		
1938		G. H. Ince Regate Grammar School University College, London			
1939					

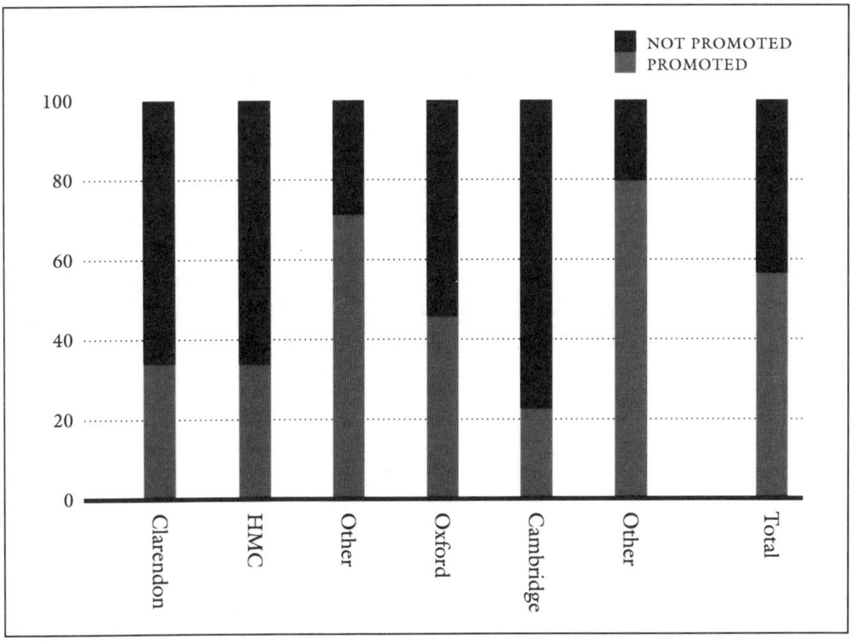

Figure 4. *Promotion and Education at the Ministry of Agriculture: Assistant Principal to Principal*

vice ministries. Although more than half of the ministry's assistant principals became principals, only one-third of the Clarendon school and Headmasters' Conference school alumni attained this promotion. Less than one-quarter of the Cambridge graduates among the assistant principals reached the next rank, although four-fifths of those who had not attended either Oxford or Cambridge received such promotions.

The inverse relationship between a Headmasters' Conference school or Oxbridge education and promotion begins to reverse itself at the next level of promotions (see figure 5). Approximately one-third of the principals advanced to the rank of assistant secretary; but 66 percent of the Oxford graduates, 57 percent of the Headmasters' Conference school alumni, and 40 percent of the Cambridge graduates received promotions. These proportions indicate a reversal of preference, but they did not necessarily change the atmosphere of the ministry. Oxford and Cambridge graduates represented 22.44 percent of the principals. This proportion increased by more than 10 percent (to 35.29 percent) of the assistant secretaries. Even so, eleven (64.7 percent) of the seventeen new assistant secretaries had not attended either Oxford or Cambridge.

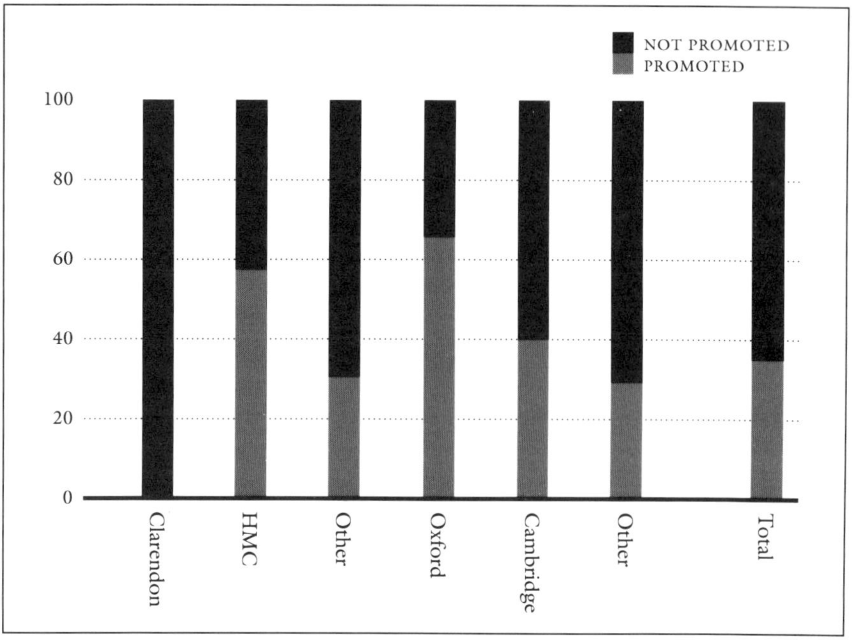

Figure 5. *Promotion and Education at the Ministry of Agriculture: Principal to Assistant Secretary*

The preference for the Headmasters' Conference school alumni and for the Oxbridge-educated asserted itself much more strongly at the next level of promotions. Seven of the ten assistant secretaries who had attended Oxford or Cambridge became principal assistant secretaries, whereas only one-half of the others (six of twelve) were promoted. These promotions to the highest levels of the ministry revealed the same preference for Headmasters' Conference alumni and the Oxbridge-educated found in the other social service ministries, although recruitment practices and promotions at the lower levels of the Ministry of Agriculture differed markedly. Despite the reversal in promotion preferences, the character of the highest levels of the ministry remained marked by the earlier opportunities granted those educated outside Oxford and Cambridge, at least in so far as University of London graduates took their place alongside Oxford graduates in the shaping of England's agricultural policy (see table 8). In the Ministry of Agriculture, as many graduates from London University as from Oxford (five each) served at the highest levels of the ministry between the wars. Together, these two groups overwhelmed the presence of the one Cambridge graduate promoted to principal assistant secretary in 1937.

TABLE 8. *Education of Ministers and Top-Ranked Civil Servants in the Ministry of Agriculture, 1919–1939*

Year	*Minister*	*Parliamentary Secretary*	*Permanent Secretary*	*Chief Scientific Officer*
1919	Lord Ernle Marlborough Balliol College, Oxford	Arthur Griffith-Boscawen Rugby, Queen's College, Oxford	A. D. Hall Manchester Grammar School Balliol College, Oxford	
1920	Lord Lee Cheltenman RME, Woolwich		F. L. Floud Cranleigh School King's College, London	A. D. Hall
1921				
1922	Arthur Griffith-Boscawen	Earl of Ancaster Eton Trinity College, Cambridge		
1923	Robert Sanders Harrow			
1924	Noel-Buxton Harrow Trinity College, Cambridge	Walter Smith Norwich		
1925	E.F.L. Wood Eton, Christ Church, Oxford	Lord Bledisloe Eton University College, Oxford		
1926	Walter Guiness Eton	Earl of Stradbroke		
1927			C. J. Thomas	
1928				
1929	Noel-Buxton	Christopher Addison Trinity College Harrowgate St. Barts. Hosp.		
1930	Christopher Addison	Earl de la Warr Eton Magdalen College, Oxford		
1932	John Gilmour Glenalmond Edinburgh University, Trinity Hall, Cambridge			
1933	Walter Elliott Glasgow Academy Glasgow University			
1935				
1936		H. Ramsbotham Uppingham University College, Oxford	D. Fergusson Berkhamsted School Magdalen College, Oxford	
1937	William S. Morrison George Watson's College Edinburgh University	Earl of Feversham		
1939	Sir Reginald Dorman-Smith Harrow RMC, Sandhurst			

Conclusion

Prior to the First World War, individual departments exercised a good deal of discretion in selecting their junior officers. Not until 1919 did open competition examination actually govern the bulk of new recruitment to the home civil service. Although departments lost much of their power over recruitment after the implementation of the MacDonnell Commission reforms,

Table 8. *Continued*

Year	*Second Secretary*	*Fisheries Secretary*	*Welsh Secretary*	*Principal Assistant Secretary*	*Principal Assistant Secretary*
1919			Cadwaladr Bryner-Jones Dolgelly Grammar School Agricultural College, Aspatria		
1920		H. G. Maurice Marlborough Lincoln College, Oxford			
1921	Lawrence Weaver Clifton				
1922					
1923					
1924					
1925					
1926					
1927					
1928				H. E. Dale St. Paul's Balliol College, Oxford	
1929					H. L. French private King's College, London
1930					
1932					
1933				A. W. Street County School, Sandown King's College, London	
1935	H. L. French			A.T.A. Dobson Clifton Emmanuel College, Cambridge	
1936					
1937					
1939		A.T.A. Dobson		E. L. Mitchell private King's College, London	

they continued to shape their own distinctive identities through their promotion practices. These naturally reflected the same concerns as had their recruitment practices.

Two of the four social service ministries—the Board of Education and the Ministry of Health—clearly favored the type of individual generally associated with English elites; that is, public school alumni and the Oxford-educated. However, the framing context provided by the departmental point of view lent different meanings to this favoritism. From the time of its inception, the Ministry of Health was imbued with the generalist philosophy set out by the Trevelyan-Northcote Report and later espoused by the MacDonnell Commission. The long tenure of Arthur Robinson as permanent secretary (1920–1935), whose own successful career embodied this principle, reinforced this approach to personnel management. The Board of Education, in contrast, identified such an educational background with a special expertise in and understanding of educational issues.

Rather different criteria operated at Labour and Agriculture. The educational background of civil servants at these ministries did not typify the image of the civil servant generally implied by the stereotype of the English elite. Both these ministries looked for something different from the open competition type, but again the meaning of the same general approach differed according to the context of each department.

W. H. Beveridge and Llewellyn Smith set the tone for the Ministry of Labour in their wide-ranging search for administrative talent to oversee the Labour Department's expanded duties in 1909 and 1911. They looked for qualities of leadership and independence of judgment. As a consequence, the Labour Department of the Board of Trade tended to employ men that had been drawn from a greater variety of backgrounds than was usually found in the civil service. These men even included some who had begun their careers in the trade union movement. For instance, Sir David Shackleton—who served as permanent secretary in 1919 and 1920 and then became chief labour adviser—had been a cotton operative until the age of twenty-nine. Shackleton had served as a trade union official and Labour MP until he entered government service in 1910.

The Ministry of Agriculture, in contrast, valued the expert in specific subject areas. In the lower ranks, where officials had to grapple with the intricacies of English agriculture and the occasional intransigence of the English farmer, a man who knew his field could make a mark. At higher ranks, however, Agriculture officials had to deal with politicians and the officials of other departments, especially the Treasury. At that rank level, the social polish associated with a public school and an Oxford education, which could smooth such interaction, proved advantageous to both the official and the department.[52]

The structure of the English educational system and the differential demand for a career in government service among the graduates of different universities together limited the range of candidates from which the whole civil service and the individual departments could select junior officers. This served to establish the basic homogeneity of the entire civil service. But the narrow range of choice did not altogether preclude all choice, and within these limits, departments did express preferences, which showed up most strongly in the recruitment of new entrants and in promotion through the middle ranks.

The interaction of these factors formed career patterns, which can be linked to social class in two ways. In general, access to the educational institutions most favored by Education and Health was closely associated with a middle-class social origin. This relationship between social structure and education would necessarily work to define the social identity of departments, while variations in recruiting and promotion practices would give shading and nuance to that identity. Also, the personal attributes esteemed by such an education constituted a culture of class, a pattern of behavior that could be learned by the socially mobile. These attributes could take on additional significance—abstracted from their position in the social matrix. Consequently, the individuals involved in making the decisions that produced these patterns did not necessarily act out of a self-conscious class bias. By the interwar period, civil servants regarded themselves as professionals who were performing important work in the service of the state. That self-identification could not, however, obviate the larger social significance of their actions, both in shaping the typical career structure for themselves and with respect to policy issues that passed across their desks.

In all four ministries administrative capacity or expertise, however understood, formed the basis for the selection and advancement of officials. The different definitions of expertise acted upon by these four departments in building their staff demonstrates the problematic nature of that concept.[53] At Education and Health, that definition coincided with the elitist tendencies of the English educational system. At Labour and Agriculture, that definition worked counter to those tendencies. Recruitment and promotion practices thus contributed to the formation of a cohesive departmental identity.[54] But this identity, also manifested in an approach to issues of policy, carried a social significance as well. Given the influence of social origin on the opportunities offered by the English educational system, recruitment and promotion practices influenced by educational criteria would necessarily have an impact on the social profile of the civil service.

In the chapters that follow I consider how departmental identity shaped the policy-making process in each ministry, treating the four social service ministries in turn. In each case, my analysis first defines their distinctive approach to policy by examining the reactions of civil servants to some of the issues that came before them during the interwar period. The study then evaluates the degree to which officials actually succeeded in shaping policy according to their vision. My approach delineates in concrete terms the extent of their official power, which varied considerably according to the context of specific events, and identifies the ends to which civil servants used the power at their command.

Part II

3 The Board of Education: Defining Secondary Education

■ *The capital fact about English educational policy is that hitherto it has been made, except at brief intervals, by men, few, if any, of whom have themselves attended the schools principally affected by it, or would dream of allowing their children to attend them.*

—R. H. Tawney

R. H. Tawney, who had a lifelong interest in educational reform, believed that the administration of the educational system by men themselves the products (and beneficiaries) of that system maintained the pattern of class bias that continued to characterize educational opportunity in England. As we have seen, examination of the educational background of Board of Education officials corroborates Tawney's observations.[1] Of all the administrative class officials who worked at the Board of Education between 1919 and 1939 (a total of 179 men), 38.5 percent were graduates of Oxford, and 60 percent were graduates of either Oxford or Cambridge. Half the civil servants at the Board of Education had attended a Headmasters' Conference school, and half of these had attended one of the nine Clarendon schools.

Recruitment to the English civil service as a whole generally favored public school old boys and graduates of Oxford or Cambridge, but two factors further accentuated this pattern at the Board of Education. The Board did not recruit its officials through the procedures of open competition examination until 1919, thus representing a last bastion of patronage appointment after the First World War. Rather than use the examination process to recruit, Board officials could secure the kind of men they sought in a less formal way. They would, for instance, avail themselves of the good offices of the Oxford Appointments Committee. In addition, promotions consistently favored public school alumni and Oxford (but not Cambridge) graduates. As a result, virtually every man who held one of the top three ranks at the Board of Education between 1919 and 1939 had attended Oxford and one of the better-known Headmasters' Conference schools.

Controversies over the organization of English education during the interwar period provide an appropriate context to evaluate Tawney's suspicions concerning the nature of the contribution of civil servants to the policy-making process. So great a predominance, among Board officials, of men educated at the public schools and at Oxford University has two implications for the Board's manner of carrying on its business. The close relationship between educational opportunity and class background virtually guaranteed a high degree of social homogeneity, both among Board officials and between Board officials and the politicians who acted as ministers to the department. This homogeneity does not by itself provide a firm basis for predicting the attitudes that civil servants might hold on a particular matter of policy, but such a homogeneous group would more likely display consensus.[2] The roles played by promotion and patronage appointment in creating this homogeneity certainly indicate some conscious predilection for a specific social type among those responsible for the selection process. The common educational experience of so many Board officials would also have provided a model of one type of education, against which other types of education could be compared and measured.

From the 1918 Fisher Act until the 1944 Butler Act, the structure of the English educational system underwent little change.[3] Even though the question of the proper position of secondary education became an increasingly contentious issue during this period, neither the growing demand for a broadening access to secondary education nor the controversy about how best to meet that demand found expression in legislation. The constraints on expenditure imposed by a Conservative fiscal policy limited the alternative policies that any of the interwar governments could implement but did not stem the debate over just what that policy ought to be. In these debates, the officials staffing the upper levels of the Board of Education revealed that they possessed so specific a vision of what shape the English educational system ought to take that any variation from that vision had to be pressed upon them most energetically. Such energy was not often found during the two interwar decades.

The civil servants of the Board of Education believed that the state should provide suitable educational opportunities for all children. But they did not believe that all, or even many, children possessed the native ability to benefit from a secondary education. Board officials preferred an elite based on merit rather than on class and wealth, but they remained committed to the concept of a small elite thoroughly schooled in a humanistic tradition. This commitment limited the scope of the measures officials believed were required to reform secondary education. Civil servants did not have the authority to develop their own program. Nevertheless, throughout the educational controversies of the interwar years, Board officials never lost sight of their own vision as to what an equitable and efficient system of education should be.

This vision led them to protect secondary schools by regulating access to them, maintaining their traditional form, and defending their privileged status.

Civil servants rarely if ever had the luxury to elaborate a comprehensive educational program. Rather, they carried on their work in a welter of particular circumstances. My analysis will reconstruct officials' views of secondary education from their responses to particular policy issues that arose during the interwar period. I will first set the administrative scene with a brief survey of the structure of the Board of Education. Examination of the officials' rôle in formulating policy on the free place system and on raising the school-leaving age reveals their views of who should enjoy the privilege of a secondary education. Their responses to suggestions that the government provide secondary education in multilateral schools and that technical education should become a recognized part of the secondary curriculum show how they defined the nature of a secondary education. I would then like to evaluate the degree of influence officials enjoyed in formulating government policy in accordance with these views.

Origins and Organization

Parliament created the Board of Education in 1899 to centralize the administration of an expanding educational system supported by the state. According to statute, the Board consisted of the President, the Lord President of the Council, the Principal Secretaries of State, the First Lord of the Treasury, and the Chancellor of the Exchequer. In practice, the Board never actually convened, and the president acted as independently as any minister. Governments used the presidency of the Board of Education to provide a position for rising young men or senior politicians who were needed to balance the Cabinet politically. As a consequence, of the nine men who served as president of the Board between the First and Second World Wars, only three—H.A.L. Fisher, C. P. Trevelyan, and Eustace Percy—had any substantive interest in educational policy.

The organization of the Board's higher-level staff followed standard Whitehall practice. The permanent secretary, as the most senior official of the department, reported directly to the minister. The Board of Education had the distinction of being the only government department with two permanent secretaries, because the head of its Welsh Department (created in 1907 by Lloyd George to appease the Welsh nationalists) also held that rank.[4] Civil servants did not regard this as a trivial distinction, as these two men were the only officials who had the right to approach the president without first being requested to do so.

The second secretary, or deputy secretary, acted in the capacity of an executive officer. Next in the hierarchy came the three principal assistant secretaries, each of whom had the responsibility for overseeing one of the three main divisions of the educational system: secondary, elementary, and technical. In addition to these senior officials, the legal adviser—with a staff of barristers—dealt with questions of law, such as those that might arise in the drafting of legislation; the chief medical officer supervised the public health duties of the Board; the accountant-general took responsibility for the expenditures of the Board; and the director of Establishments dealt with personnel matters within the Board's staff. Assistant secretaries, like principal assistant secretaries, developed an expertise in a particular educational topic. In contrast, the duties of the two lowest ranks, principal and assistant principal, were organized geographically. Each officer at this level dealt with all types of education in a particular area, referring any problem to the senior officer with the appropriate specialty (see table 9 for the departmental organization as it stood in 1926). For instance, a junior official might take a question about the secondary school in the locality under his charge to the principal assistant secretary in charge of secondary education.[5]

The Board of Education employed a body of inspectors to evaluate the effectiveness of schools receiving state aid as well as to ascertain their compliance with Board regulations. Three chief inspectors—one of whom held the position of senior chief inspector—controlled and coordinated the work of the entire inspectorate. Under them, nine divisional inspectors supervised all the inspectors in each territorial division of England. Divided into five groups within the territorial divisions, separate staffs inspected the five types of schools recognized by the Board: elementary, secondary, technical, teacher training, and art. The Welsh Department had its own chief inspector, who directed still another staff of inspectors.[6] In addition, the Board had attached to it an advisory body called the Consultative Committee. Its members appointed by the president of the Board, the Consultative Committee investigated and reported on broad questions of policy referred to it by the Board.

Policy Making in Secondary Education

Free Places

The problem of determining who should have the privilege of attending secondary schools engaged the attention of the Board in several forms during the interwar decades. The growing demand for a secondary education translated into pressures both to increase the number of places available at secondary schools and to raise the school-leaving age. Because the demand for secondary school places (a large number of which remained in the private sector) greatly exceeded the supply, the Board of Education had to devise criteria to determine who had the right to those places and had to decide

TABLE 9. *Board of Education, 1926*

PERMANENT SECRETARY
Sir Aubrey V. Symonds

DEPUTY SECRETARY
Sir Edmund B. Phipps

Private Secretaries to the President:
R. S. Wood, J. Wilkie
Private Secretary to the Permanent Secretary:
B. L. Peasron *(Asst. Principal)*
Private Secretary to the Parliamentary Secretary:
W. R. Richardson *(Asst. Principal)*

ELEMENTARY SCHOOLS
Principal Assistant Secretary:
E. H. Pelham
Assistant Secretary: R.E.S. Hart

SECONDARY SCHOOLS
Principal Assistant Secretary:
M. G. Holmes
Assistant Secretary:
C. W. Maudsley

TECHNICAL AND CONTINUATION SCHOOLS
Principal Assitant Secretary:
W. R. Davies
Assistant Secretary: F. E. Douglas

TERRITORIAL DIVISIONS

	I London & Middlesex	II Outer London	III S.E. & S.W.	IV E & E.C.	V W.C.	VI N. & N.E.	VII N.W.
Principals	A. Maxwell-Lyte G. G. Williams	W. C. Cleary T.H.H. Walrond	E. L. Heath A. R. Guest	H. E. Mann G. D. Rokeling	P.H.B. Hughes A. T. Baines	S. H. Wood G.H.V. Sutherland E. L. Turnbull	D. du B. Davidson E. D. Marris
Assistant Principals	—	A.W.C. Mitchell —	A. McL. Currie	Miss K. W. Elliott		G.A.N. Lowndes	A. F. Sharam J. Rhodes
Assistant Administrative Officer	—		—	—	S. Lukey	—	—

TRAINING OF TEACHERS, etc. DIVISION
Assistant Secretaries: R. R. Campbell, W. H. Fawkes, A. P. Oppé
Principal: A. J. Finny
Assistant Principals: R. Heath, E. N. Strong

PENSION AWARDS DIVISION
Assistant Secretary: L. J. Morison
Principals: H.A.S. Ferris, J. C. Gravestock

PROGRAMMES, STAISTICS, etc.
Assistant Secretary: C. E. Sykes

WELSH DEPARTMENT
Permanent Secretary: Percy E. Watkins
Assistant Secretary: J. E. Talbot
Principal: T. G. Roberts
Assistant Principals: A. E. Thomas, H. E. Weston

Source: Public Records Office, ED 23/261/115260

FINANCE BRANCH
Accountant-General: Sir Hugh W. Orange
Deputy Accountant-General: B. P. Moore
Principal Finance Officer: J. G. Rhodes
Finance Officers: H. W. Buckley, F. J. Gardner

ESTABLISHMENT BRANCH
Director of Establishments: K. G. Howarth
Principal: L. G. Duke

LEGAL BRANCH
Legal Advisor: H. J. Simmonds
Assistant Legal Advisers: W.G.B. Ritchie, J. H. Lincoln, D. Vesey
Legal Assistants: E. L. Hopkins, A. C. Dawes, B. L. Gordon, W.V.S. Sinclair

MEDICAL BRANCH
(54 Victoria Street)
Chief Medical Officer: Sir George Newman

MEDICAL STAFF
Senior Medical Officer: R. H. Crowley
Chief Woman Medical Adviser: Dame Janet M. Campbell
Chief Medical Inspector: A. Eichholz
Medical Officers: R. P. Williams, H.C.T. Langdon, Miss L. E. Wilson, Miss M. C. Bywaters, J.E.A. Underwood

ADMINISTRATIVE STAFF
Assistant Secretary: W. C. Eaton
Principals: N. D. Bosworth-Smith, J. R. Warberton, D. W. Corrie
Assistant Principals: H. D. Healiff, G. N. Flemming

OFFICE OF SPECIAL INQUIRES AND REPORTS
Assistant Secretary: A. R. Ainsworth
Assistant Principal: J. H. Burrows

CONSULTATIVE COMMITTEE
Secretary: R. F. Young (Principal)

EMPLOYMENT COMMITTEE
Secretary: H. B. Wallis (Principal)

ADULT EDUCATION COMMITTEE, LIBRARIES COMMITTEE AND JUVENILE ORGANIZATIONS COMMITTEE
Secretary: C.O.G. Douie (Assistant Principal)

COMMITTEE ON WELSH
Secretary: P. A. Lewis (Assistant Principal)

ARCHITECT'S OFFICE
Architect: G.F.N. Clay

how to finance the education of those students whose families could not afford to pay school fees. Raising the school-leaving age entailed the development of a curriculum that was suitable for the much larger numbers of older students remaining in the classrooms of the already existing state-supported elementary school system.

The free place system, devised in 1907 under the aegis of Sir Robert Morant, had originally reserved a minimum of 25 percent of school places at grant-aided secondary schools to qualified ex–public elementary school students. Throughout the interwar period, the Board continued to rely upon free places to enable academically talented elementary school pupils to take advantage of a secondary education. Consequently, Board officials had to adjudicate requests to increase (or decrease) the proportion of free places made available by particular schools. In dealing with these questions, civil servants balanced what they regarded as a legitimate demand for equity of access to a secondary education against their desire to maintain a high academic standard in secondary schools. This, they thought, necessitated protecting secondary schools from an influx of students who, they feared, would be ill-prepared for and unsuited to benefit from a secondary education.

In the closing years of the First World War, civil servants urged that secondary schools be made more accessible to a broader range of the population. In 1917, when the Ministry of Reconstruction's Committee on Education recommended raising the school-leaving age to fourteen and the establishment of continuation schools to provide further education for those who had stopped attending full-time school in order to work, E. K. Chambers (see appendix) suggested instead "a vast extension of the present Secondary School system, together with infinitely more free access to that system."[7] It is ironic that Chambers later found himself responsible for the administration of continuation schools during the abortive attempt to implement this proposal as a part of H.A.L. Fisher's package of educational reform after the war. The failure of these continuation schools evidently embittered Chambers's remaining years at the Board.

The son of an Anglican minister who was a Fellow and Tutor at Worcester College, Oxford, Chambers had himself attended Marlborough and Corpus Christi College, Oxford. He began his career at the Board of Education in 1892. In those days the pace of work at the Board was so leisurely that Chambers spent part of each day at the British Museum doing research for a scholarly work on medieval literature, *The Medieval Stage,* which appeared in 1903. Then Robert Morant's leadership as permanent secretary of the Board caught Chambers's imagination, and he wholeheartedly entered into the enterprise of educational reform begun by Morant—work that engaged his attention for twenty years. With the failure of the experiment in continuation schools, Chambers lost interest in the Board's work. He took up his scholarly research again and published *The Elizabethan Stage* in 1923, a year after becoming the Board's second secretary.[8]

Chambers's enthusiasm for expansion was not an isolated sentiment among Board officials in the immediate postwar period. In 1923, L. A. Selby-Bigge wrote to the president of the Board, Edward Wood, pointing out the much increased demand for secondary education and noting the diminishing admissions due to the economy measures the Board had had to take at the behest of the Treasury during the financial emergency of the previous two years. (Wood, better known as Lord Halifax, had replaced H.A.L. Fisher as president of the Board after the collapse of Lloyd George's coalition left the Conservative party in power.) In his memorandum Selby-Bigge, who had become permanent secretary in 1911, lamented the inability of the country to meet this demand. Selby-Bigge warned that "unless a considerable development of Secondary Schools can be allowed and even encouraged at a fairly early date, a great opportunity will have been lost and the country will suffer." E. H. Pelham (see appendix), principal assistant secretary in charge of secondary schools, prepared a detailed program for the expansion of secondary education to submit to Wood.[9]

Board officials did not long sustain their enthusiasm for a policy of expansion, however. The very next year, Pelham cautioned C. P. Trevelyan, the first Labour president of the Board of Education, against a too rapid expansion of free secondary education.[10] This apparent turnabout in official advice might be explained as an effort to counterbalance the known predilections of the Board's political leadership—the Conservatives for retrenchment, Labour for expansion. By the end of the interwar period, however, civil servants agreed that the secondary school system had expanded sufficiently, and they decided to discourage the founding of new secondary schools. In 1937, R. S. Wood (see appendix) argued that the widespread demand for and growth of secondary education had led to the admission of too many pupils incapable of meeting the academic standard that a secondary school should maintain. Board officials believed that this had led to a lowering of the school-leaving age among secondary school pupils, which in turn further diluted the quality of secondary education.[11]

Civil servants feared that any large increase in the number of students would lead to a deterioration in the quality of secondary education. The prestige of England's secondary schools rested in part on the rigorous educational standards they upheld. When faced with requests to increase the proportion of free places allowed in state-aided secondary schools or to completely abolish fees for secondary education, Board officials reiterated the need to maintain these standards. In a policy-setting minute written in response to a request from Durham for the Board of Education to authorize the raising of the proportion of free places in Durham schools to 60 percent, H.A.L. Fisher spoke for them all when he commented: "I doubt whether the Labour men who control educational policy in Durham realize the great importance of insisting upon a high standard of quality in the Secondary Education of the Country." E. H. Pelham was to voice the same concern in 1924 when he warned C. P. Trevelyan against the dangers inherent in the rapid expansion of free secondary education.[12]

The interest in upholding the quality of secondary education sustained the official view that only the best-qualified pupils should go to secondary school. Since Board officials never accepted the proposition that every student should by right enjoy a secondary education, they were constantly contending with the problem of determining who was entitled to a secondary education and who was not. This problem grew more acute as the demand for secondary education increased. E. H. Pelham wrote, on January 20, 1922: "Broadly speaking we have got to work on the principle that as there are not enough places to go round selection must be on merit and by competition." The system of free places guaranteed that some qualified but needy student could enjoy the advantage of a secondary education. Pelham argued against the reduction of free places as an economy measure—recommended by the 1922 report of the Geddes Committee, which had been appointed the previous year to affect reductions in government expenditure—on the grounds that secondary school places would then go to less qualified fee-payers.[13]

The threat of the "Geddes ax"[14] necessitated that the Board set priorities in the state funding of education. E. K. Chambers revealed the different values civil servants placed on the schools they administered in his opposition to the implementation of the budget cuts for secondary education recommended by the Geddes Committee. He suggested that industry could (and should) bear the entire cost of technical education, and he insisted that the salaries of elementary schoolteachers should be cut rather than those of secondary schoolteachers. These suggestions clearly indicate Chambers's notions of what order the state should follow when allocating funds for these different types of education: secondary, first; elementary, second; and technical, last.[15]

Although civil servants wanted to preserve free places as a means of ensuring that bright pupils from poorer homes could have a secondary education, they regarded the restriction of free places to students who had attended public elementary schools as an anachronism. Pelham, Selby-Bigge, and H. W. Orange (see appendix), the Board's accountant-general, all put this view to Trevelyan in 1924. Orange asserted that this restriction should be removed altogether if the proportion of free places was raised to 40 percent. Pelham argued that the government had the responsibility to promote secondary education among all segments of the population, not just that segment represented by public elementary school pupils. Selby-Bigge suggested that, since public elementary schools had become securely established as a feeder to secondary schools (in 1922 Pelham had estimated that one-third of the pupils at grant-aided secondary schools occupied free places), the need for this restriction on free places no longer existed. Selby-Bigge did concede, however, that the Board should continue to require each school to take a minimum number of pupils from public elementary schools, "in order to guard against any reversion to 'aristocratic' tendencies."[16]

In 1929, M. G. Holmes (see appendix), who had been principal assistant secretary for secondary education since 1926, took these arguments one step further by suggesting the "ideal arrangement" of selecting pupils according to their merit and then assessing fees according to the means of the student's family. This view did not find favor either with Holmes's minister, C. P. Trevelyan, or with the Labour government, which opposed on principle any measure that smacked of a means test. Holmes had another opportunity to put forward this idea when the Committee on National Expenditure (better known as the May Committee), appointed to report on the 1931 financial crisis, recommended the abolition of free places as an economy measure.[17]

A coalition calling itself a National government replaced the Labour government in August 1931, but it feared an adverse public reaction and would not drop the public elementary school requirement for free places in 1932. Something approaching that policy, however, found its way into an explanation of government policy that the Board prepared in 1933 for a Conservative candidate for Parliament. An answer proposed for a hypothetical question on free secondary education asserted: "We ought to admit to the schools pupils who have shown themselves qualified for secondary education, as fee-paying pupils in the case of those whose parents can afford to pay fees, and as free pupils in the case of the remainder."[18] The argument for the abolition of the public elementary school restriction on free places rested on the (probably correct) assumption that a pupil's attendance at a public elementary school no longer signaled the poverty of the student's family. The restriction nevertheless still had some validity. Although some of the middle class had begun to send their children to public elementary schools, the working class still did not have access to England's private preparatory schools.

The May Committee put forward other suggestions to increase fee income in secondary schools by raising fees or by the government's grant to secondary schools based on the assumption of a minimum tuition. The Board's civil servants firmly opposed such expedients, however. M. G. Holmes, now deputy secretary, outlined the objections to these proposals, pointing out that raising fees a standard 25 percent or paying grants to schools based on a presumed standard tuition fee left local revenue to make up the difference. He argued that implementation of these proposals could not accommodate local variation and would certainly penalize poor areas. In contrast, Holmes found the idea that free places be subject to a means test "incontrovertible in principle." Holmes concluded: "It might be possible to admit on merit and then administer a means test before exacting payment."[19] C. P. Trevelyan had rejected this very same proposal when Holmes advanced it in 1929.

E. H. Pelham, who had become permanent secretary in 1932, responded to the May Committee's attacks on the free place system as he had responded to similar attacks by the Geddes Committee ten years before. Pelham expanded on Holmes's suggestion, urging a reform that would link educational and fiscal goals by instituting standards of admission according to merit and charging fees according to the means of the students family. The present system did not guarantee the best-qualified children admittance to secondary schools, Pelham argued. The number of children qualifying for free places could (and did) exceed the number of free places available. Children who were less qualified academically but with greater financial resources than free place students took the remaining school places. The anomalies of the free place system, according to Pelham, included a lack of inquiry into the means of the families of free place winners, the lack of any "ascertainable principle" by which schools assessed fees, and the lack of any provision for a partial rather than total remission of fees.[20]

Throughout 1932 the Board grappled with the proposed abolition of free places and their replacement by "special" places subject to a means test. The attempt of Board officials to reconcile the contradictory goals of the Treasury (to increase fee revenue) and the Board of Education (to maintain educational opportunities for the children of poor parents) suffered a setback when the local education authorities (LEAs) rejected the suggestion that admission to secondary schools be predicated on merit alone. These governing bodies, which administered and contributed to the funding of state-supported schools, believed that admission by merit combined with fees assessed according to the means of the student's family would result in a loss of fee revenue.[21]

The LEA view accords with Pelham's contention, that restrictions on the free place system permitted the admission to secondary schools of pupils that were less qualified but more affluent. Rectifying this inequity, however, would require increased expenditure, not less, and in a time of financial exigency officials could only make the best of this blow to the department's efforts to guarantee admission by merit. N. D. Bosworth-Smith (see appendix), a newly promoted assistant secretary, argued weakly that special places would still increase secondary school accommodation for poor pupils because a means test would eliminate those who were not poor.[22] R. S. Wood, director of Establishments for the Board, devised an awkward scheme to preserve some semblance of the Board's original proposal, suggesting that some minimum percentage of secondary school places be reserved as special places, that the balance of places be filled with qualified fee payers, and that any remaining places be added to the quota of special places. Wood did not approve of the proposal that LEAs be allowed to award maintenance allowances to pupils not in possession of a special place. He contended that such awards, made outside the control of the Board of Education, would lead to anomalies.[23]

In the fall of 1932, Board officials made another attempt to effect reform in the revision of Board regulations regarding free (now called special) places. The civil servants suggested to their minister, Lord Halifax, that, for special places, a student qualifying for a free place no longer be required to be a pupil of a public elementary school. Holmes, with Pelham's support, argued that attendance at a public elementary school no longer indicated the poverty of the student's family, as it had done in 1907 when the regulations were first written. Accordingly Holmes concluded: "To retain the ex-P.E.S. qualification would be to graft an unscientific excrescence on what under the Draft Regulations is for the first time a scientific system."[24]

Halifax—after consultation with Harold Ramsbotham, his parliamentary secretary—rejected this advice, for political reasons. Both Halifax and Ramsbotham suspected that the change would arouse opposition among urban working-class constituencies. In these areas many parents saw the free place system as the only hope for their children to go on from a public elementary school to a better life. After this round of discussion Halifax concluded: "I should prefer to decide to keep the P.E.S. qualification, illogical and untidy as it is."[25]

All these discussions manifest a vision of a meritocratic educational system that would allow all bright children, regardless of family background, the opportunity to attend a secondary school. However, the terms of the debate also assume that children bright enough to benefit from a secondary education constituted a relatively small proportion of the population. The meritocratic ideal led civil servants at the Board of Education to encourage the development of secondary education after the First World War and to attempt repeatedly to make the free place system function in a more equitable way. Civil servants believed that opportunity should be based on merit, but they insisted that opportunity should be limited to the most talented. R. S. Wood expressed a concern in 1937 that the growth of secondary education had led to the admission of many pupils "not of a capacity to receive the type of education . . . a Secondary School should offer." After considering Wood's report, Board officials concluded that the country had reached the saturation point for secondary education (although at that time far less than one-third of England's children attended a secondary school), and that the Board of Education ought to discourage new secondary schools.[26]

The School-Leaving Age

Raising the school-leaving age represented another way to broaden educational opportunity. Such a measure would bring secondary-type education within the reach of larger numbers by retaining older pupils in the classrooms of elementary schools. This approach received a resounding endorsement in 1926 when the Consultative Committee (an expert body appointed to give advice to the Board of Education on questions of policy referred to it by the Board) under the chairmanship of Sir Henry Hadow issued its *Report on the Education of the Adolescent* (better known as the Hadow Report). Labour opinion hailed the report as official and impartial endorsement for their policy of "secondary education for all." R. H. Tawney, who formulated this policy for the Labour party, had also been a member of the Consultative Committee that composed the Hadow Report.[27]

The Hadow Report's most important recommendation, to raise the school-leaving age to fifteen, did not generate much support among civil servants at the Board of Education. The accommodation of larger numbers of older students at elementary schools would have necessitated an expansion of physical facilities and the creation of a suitable curriculum. In 1927 Eustace Percy, president of the Board, insisted to the Association of Education Committees that other reforms must be accomplished first. Within the Board, however, E. H. Pelham expressed doubts that the government would ever take such a step.[28] The Board readily undertook the implementation of other recommendations made by the Hadow Report, such as reducing class size, repairing or replacing decrepit school buildings, and devising a separate curriculum for pupils kept in the classroom until the age of fifteen.

Despite the enthusiasm of Labour supporters, none of these proposed reforms actually touched the secondary schools. The Hadow Report, although it had been intended to initiate substantive reforms in secondary education, did not actually treat secondary schools as such. Key ambiguities in the report itself allowed alternate interpretations of it. Although the report's tone implied a commitment to the creation of a more egalitarian system of education, the Consultative Committee's terms of reference limited the report to an examination of nonsecondary schools only. Secondary schools, including the prestigious public schools, remained beyond the study's purview. The distinction between elementary and secondary schools was legal as well as social. The Board of Education administered secondary and elementary schools according to two different sets of regulations. The Consultative Committee wished to erase the social difference between the secondary and elementary school systems, but they could not deal with the legal differences between the two. The committee respected the limitations placed upon it, expressing its aspirations only in terms of the educational system then in existence.

The Hadow Report's specific recommendations included raising the school-leaving age to fifteen in 1932, calling all education received before the age of eleven "primary" and all education received after the age of eleven "secondary," and constructing selective "central" schools to provide a separate course of study for pupils in the elementary schools aged between eleven and fifteen. These recommendations, even if they had been carried out immediately, would not have radically changed the nature of the English school system. To call these central schools secondary, as the committee recommended, would not (and did not) confer secondary status upon them.[29]

The need to reorganize elementary schools along the lines recommended by the Hadow Report and Charles Trevelyan's efforts to raise the school-leaving age kept the issue of curriculum before the Board. Civil servants' views of what sort of postprimary education elementary schools should provide underlined the distinction they reserved for secondary education. According to the civil servants, older students in elementary schools should follow a "practical" course of study. Both H. E. Mann and D. du B. Davidson (see appendix for both) stressed this point in their discussions of raising the school-leaving age in the division under their supervision. Trevelyan himself, in a 1929 meeting with the LEAs, emphasized "the need of a varied curriculum for the older children and the importance of practical instruction." Trevelyan here repeated, almost verbatim, the sentiments expressed by Henry Richards (see appendix), a chief inspector at the Board. Richards had explained this view when Trevelyan met with his officials to prepare for the conference with the LEAs. Richards returned to this theme at a meeting of divisional inspectors, held the following autumn, when he identified "the real problem" as "giving further and appropriate education to *all* unselected children." The solution to this problem, Richards argued, did not lie in the further education offered selected children: "It must be borne in mind that the development of a proper type of education for such non-selected schools involved laying considerable stress on games, the cultivation of teamwork and everything that was meant by the much abused word 'citizenship.' " To this end, Richards recommended that all such schools should be provided with playing fields.[30] The wide gap separating children in elementary schools from children in secondary schools—a gap reinforced by their educational experience—would thus remain, even if both types of school educated the same age groups.

The recommendations of the Hadow Report appealed also to those who wished to put English education on a more efficient and productive footing. In a note on education policy sent to the Chancellor of the Exchequer in 1928, Eustace Percy included Hadow reorganization as a first step in the construction of a system of education "to select and train a sufficient body of men (and women) to manage the mechanized civilization of today."[31] For

Percy the English educational system with its inefficiencies and injustices did not adequately serve English society because it failed to prepare people properly for their role in society. This view differs markedly from the Hadow Committee's ideal of an educational system that might better serve not only the needs of the state but also those of individuals.

The question of raising the school-leaving age colored discussions of education policy throughout the rest of the interwar period, but Board officials never evidenced enthusiasm for this step. After enumerating the many obstacles to taking such action immediately, they bowed to C. P. Trevelyan's desire to raise the school-leaving age during his second tenure as president of the Board under the second Labour government. They strenuously rejected the various suggestions to use this mechanism to ease unemployment. Even after the passage of the Education Act of 1936, civil servants remained skeptical about the prospects of actually implementing this reform. Their discussions of postprimary education in 1937 record their apprehension that "there is no assurance that the reorganization of Elementary Schools and the raising of the school age to 15 + will be completed." In the end their doubts proved justified. The day appointed by the 1936 Education Act for the raising of the school-leaving age coincided with the outbreak of the Second World War, and M. G. Holmes, then permanent secretary, decided that the country could not undertake that task under wartime conditions.[32]

At the same time, Holmes—who was on the board of governors of Wellington in addition to his official duties—was engaged in correspondence with Spencer Leeson, headmaster of Winchester and also a former civil servant at the Board of Education (see appendix). These two men wanted government to come to the aid of public schools, which were at that time in serious financial straits because of falling enrollments. Holmes and Leeson decided that the Headmasters' Conference or the Governing Bodies Association ought to ask the government to appoint a royal commission to investigate the problem.[33] In 1942, the government appointed a departmental committee chaired by Lord Fleming to consider this issue. The contrast between Holmes's reactions to the plight of the public schools and the prospect of extending the scope of elementary school education suggests that he was concerned more about the fate of the public schools (most of which remained in private hands and provided a postprimary education for only a small proportion of the population) than about the fate of the state-supported elementary school system.

Those who hailed the Hadow Report as a great advance for English education could hardly fail to be disappointed when the recommendations of the report, as implemented by the Board, did not serve the ends envisioned by the Consultative Committee. The issues were further confused because Percy's version of the Hadow reorganization still represented some improvement in terms of equality of education and increased educational opportunities. However much the ideals expressed by the Hadow Report might have raised hopes, the Hadow reorganization could not, by itself, guarantee secondary education for all.

Multilateral Schools

Board officials agreed upon the need for certain kinds of education reform, especially reform that might guarantee meritocratic recruitment, but it is clear they never envisioned any general reorganization of state-aided secondary schools. Although Board officials did not themselves put forward any alternatives to the existing organization of England's secondary schools, suggestions from other quarters appeared upon their desks from time to time. Indeed, the evaluation of such suggestions constituted an important part of their duties. One suggestion—the concept of multilateral (later termed comprehensive) schools—received a rather unsympathetic appraisal. Their determined resistance to this idea delayed its implementation by many years.[34]

In 1929, Board officials prepared an analysis of this method of structuring secondary education when Morgan Jones, parliamentary secretary at the Board of Education during the second Labour government, circulated a memorandum to the Board's staff proposing just such a school system. Later the same year the Labour party Research Department Education Advisory Committee sent the Board of Education their "Report on a Unified System of Post-Primary Education." This document contained a more elaborate exposition of a secondary school system composed of what we now call comprehensive schools. The report indicated Labour's concern with the social implications of different school systems for different types of education and asserted unequivocally: "We are opposed to a system which differentiates between a type of school where the pupils are retained until university age and other types where the pupil is expected to leave at 15 or 16. A division on these lines can only tend to accentuate undesirable social distinctions."[35]

Board officials did not approve of this approach to secondary education. M. G. Holmes, at that time principal assistant secretary in charge of secondary education, argued that these schools would become "anaemic reflections" of already existing secondary schools and would limit the variety of courses available to pupils. S. H. Wood (see appendix), the president's private secretary, wrote ominously that the development of just one type of postprimary school was "dangerous . . . and not in the best interests of education or the children," but he did not elaborate on this warning. Francis Stead, chief inspector of secondary schools at the Board from 1926 until 1933, also opposed such schools. He argued that the academic stream of comprehensive schools would get too much attention, an argument resting upon the assumption that separate schools were more likely to ensure equal treatment of the different courses of study. Holmes also presented Jones's suggestion to a conference of divisional inspectors, which group concluded that "the desired object would be much more satisfactorily obtained by the provision of greater facilities for interchange and promotion from modern to Secondary Schools."[36]

Civil servants believed that parity among different courses of study, equal opportunity for pupils, and educational quality could all be served best by allowing the transfer of pupils from one type of school to another. Even more radical educational reformers like R. H. Tawney had to content themselves with this position as the most progressive possible at the time.[37] Comprehensive education did not become official policy until some years after the Second World War.

Technical Education

The question of the proper place of technical education required civil servants to make judgments about the appropriate curriculum and organization for secondary schools. In 1937 Board officials had to deal with the Consultative Committee's recommendation that the state provide technical high schools. Many people both inside and outside the Board agreed that England needed to encourage technical education—this had been one of Lord Eustace Percy's pet projects when he was president of the Board of Education during Baldwin's Conservative government between 1926 and 1929. Despite the widespread acceptance of the need for such schools, the question still remained, Would they be secondary schools? The answer to this question was important, since the Board of Education administered secondary schools according to separate regulations setting different, and higher, standards for facilities and staffing than did either the elementary or further education regulations. The Consultative Committee wished the Board to identify them as secondary schools in order to enhance their prestige.

Civil servants met to discuss this issue in October 1937. At the same time, they considered several other suggestions for changing the curriculum the Board required for a secondary school. The Consultative Committee as a body had recommended that the Board allow a greater variety in the secondary curriculum. The chairman of the Consultative Committee, Sir Cyril Norwood, also took this view in his pamphlet "The Curriculum in Secondary Schools." The Association of Education Committees had pressed the Board to drop the requirement for math and modern languages and to upgrade the standing of art, music, and other "practical" subjects.[38]

Board officials perceived all these proposed changes as threats to the quality of secondary education. As for technical schools in particular, the Board had hitherto discouraged LEAs from setting up such schools, but as the assistant secretary who summarized the discussion, G. G. Williams (see appendix), pointed out to his colleagues: "We can hardly maintain this attitude if the Consultative Committee is likely to recommend schools on similar lines." Williams himself, who had attended Westminster and Christ Church, Oxford, argued that if the Board adopted the technical high school in principle, then the Board should give it a good sendoff by including it under the regulations for secondary schools.[39] The chief inspector for secondary schools, Francis Duckworth (see appendix), also recommended this course of action. Duckworth, who had been a master at Eton prior to entering the Board's inspectorate in 1920, maintained that the opposition between vocational and general education had been greatly exaggerated and that changing the secondary curriculum would not necessarily lower its standard.[40]

Robert Wood, principal assistant secretary for technical education, took the opposite view. He argued that the leaving age for technical schools would in practice probably be less than sixteen, thus making their inclusion under secondary regulations inappropriate. A leaving age of fifteen precluded the more advanced curriculum that justified the separate existence of secondary schools. Wood pointed out the far-reaching consequences of violating this principle. "Unless the Secondary school course is more advanced than that of a good Senior School," he warned, "then there would appear to be no occasion for selective entry and no justification for fees." In different ways, both Williams and Duckworth conceded this point. According to Williams, the Board would have to insist that those schools recognized as technical high schools recruit selectively at eleven plus, keep their pupils until sixteen plus, and offer a high type of curriculum to justify their status. Duckworth simply commented: "I recoil from the idea of a Secondary school with an 11–15 age range."[41]

After this exchange of memoranda, Board officials held another general meeting. In this discussion they reached a consensus about the minimum attributes of a secondary school. These included recruitment by examination at eleven plus, an extended course of study lasting at least five years that prepared the student for university, and a professional staff. G. G. Williams had noted earlier that the technical high schools would lack a sixth form (another traditional characteristic of secondary schools). R. S. Wood argued that secondary schools did not provide "vocational" education, and that technical high schools would do just that. After they had deliberated these distinctions, Wood's view prevailed, and Board officials concluded that technical high schools should be administered by further education rather than secondary education regulations. In the years immediately prior to the outbreak of the Second World War, this attitude undoubtedly undercut new efforts made by the Board to encourage LEAs to provide technical education.[42]

The tenor of these discussions at the Board of Education show that secondary education meant a special curriculum (academic), a course of a certain length (five or six years), a particular entry age (eleven plus), and selective recruitment. All of these characteristics had originated with public schools. In addition, the civil servants' strong opinions that vocational training was not the proper function of secondary education recalled the amateur ideal associated with the public schools. Despite the alternatives pressed upon them throughout the interwar decades, Board officials maintained a consistent vision of what constituted a secondary education, and they never came to see it as a chronological stage through which every child should pass.

The Purpose of Secondary Schools

Board officials obviously recognized the class bias of the secondary school system, but they thought that democratization of secondary education meant no more than the equalization of the opportunity for secondary education. In testimony before the Consultative Committee, Board officials Holmes and Duckworth asserted that "social differences" tended to diminish as the proportion of pupils from public elementary schools increased in secondary schools. At another point in their testimony, they noted: "The heads of Secondary Schools as a rule desired a definite proportion of pupils from the better class homes for the purpose of maintaining a reasonable standard in speech, manners, etc." Holmes and Duckworth show here that they understood the process by which secondary education served to give a leg up to the upwardly mobile lucky few.[43]

Secondary schools thus provided much more than an academic education leading to university and to a professional career; they provided also the training necessary for a complete change in social identity. In his 1937 analysis of the state of postprimary education, Robert Wood astutely observed: "The whole approach to the problem of post-primary education has been poisoned by the false notion that its main object is to educate a few more people out of their class, thereby actually strengthening instead of diminishing class distinctions."[44] The changes in recruitment for secondary schools that were encouraged by the Board of Education might have made secondary schools a vehicle for social mobility; but social mobility does not, by itself, necessarily break down distinctions among classes. Indeed, the concept of social mobility necessarily presupposes some system of class hierarchy.

With their continuing concern for the standard of education that was provided by secondary schools, the civil servants at the Board of Education tried to ensure that the brightest children received the best education. Characteristics of this education bore a resemblance to the public school education received by the civil servants themselves. The curriculum, for instance, was totally academic and did not include technical, "practical," or vocational subjects. Although the secondary schools under the administration of the

Board of Education largely catered to day students rather than boarding students, Board officials insisted that secondary schools be separate from schools providing other types of education, thus isolating the students from their contemporaries. As their discussion of technical high schools revealed, the characteristics that Board officials thought defined what a secondary education ought to be—even in details such as beginning age, length of course, and presence of a sixth form—closely resembled a public school education.

Under the supervision of the Board of Education, English secondary schools continued to carry out the traditional function of public schools—the training of an elite. The definition of the proper method of recruitment to that elite began to change from hereditary (or aristocratic) to meritocratic, but the number of the elect remained small. The Board's civil servants believed that the best interests of the nation depended upon the proper funding of secondary education by the state, the accurate selection of the brightest children to attend secondary schools, and the maintenance of the highest standards by those schools. The civil servants of the Board of Education therefore took a special interest in all these issues.

Board officials tried to ensure that the education given by the nation's secondary schools provided a suitable preparation for the country's future leaders. This education, they believed, should consist of an academic, nonvocational course of study that would mold the character as well as train the mind. In short, they thought that the ideal curriculum should be as much like that of the public schools as possible, and that this curriculum should be provided by schools structured as much like the public schools as practicable.

Ministerial Leadership in the Board of Education

The memoranda left by Board of Education civil servants do more than record their views of policy issues, they also reveal how Board officials tried to shape policy in accordance with their views. Defining the extent of the civil servants' influence depends upon an understanding of the resources available to them and how they used these resources. In the end, the most crucial factor in evaluating the influence of the Board's officials remains the degree of their success in achieving their ends. If civil servants at the Board of Education never had any effect on what the Board did, then it does not much matter what they thought or, indeed, who they were.

The civil servants' constitutional position did limit their range of action. No matter how much a civil servant might favor a policy, if its implementation depended upon either the appropriation of funds or a change in the law, the Cabinet had to act. The minister of a department held the key to the relationship between a department's civil servants and the political arm of the government. A department could have either a sympathetic or an adversarial relationship with its minister, and a minister could command a strong or a weak position in the Cabinet. Within this context, officials might take four different stances toward policy. Civil servants themselves might propose a change in policy—the most aggressive attitude a civil servant could take. When some other agent suggested a new policy, the civil servants could oppose it, support it, or remain indifferent to it (although in practice indifference often amounted to opposition).

The civil servants at the Board of Education did occasionally try to initiate policy. For instance, they suggested that the government remove the restriction of free places to pupils from public elementary schools. They put forward this proposal several times (in 1924, 1929, and 1932), but they never managed to gain any support for their suggestion, either from their ministers or from the government. The restriction that the civil servants opposed was written into the law. Under these circumstances they had no independent power. If they failed to marshal support among those with the power to act, they could do little but wait for the government to change and try again. As a result, the restriction of free places to public elementary school pupils remained in force throughout this period, despite the disapproval of Board officials.

Even if the civil servants managed to persuade their minister to adopt their point of view, the minister then had to persuade his colleagues in the Cabinet to approve the proposal. Cabinet approval depended upon many circumstances beyond the control of the civil servants. A minister's status in the Cabinet had a direct bearing on his chances of acting as a successful advocate for his department. Because the Board of Education was not an important Cabinet post, education did not always have a strong advocate in the Cabinet.

Civil servants had a better chance of seeing a policy implemented when they worked with an active minister who had an independent commitment to the policy. When C. P. Trevelyan became president of the Board of Education under the first Labour government in 1924, for example, Board officials immediately approached him with recommendations to increase educational expenditure, recommendations they had brought to Halifax only the year before. Unlike his predecessor Trevelyan did not need to be persuaded of this point of view for he had a deep interest in education policy and had come into office with positive ideas of what he wanted done. And on the matter of increased expenditure for education Trevelyan and his officials agreed. Trevelyan had some success in persuading his prime minister and Chancellor of the Exchequer of his point of view, a reflection of Trevelyan's standing among his colleagues and (probably more important) of the Labour party's commitment to support social services, which contrasted with the Conservatives' drive to reduce government expenditure.

The most striking case of a partnership between minister and civil servants occurred at the beginning of the interwar period. H.A.L. Fisher, whom Lloyd George had brought into his Cabinet to develop a new educational policy, worked with his civil servants to achieve one of the few successes of postwar reconstruction, the Fisher Act of 1918. Although the support of the civil servants was not crucial to the original passage of the act—Fisher's position in the Cabinet was the vital factor in that accomplishment—their loyalty to Fisher and their support of this policy came into play when the government began to back away from implementing Fisher's programs because he could not defend himself in person.[45] While Fisher was attending the League of Nations Conference, Selby-Bigge, then permanent secretary of the Board, had to defend the Board's (and Fisher's) policy, taking upon himself a larger role in the councils of state than ordinarily allowed a civil servant. The correspondence between Selby-Bigge and Fisher shows how they worked together to avert the threat to their policy. Selby-Bigge, when pressured, could reply that he could make no move without Fisher's knowledge and approval. Fisher, for his part, although willing to compromise, made known his firm intention to resign if the government attempted to abandon his policy.[46]

The civil servants of the Board must have found it difficult to cope with the unaccustomed experience of direct political pressure. Selby-Bigge revealed the strain he felt in a letter bringing Fisher up to date on recent events when he added, rather wistfully, "I wish you could come back and smite the philistines with the jawbone of the Secretary of the Middle Classes Union. It is very difficult for us to keep up our end."[47] The combination of Fisher's position in the Cabinet, his willingness to use that position to protect his department, and the arguments marshaled by Fisher's civil servants, all helped to preserve the basic elements of his policy.

Lewis Amherst Selby-Bigge epitomized the combination of academic achievement and administrative acumen for which the Board of Education's staff was so well known. He had been a Fellow and Lecturer in Philosophy at University College, Oxford, before he entered public service in 1894 as an assistant charity commissioner. Selby-Bigge edited several editions of eighteenth-century British philosophers (including one, *British Moralists*, that is still in use). Selby-Bigge moved to the Board of Education in 1902 where his tact and low-key manner later made him the logical successor to the more volatile and abrasive Robert Morant. (In 1911 Morant was forced out of the Board by a furor over a memorandum containing an unfortunately worded evaluation of elementary schoolteachers.) Selby-Bigge and H.A.L. Fisher had been at Winchester together and this probably cemented their close working relationship, but other political appointees also found him a congenial colleague. The Duchess of Atholl—Eustace Percy's parliamentary secretary between 1924 and 1929—remembered: "I soon came to value Sir

Amherst's great knowledge and balanced judgment; and after his time at the Board came to an end I spent some delightful weekends with him and his wife in their charming house in Sussex." On the other hand, John Dover Wilson, a subordinate official who very much admired E. K. Chambers, considered Selby-Bigge's gentlemanly and less forceful approach to administration a betrayal of the ideals Morant had set for the Board.[48]

When civil servants tried to oppose a policy supported by their minister, they enjoyed a much weaker position than when minister and officials worked together to oppose a policy imposed upon them from outside. At the beginning of Eustace Percy's tenure as president of the Board of Education under Baldwin's Conservative government of 1925, Percy, without consulting his civil servants, reached an agreement with the Cabinet on the restriction of the Board's expenditure. He then composed a circular for the LEAs, informing them of the changes in policy that would result from the reduced budget. Although every one of his senior officials opposed the wording of Circular 1371—and some expressed their opposition in very strong language—Percy went ahead with its issuance. The second secretary, E. K. Chambers, whose approaching retirement evidently weakened normal official discretion, used unusually strong language:

> It is my duty to co-operate loyally in carrying out any policy upon which you may decide. I hope you will forgive me, if I am wrong in thinking that in the present circumstances of the office it is also my duty, with all submission to tell you as clearly as possible what I feel about the policy expressed in the Draft Circular to Local Authorities. It fills me with serious dismay. I am convinced that it will be regarded, and justly regarded, by progressive Authorities, by the teaching profession, and by all interested in promoting education development, as a reversion to the policy of restricting that development which the Prime Minister was believed to have abandoned at the time of the General Election, and as completely inconsistent with that continuity of policy to which you are committed.

Chambers went on to characterize Percy's draft circular as less than straightforward in its justification of the cuts in expenditure. He criticized the plan to ration the state's share of local education expenditure because he thought it unfairly distributed the burden of economy measures among the LEAs. He deplored the use of the programs, which had been originally submitted to the Board by LEAs in order to facilitate planning for future development, as the present basis for restricting expenditure. Chambers predicted that LEAs would think these programs had been solicited in the first place to prevent progress rather than to evaluate educational development. Chambers, at the end of his memo, again assumed the submissive role of a neutral official: "I can only repeat in conclusion that the responsibility for policy is yours, and that I shall do my best to help in carrying out any policy you may adopt."[49]

Percy was not moved by the reservations so strongly expressed by his officials. At the end of November 1925, he issued Circular 1371 to the LEAs, informing them of new spending ceilings. The circular elicited an immediate, and very critical, response from the public. The volume of protest soon grew so great that the government could not ignore it. The public outcry gave Percy considerable leverage in the Cabinet when a final confrontation took place between Percy and Churchill at the end of February 1926. Baldwin, called in to arbitrate their differences, decided in favor of Percy, who recorded in his autobiography: "My circular was drowned in the flood of protests and my colleagues left me free thereafter to pursue my policy as best I could." Winston Churchill, who as Chancellor of the Exchequer had an interest in containing education expenditure, entertained suspicions that Percy had engineered the entire incident in order to get his own way, but Percy denied any such duplicity.[50] In March 1926 Percy withdrew Circular 1371. Although the Economy Bill passing through the House of Commons at this time permitted the Board of Education to disallow "excessive" expenditure of the LEAs, the government reluctantly retained the principle of the percentage grant (the system whereby the state underwrote a set proportion of local education expenditure) for financing state education.[51]

In this case, a strong adverse public reaction (a reaction that Board officials had predicted) forced Percy to modify his position. Percy's habit of addressing memoranda to his civil servants rather than soliciting memoranda from them best illustrates the difference between Percy's ministerial style and the styles of others who held the position of president of the Board of Education. Percy figured as "the only Minister who is his own Permanent Secretary" in a now standard history of English education written by G.A.N. Lowndes, who had good reason to know, having served in Percy's private office while a junior official at the Board of Education.[52] Percy's actions during this crisis demonstrate that he was quite capable of carrying out his decisions in the face of sustained opposition from his officials, although in this particular case the analysis of his officials proved accurate. Percy regularly went without the official support that H.A.L. Fisher, Lord Halifax, and Charles Trevelyan had relied upon. He also reduced the civil servants' role in policy making, and Board officials later looked back on his tenure in office as one that inflicted long-term damage on the department's authority and efficacy.[53]

A resolute minister could undoubtedly reject the advice of his officials. A strong and consistent stand by officials could either provide crucial support to a minister whose views civil servants found congenial or sway a minister whose views were unformed. A third situation often obtained when individuals or groups outside the government brought suggestions to the Board. During the second Labour government both the parliamentary secretary of the Board and a research group associated with the Labour party proposed multilateral or comprehensive schools as an alternative direction for English secondary education. Trevelyan apparently took no interest in this suggestion; and as we have seen, Board officials opposed it. With no sponsor inside the Board the idea made no headway until comprehensive schools became a part of Labour education policy after the Second World War. If Trevelyan had taken up the idea, he could have forced his civil servants to consider it seriously. If the civil servants had adopted the idea, they could have kept it alive inside the Board (as they had with the dispensing of public elementary school restrictions on free places), until they could persuade a sympathetic minister of its validity.

Civil servants were more successful at halting the progress of policies they opposed than they were at implementing policies they supported. The initiation of policy is a special kind of support; presumably one would not suggest a policy one did not support. The implementation of policy depended upon too many factors outside the control of the civil service, however, whereas successful opposition to a policy depended mainly on the attitude of the minister. Of the three attitudes a minister could take toward a policy (support, opposition, or indifference), two (opposition and indifference) allowed civil servants the opportunity to impose their own point of view. The officials faced certain defeat only if their minister actively supported the policy that they opposed. What effect could official "indifference" have on the development of education policy?

When C. P. Trevelyan became president of the Board of Education for the second time in 1929, he came into office determined to see the school-leaving age raised from fourteen to fifteen. After three years of struggle and the defeat of three different bills, Trevelyan resigned. His failure became a part of the larger failure of the second Labour government, a failure that many have claimed the civil service contributed to. The memoranda of Board officials reveal an attitude toward this issue as close to "indifference" as any evidence they left. This "indifference" was a studied, official neutrality that barely masked outright hostility.

Although the civil servants at the Board of Education had never really supported the raising of the school-leaving age to fifteen, they had never opposed it in principle. Officials invariably took the position that the time was not yet right for such a move. As early as 1917, the Reconstruction Committee on education had recommended that the school-leaving age be raised to fifteen, within five years of its being raised to fourteen. W. R. Davies (see appendix) and E. K. Chambers both wrote critiques of the Reconstruction Committee's proposals. The two civil servants did not agree on the proposal's overall merit. Davies believed the proposed policy "rash"; Chambers thought it amounted to secondary education for all and expressed sympathy for that ideal. Both agreed, however, that the elementary school system lacked teachers to handle the increased numbers that would result from raising the school-leaving age. In addition, they argued, elementary teachers could not cope with providing the curriculum necessary for older students. Rather than take what he characterized as "a leap in the dark," Davies recommended that they study the results of Fisher's proposed legislation (which would raise the school-leaving age to fourteen) before they took action to raise the school-leaving age any further.[54]

The issue came up again during Eustace Percy's tenure as president of the Board. The civil servants' view remained unchanged, and their opinion that the schools were not ready to deal with large numbers of older students found a congenial champion in Percy. When a deputation from the Association of Education Committees visited the Board in 1927 to express support for the Hadow Report and to urge that the school-leaving age be raised in 1933, Percy replied that he supported the Hadow Report but that the reorganization of the elementary schools also recommended by Hadow must precede the raising of the school-leaving age.[55]

With Trevelyan's return to the office only two years later, Board officials had to face the prospect of raising the school-leaving age immediately. At a meeting of the principals in charge of the territorial divisions, only E. L. Heath (see appendix), who administered the Southwest Division, foresaw no great difficulties in implementing Trevelyan's policy. H. E. Mann, who had responsibility for the Northeast Division, prefaced his detailed analysis with the assertion: "There are very obvious objections to raising the school age now at short notice." His enumeration of these included the shortage of teachers and accommodations and the inadequacy of the curriculum for older students. Mann's views were echoed by the observations of D. du B. Davidson and A. Maxwell-Lyte (see appendix), who had charge of the Northwest and Southeast Divisions, respectively. Mann, Davidson, and Maxwell-Lyte all pointed out the problem posed by church-supported voluntary schools.[56] The issue attracted the attention of Selby-Bigge who, although he had retired from the Board several years before, not only wrote Trevelyan to voice his opposition privately but even made his views public. He asserted that neither schools nor parents would readily adjust to such an abrupt change because the Hadow reorganization had not sufficiently progressed, arguments that echoed those of his former colleagues.[57]

Despite their objections, the civil servants at the Board recognized Trevelyan's determination to carry out his goal. Aubrey Symonds (see appendix), permanent secretary between 1926 and 1931, reported that the Board's inspectors thought that "if the Government came to the decision to raise the school-leaving age immediately the difficulties might be acute in some areas, but the proposal was not impracticable."[58] After this somewhat less than enthusiastic endorsement, Board officials set to work devising plans to carry out Trevelyan's policy should it become law.

Trevelyan's bills foundered on the problem posed by voluntary schools. These schools, primarily supported by religious groups, could not afford to provide education to their pupils for an extra year without financial aid from the state. Nonconformists opposed such state aid, whereas Roman Catholics insisted upon it. Since both nonconformists and Catholics represented important constituencies for the Labour party, Trevelyan found himself in a difficult dilemma. His civil servants did nothing to help him out of this difficulty.[59]

Although well aware of the intricacies of the problem, Board officials did not offer the constructive advice that might have been expected of them. A memorandum describing a meeting to consider the various difficulties in raising the school-leaving age ended with a note that the president of the Board was "reminded" of the connection between raising the school-leaving age and the problem of voluntary schools. The Board's deputy secretary from 1926 until 1929, E. B. Phipps (see appendix), composed a memorandum on aid to voluntary schools in which he discussed the possibility that, under special circumstances, the LEAs might give funds to church schools. In cases where a voluntary school was the only school serving an area and, therefore, would be required to accommodate additional students, Phipps believed that the school had a claim on public support. Phipps offered a straightforward solution to the problem of voluntary schools with substandard facilities; they had a choice between meeting a deadline to make repairs and releasing their school to the LEA. If the school did not elect one of these options then Phipps would condemn the school. "The mere effect of such action would probably bring a large proportion of Church School Managers to reason," Phipps predicted, adding disingenuously, "it would no doubt exasperate the Roman Catholics." Phipps's comments reveal an attitude not conducive to compromise.[60] Before the passage of the Education Act of 1936, Lord Halifax, who served as president of the Board of Education in the 1931 national government, managed to reach an agreement with the churches about their schools before the bill was introduced into Parliament.

The reaction of Board officials to Trevelyan's problems makes a striking contrast to their reaction to Fisher's difficulties ten years earlier. Trevelyan encountered many obstacles to the passage of his bills, and it is impossible to determine whether the civil servants' failure to help was a crucial factor in his defeat. The civil service must bear a measure of the responsibility for the disaster that overtook Labour's educational policy, however. If Trevelyan's officials had taken the aggressive and positive stance adopted by Fisher's officials, they might have been able to salvage some of Trevelyan's efforts, as they had for Fisher's policy. But Board officials did not agree with Trevelyan's policy. Trevelyan did not have at his command the strong support that H.A.L. Fisher had called upon from Selby-Bigge, for example. Before his promotion to permanent secretary at the Board of Education, Trevelyan's permanent secretary, Aubrey Symonds, had spent his entire career, from 1896 to 1926, at the Local Government Board and the Ministry of Health. Not only did Symonds lack Selby-Bigge's expertise but the precarious state of his health prevented him from taking a similarly leading role in the formulation of policy at this critical juncture.[61]

Conclusion

The outbreak of the Second World War marked the end of a singularly frustrating period for those interested in education. After almost twenty years, the school-leaving age remained at fourteen. Although the demand for secondary education had increased dramatically since the First World War, special (free) places still accounted for less than half of the secondary school places. Education estimates had suffered massive cuts during the economy drives of 1922, 1925, and 1931. The Board of Education implemented only one positive measure between the Fisher Act of 1918 and the Butler Act of 1944, which was the reorganization of elementary schools along the lines recommended by the Consultative Committee in 1926. This had allowed LEAs to develop an expanded and more advanced curriculum for students who voluntarily remained in these schools beyond the school-leaving age of fourteen.

Any assessment of the civil servants' role in this history must take into consideration the sphere of influence available to them. We cannot hold officials responsible for the worldwide depression of the 1920s or even the fiscal philosophy of the Treasury—a philosophy so pervasive that it could be shared by Labour's Chancellor of the Exchequer Philip Snowden and Conservative minister of health and party leader Neville Chamberlain. Brian Simon has described the conflicts with the Cabinet and the pressures of public opinion that buffeted the Board of Education.[62]

Yet Board officials were not mere ciphers. They had enthusiastically supported H.A.L. Fisher in his attempts to reform English education. They stubbornly and, in some cases, effectively opposed Treasury attacks on the education estimates. Within the fiscal, statutory, and political constraints imposed upon them, civil servants shaped the character of state-supported education. Under the supervision of the Board of Education, English secondary schools continued to carry out the traditional function of English secondary education. The training of an elite, previously the exclusive province of the public schools, became the mission of state-aided grammar schools.

Board officials tried to ensure that the education offered in the nation's secondary schools provided a suitable preparation for the country's future leaders. In doing so they certainly did not present a monolithic stone face of unanimity.[63] Nevertheless, a general consensus pervaded the Board that this education should consist of an academic, nonvocational course of study that would mold the character as well as train the mind. Civil servants might believe that the state should draw secondary school students from a broader range of the population, but they retained the notion that only a small proportion of the population deserved a secondary education.[64] Civil servants also opposed every suggestion to change the basic nature of the education provided by these schools, which at that time gave a university-preparatory course of study patterned after the education offered by the public schools.

Despite the constitutional, political, and economic realities that circumscribed the civil servant's scope of action, Board officials managed to shape the English education policy in accordance with their views. Their policies in turn encouraged the development of an educational system geared for the selection and sustenance of a small, meritocratic elite remarkably similar to the small, aristocratic elite that had successfully governed England for so long. As R. H. Tawney remarked, the civil servants of the Board of Education were themselves the products of this system, a system they consciously and purposefully utilized to staff their department. In carrying out their duties Board officials strove, by and large successfully, to defend and to sustain this system.

The characteristic education shared by Board of Education civil servants thus did not belong only to the remote childhood years of these men. Their educational credentials did not simply provide them with the means to obtain congenial employment. Their experience of a public school and Oxford education continued to bear upon their careers, both by enhancing their prospects for success and by providing them with many of the framing concepts they used to carry out their work. In this way social identity and professional identity became inextricably intertwined, providing, at least in this case, the mechanism that linked the processes of social class sustained by educational institutions to the formulation of education policy. At the Ministry of Agriculture, in contrast, the development of a professional identity served to mitigate the influence of social class on government policy.

4 The Ministry of Agriculture: Friend to the Worker

■ *The farmer strolling 'round his paddock*
The fisherman in quest of haddock,
Unite to sing with grateful glee
The praises of their Ministry.
Rude simple souls, they lack that store
Of expert scientific lore
On which alone success depends
And this their kind Department
sends.
For, if calamities befall
The men who till, the men who trawl—

. . . .

The staff is ready in a trice
To help them with its best advice
On land or sea, in drought or storm,
Sent free of charge in pamphlet form.

English agriculture suffered a series of calamities immediately after the First World War. Foreign supplies of grain flooded the world market and financial crisis gripped the country—a combination that devastated the agricultural community. The Lloyd George coalition's agricultural policy collapsed along with the price of wheat, which fell by almost half between 1920 and 1923.[1] That policy, embodied in the 1920 Agricultural Act, had committed the state to maintain a minimum price for cereal crops and to protect the wages paid to agricultural workers through a wages board that negotiated and ratified wage agreements.

The expense involved in actually providing subsidies to farmers in the face of such a drastic decline in prices proved too great a shock for the policy to survive. Although the 1920 act contained a provision guaranteeing a four-year grace period before its repeal, the government repealed it within eighteen months of its passage.[2] The abrupt return of a laissez-faire policy would test the ability of the agricultural sector to respond to market forces unprotected by government intervention. Farmers coped with falling prices by cutting costs, and reducing wages most speedily accomplished that. Agricultural laborers, after 1921 lacking the protection guaranteed them by the wages boards, therefore shouldered the burden of the interwar collapse of English agriculture.

Throughout the interwar period civil servants had to consider the policy questions raised by the situation of agricultural labor. The energy that officials brought to this task does not conform to the negativism popularly ascribed to the civil service. At a time when successive governments remained wedded to fiscal retrenchment and laissez-faire policies despite widespread suffering and hardship caused by the depression, Agriculture civil servants did what they could to mitigate the predicament of agricultural workers. Officials pressed successive governments to take steps to redress workers' grievances with respect to a range of issues including the regulation of agricultural wages, the place of tied cottages in rural life, and the proper governmental response to rural unemployment.[3]

Recruitment and promotion practices unique in the civil service sustained the activist tradition adhered to by Agriculture officials. Prior to 1919 Agriculture used both patronage appointment and special examination rather than open competition to fill vacancies. In addition, unlike most other ministries, Agriculture routinely utilized promotion from the lower ranks to recruit junior officials. As permanent secretary Thomas Elliott had explained to the 1912 Royal Commission on the Civil Service, the department's interest in filling its ranks with those knowledgeable of the practice of agriculture led them away from the open competition type. The men recruited by the department had very different educational credentials from those who entered Agriculture by open competition after 1919. Open competition produced three-quarters of the Oxbridge graduates and two-thirds of the Headmasters' Conference school alumni among Agriculture officials (see figures 4 and 5 and table 8).

Agriculture's recruitment practices before 1919 created a broader social ambience among its officials than in other ministries. The appointment of Rowland Prothero (later Lord Ernle) in 1916 and Daniel Hall in 1917 as, respectively, president and permanent secretary of the Board of Agriculture (see appendix for both) reinforced the cult of the expert that suffused the department. With credentials both scholarly and scientific, Prothero and Hall oversaw the development and implementation of the policies of subsidies and wage regulation that produced such bountiful wartime harvests. Their success stood as an inspiration to the officials who came after them.

The sustained efforts of Agriculture civil servants to achieve their clearly defined ends demonstrate that, despite occasional disagreement among themselves, they had a consistent vision of what government policy ought to be. As in the case of the Board of Education, the combination of persistence and consistency on the part of permanent officials enjoyed a measure of success in shaping that policy. But Agriculture officials, unlike Education officials, did not identify with or profit from the agricultural system as it stood. Rather, their position as expert outsiders allowed the development of a vision of an English agriculture, both efficiently productive and humane, that did not reflect the perspective of either farmers or landlords. They did not hesitate to employ the power of the state to help make that vision a reality, but the state did not readily extend that power to them, especially during the 1920s, a decade when fiscal considerations outweighed all others.

The analysis below falls into three parts. First, a description of the development of the Ministry of Agriculture outlines its administrative structure. Next, an examination of the civil servants' discussion of wages boards, rural unemployment, and tied cottages shows their distinctive view of rural labor relations and the consistency with which they pressed their views on successive governments during the interwar decades. Finally, an assessment of the ministry's leadership defines the extent to which the energy and consistency of civil servants actually shaped the development of government policy.

Origins and Organization

The repeal of the Corn Laws in 1846 committed England to a policy of free trade in agriculture that lasted virtually unchallenged until the twentieth century. Even so, within two decades the state began to take upon itself powers and duties to regulate agriculture, at first chiefly to control animal and plant diseases. The Board of Agriculture, formed in 1889, combined the administration of the Contagious Diseases (Animals) Act and the Destructive Insects Act (tasks previously discharged first by the Home Office and then by a committee of the Privy Council) with the collection of agricultural statistics and the supervision and coordination of agricultural research and education. In 1903 the Board acquired the administration of Kew Gardens and the oversight of the nation's fisheries as part of its duties. After the First World War the Board became the Ministry of Agriculture and Fisheries, absorbing the duties of the Food Production Department (which originally had been set up to deal with the difficulties of feeding England during the war) but losing its responsibilities for forests with the creation of the Forestry Commission.[4]

The Board of Agriculture, like the Board of Education, developed first out of a piecemeal accretion of the state's powers during the nineteenth century. The state's relationship to agriculture then underwent a drastic transformation during the First World War. England's dependence on imported food combined with the efficacy of Germany's submarine warfare compelled the government to intervene in the conduct of agriculture in order to expand food production. Under the supervision of the Food Production Department (created in 1917, this semi-autonomous department reported to the president of the Board of Agriculture) farmers plowed under thousands of acres of pasturage and planted wheat and oats, leading to a tremendous increase in cereal production. The Corn Production Act of 1917 administered by the Board of Agriculture produced this dramatic result by providing subsidies for farmers and regulating wage settlements for agricultural workers.[5] The success of this program in wartime led the Lloyd George coalition to include it in their postwar program of legislation; it was passed into law but then was almost immediately repealed.

The Ministry of Agriculture and Fisheries had responsibility for a wide range of programs from the West Mersea Shell Crushing Station to women's institutes. The bulk of the ministry's duties, however, involved the compilation and dissemination of information on topics of special interest to the agricultural communities. The problems posed by plant and animal diseases, for instance, had always been counted among the department's responsibilities. In common with all ministries, Agriculture had a Finance Division to supervise departmental expenditure and an Establishment Division to administer personnel matters. A Fisheries Division took charge of all questions related to fish and fishing. Agriculture also had a separate Welsh Office, although their Welsh secretary did not hold so high a position in the ministry's hierarchy as did the Board of Education's Welsh secretary.

The Ministry of Agriculture organized its various other duties into divisions that roughly corresponded with the general topics of agricultural economics, agricultural land, and agricultural research and education (see table 10). At the beginning of the period, the permanent secretary, the second secretary, and the chief scientific adviser each administered one of these divisions. Not until 1928 did the addition of principal assistant secretary positions permit a more specialized organization within the ministry. In the 1930s the ministry's responsibilities expanded to include marketing schemes and trade relations. It carried out all these duties with a relatively small staff. The number of administrative class officials stood at only thirty-five in 1927, increasing to forty-five by 1937.[6]

The pre-First World War Board of Agriculture, like the Board of Education, did not recruit its administrative staff through open examination. Instead, Agriculture used patronage appointment and special examination to fill vacancies but, unlike most other departments of state, often turned to promotion from the lower levels of the civil service as well. The Board of Agriculture thus offered a greater prospect for advancement to the bright and ambitious among the department's Second Division staff. This must have enhanced morale within the department, but it also must have lowered the standing of the department within the civil service. H. E. Dale, a former Agriculture official who wrote on the civil service, thought that the status of

TABLE 10. *Ministry of Agriculture and Fisheries, 1920*

Agriculture Advisory Council — Minister — Administrative Council[a]

Minister
↓
Parliamentary Secretary

Deputy Minister of Fisheries

Fisheries Secretary: H. G. Maurice	F.L.C. Floud	Sir Lawrence Weaver	Sir Daniel Hall	Welse Secretary: C. Bryner Jones
Fisheries Division	Secretariat, Finance, and Economic Division	Land and Supplies Division	Intelligence Division	Welsh Office
All fisheries business	1. Establishment Division a. Registry, typists, messengers, charwomen b. All staff questions, appointments, and promotions c. Accomodations 2. Finance Division 3. Economic Division a. Statistics b. Publications c. Rural industries d. Farm workers 4. Woman Adviser, Women's Institutes	1. Land Settlement and Supplies Division a. Small holdings and allotments b. Buildings c. Supplies d. Estate management e. Purchases 2. Land improvement a. Cultivation of land b. Land drainage and reclamation c. Tithe, copyhold, and commons	1. Education and Research Division a. Country educaton b. Research and technical advice c. Training of ex-servicemen 2. Livestock Division a. Improvement of livestock and horse breeding b. Dairying c. Small livestock d. Rats 3. Animal Diseases Division	Welsh business in commenction with: a. Land settlement b. Education c. Cultivation of land

Source: Reports of committees appointed to investigate the staffing and methods of work in the Ministries of Labour, Agriculture, and Fisheries, and the Royal Commission of Sugar Supplies, Appendix A, 32, Cmd. 1069 (1920).

Note: The Royal Botanic Gardens, Kew, and the Agriculture Wage Board are extradepartmental, except as regards questions of staff and finances, which are dealt with by the Secretariat of the Ministry.

a. For legal business only: F. A. Jones, Legal Adviser; for Welsh business only: C. Bryner Jones.

the Board's First Division staff, compared to that of other departments' staff recruited in a more orthodox manner, suffered as a result of such promotions.[7] The personnel policies of the Board of Agriculture, unlike those of other departments of state and open competition recruitment, rewarded expert rather than general knowledge. Consequently, Agriculture's staff had a broader social base than was generally characteristic of the civil service as a whole.

The Ministry of Agriculture and Agricultural Workers

The plight of the agricultural worker worsened during the interwar period as depression eroded hard-won gains. Agriculture officials strove to soften the blow of depression and to secure for agricultural labor a more equitable position within the agricultural community. Civil servants advanced and defended measures to provide agricultural workers with unemployment relief and unemployment insurance. They attempted to bring an end to the system of tied cottages, which made workers answerable to the farmer as both employee and tenant. Civil servants also worked for the reinstatement of wages boards. This mechanism for the negotiation and enforcement of wage agreements had been part of the 1917 Corn Production Act, and the 1920 Agricultural Act had supposedly put the earlier reforms on a permanent footing. Thanks in part to the efforts of civil servants, the repeal of the 1920 act did not mean the permanent loss of this measure, which had so improved the lot of the agricultural worker.

The Regulation of Wages

Agriculture officials had supported the regulation of wages through the mechanism of a wages board first created by the 1917 Corn Production Act. The Agricultural Policy Subcommittee of the Reconstruction Committee had originally recommended this measure. The Selborne Committee (as it was known) numbered among its members later permanent secretary and chief scientific adviser at Agriculture, A. D. Hall, and its report has been described as "a sort of Bible for the Board of Agriculture."[8] Ministry officials believed that the dismantling of this apparatus in 1921 and its replacement by the far less effective mechanism of conciliation committees—without the power to enforce anything but unanimous agreements—left the worker at the mercy of the farmer. Weekly wages, which in 1921 had reached a high of over 46s, fell by some 25 percent (to 31s) during 1922, the first year that the conciliation committees came into operation.[9]

In 1923 when a senior staff officer, Russell Edwin Stanley (see appendix), reported on the operation of the conciliation committees, wages had fallen to 28s.[10] The work of the committees had come to a standstill in many places, according to Stanley, who blamed this on the interference of the National Farmers Union (NFU) in jurisdictional disputes between the National Union of Agricultural Workers and the Land Workers Union. The committees' difficulties in reaching agreements during 1922 stemmed from the farmers' desire to cut weekly wages further. The ministry had trouble persuading the committees even to meet in 1923 because of the impasse of the previous year.

Neither the carrots nor the sticks at the ministry's command could bring much pressure to bear upon farmers. After the passage of the Agricultural Rates Act, which gave tax relief to farmers, a Ministry of Agriculture letter to farmers urged them to raise wages and warned that similar legislation favorable to farmers might otherwise be more difficult to obtain in the future. Stanley observed: "This communication seemed to produce no effect whatever on the employers' attitude on the Conciliation Committees." In his review of the situation in those areas where agreements had not been reached, Stanley cited the example of south and east Berkshire, where "the employers have made exceptionally drastic cuts since the Wages Board was abolished, reducing wages from 42s to 33s within only two months of that event, and only a month later bringing their proposal to the Conciliation Committee down to 30s."[11] Stanley's analysis outlined a rapidly deteriorating situation where the government had no authority to resolve the deadlock between farmers and farmworkers. At that time, however, both the government and the minister of agriculture opposed wages boards.[12]

With the formation of the first Labour government in 1924, ministry officials could look forward to a return of the wages boards. Given their attitude toward the conciliation committees, their approval of wages boards is not surprising. Early on, Stanley recommended a structure that consisted of local boards with a central board of appeals, and this concept gathered a good deal of support within the ministry. R. J. Thompson, an assistant secretary (see appendix) who noted the farmers' opposition to any centralized body with the power to fix wages, also endorsed local boards with a central board of appeals. Without exception, civil servants opposed giving the minister responsibility over the wage settlements achieved by wages boards. Stanley pointed out that such an arrangement would allow a reactionary government to obstruct the work of the wages boards. Stanley recommended instead that the government should enforce the penalties for breaches of wage rates, because a worker seeking satisfaction through the courts would be too vulnerable to victimization. He warned: "In the present state of the N.F.U. [National Farmers Union], the worker bringing a case against his employers would undoubtedly be a marked man throughout his area and would probably never again obtain a job in agriculture." Stanley also opposed exemptions to permit lower wages for "slow" workers, both because the administrative apparatus required to administer such a loophole would be too complicated and because the misuse of such a provision might lead to a "speed-up."[13]

Ministry officials did not support a statutory minimum wage. Thompson argued that some farmers might not be able to pay it, a situation that would lead to their reducing their workforce. He worried as well that the impact of a 30s minimum in some areas could lead to more use of part-time labor and the increasing casualization of workers. He also believed that such state action could weaken union organization. Stanley recommended that the government include a minimum wage in their bill but be prepared to drop it if too much opposition materialized.[14]

The chief concern of officials was to protect agricultural workers from low wages. Even the ministry's permanent secretary Sir Francis Floud (see appendix), a man who consistently opposed government intervention in the mechanisms of the marketplace, urged the government to take a "bold line." He agreed that "a reasonable rate of wages must be regarded as a first charge on any industry," and that agricultural wages were too low. A.G.L. Rogers, a first class clerk (see appendix), detailed many examples of how farmers abused their workers: "I was told how pigsties and cowhouses are concreted and made weatherproof," he reported, "while labourers' cottages are neglected and allowed to fall out of repair." Stanley best summarized the position of the agricultural labor as understood by Ministry of Agriculture officials when he wrote: "Agricultural labourers are now back to pre-war conditions of working merely for body-and-soul minimum of shelter and food. Inarticulate and unorganized, he is at the mercy of the powerfully organized and still fairly prosperous farmer."[15]

Noel Buxton, Labour minister of agriculture, did not balk at these recommendations urging him to do something for agricultural workers, who formed an important part of his constituency in Norfolk. In addition, Buxton's parliamentary secretary, Walter Smith, was president of the National Union of Agricultural Workers. The Agricultural Wages (Regulation) Act passed under Buxton's leadership reestablished a central wages board and county wages committees. The county wages committees consisted of equal members of representatives of workers and farmers augmented by two appointed members and an independent chairman. A Liberal party amendment supported by the Conservatives took away the power of the central wages board to amend the wages rates and hours set by the county committees. Even so, the passage of this measure constituted one of the few successes of the first Labour government.[16] Permanent officials actively supported this achievement, which worked to sustain a gradual increase in wages during the remainder of the interwar period.

Rural Unemployment

The operation of wages boards protected the earnings of farmworkers, but they could not assist the man who did not have a job. Unemployment dominated discussions of the condition of agricultural workers, constituting the most important feature of rural, as well as urban, labor relations during the 1920s and 1930s. Since agricultural workers did not enjoy the benefits of unemployment insurance, they did not have to register at labor exchanges. As a consequence, statistics on rural unemployment are scattered and unreliable. The number of those regularly employed in agriculture, however, dropped steadily: from 685,000 in 1921 to 620,000 in 1923, rebounding to 650,000 in 1927, and declining again to 616,000 in 1931 and 511,000 in 1939. High unemployment in urban areas precluded the ready assimilation of agricultural workers by industry.[17]

Officials encountered the effects of large-scale unemployment in a variety of guises. The civil servants of the Ministry of Agriculture considered policies both to mitigate the effects of unemployment and to reduce the incidence of unemployment. These included public works schemes, the inclusion of agricultural workers in unemployment insurance to relieve rural unemployment, and land settlement to relieve urban unemployment.

Chief scientific adviser Sir Daniel Hall insisted that one of the weaknesses of British agriculture consisted of its inability to absorb large numbers of workers. Efforts to make agriculture an economic industry, as Sir Francis Floud so often urged, would inevitably have led to a decrease in the numbers employed on the land. Ministry of Agriculture officials supported schemes to settle men on their own holdings because they considered owner-occupiers both better farmers and better citizens. Civil servants, however, did not believe that programs to encourage this class could make any great impact on unemployment. The chief beneficiaries of such programs would have to be tenants who would be able to purchase the farms they leased. However, aiding this group would not reduce unemployment because they already made their living on the land.

If agriculture, unaided, could not absorb its own excess labor, then it could hardly make any appreciable dent in the burgeoning urban and industrial unemployment. Writing in 1926, Sir Francis Floud pointed out that only a substantial increase in the acreage under cultivation would enable agriculture to employ many more workers. An increase of the requisite magnitude would necessitate government subsidies to stimulate and to support increased agricultural production. Not only would such a program be open to the objection of expense, but Floud questioned the fundamental feasibility of resettling urban workers in a rural environment. Agriculture is skilled work, Floud argued, and consequently "it is madness to expect any large number of urban unemployed can or would wish to be absorbed on the land without previous experience or knowledge."[18]

Ministry of Agriculture officials remained skeptical that agriculture could make any significant contribution to the reduction of urban unemployment.

However, they were favorably inclined toward public works schemes to relieve distress caused by unemployment and underemployment among rural workers. In 1922 Ministry officials forcefully defended state-funded drainage schemes, which they thought had relieved much distress in rural areas. Opposition to this program came from both the Treasury and the Ministry of Labour. Assistant secretary A.T.A. Dobson (see appendix), the ministry's representative on the interdepartmental Committee on the Relief of Unemployment, reported that Horace Wilson of the Ministry of Labour (see appendix) objected to the possibility that such programs might lead farmers "to suppose that they can unload their spare labour on unemployment schemes." In the face of this opposition, the best Dobson could do was to have Agriculture's views of this rural public works program included along with Labour's in the committee's final report. In bringing his minister (at that time, Arthur Griffith-Boscawen)[19] up to date on this matter, Dobson stated the department's support of the drainage schemes in very strong terms:

> There is no doubt whatever that it has, in a most complete way, relieved rural unemployment—and that there is rural unemployment cannot for one moment be denied whatever line the officials of the Ministry of Labour may take as to the previous unwillingness of employers and employees to come into the Unemployment Insurance Act.[20]

Public-funded land drainage is easily defended. Relatively inexpensive, almost all its expense consisted of labor costs, so it was an efficient form of unemployment relief. And drainage is absolutely necessary to the conduct of agriculture in many parts of England, particularly East Anglia (where even the Romans financed large-scale drainage projects).[21] Although farmers had to be responsible for the ditching necessary to drain their own land, their work would serve no useful purpose if the region also was not drained, which required construction on a scale beyond the means of individual farmers. In order for this work to get done at all there had to be some kind of support from the state. The Cabinet approved continuation of the land drainage program.

Land drainage remained a feature of government policy throughout the interwar period, representing a successful, though small-scale, exercise in public works. Between 1919 and 1926, the ministry made grants totaling £850,000 to carry out much needed improvements in land drainage that cost £1,250,000. Less than 1 percent of Unemployment Grants funding, the auspices under which such projects fell, went to drainage schemes, however. The elements of the argument for state-funded drainage had so much force that the Drainage Act—which consolidated drainage problems implemented by the state in the 1920s—was in 1930 carried through Parliament by Christopher Addison with the support of all parties. In order to make this argument in the first place, however, civil servants had to be at least as attuned to the needs of agriculture as to the needs of the state. Agriculture officials, even Floud, did not reject state intervention in agriculture when it took the form of land drainage.[22]

Unemployment Insurance

To provide work is one obvious way for government to alleviate unemployment. Providing relief is another response. Agricultural workers had not been included under the original 1911 scheme of unemployment insurance, which had applied only to building, engineering, and shipbuilding. They had also been excluded from the much more comprehensive 1920 act (along with domestic servants and civil servants), largely because both farmers and laborers remained opposed to inclusion.[23] In 1920 high grain prices and full employment in agriculture still obtained, and no one wanted to bear the cost of agriculture's participation in the national system of unemployment insurance. This left unemployed workers dependent upon the mercy of the local Boards of Guardians that administered poor relief and private charity. The continued distress in rural areas after 1920 because of unemployment and underemployment began to move opinion within the Ministry of Agriculture and among agricultural laborers themselves toward accepting the need to include them among those groups covered by unemployment insurance.

Opposition still persisted in many quarters, however, including the Ministry of Labour. In February 1931, H. L. French objected to the indecisive tone of a memorandum on the subject prepared jointly by Agriculture and Labour, but his counterpart at the Labour Ministry, J.F.G. Price, unsympathetically suggested that the disagreement be ironed out at the ministerial level or taken to the prime minister. In response to this challenge, Agriculture's permanent secretary, Francis Floud, then wrote H. B. Usher in the Prime Minister's Office, setting out the Ministry of Agriculture's view of the memorandum of evidence prepared with the Ministry of Labour. He pointed out that the workers were pressing harder for the government to do something and warned that "there is no doubt that the absence of any promise by the Government to deal with the matter is keenly resented in the rural areas and is creating a difficult situation for the Party."[24]

In the end, nothing came of all these discussions. The Unemployment Insurance Act of 1931 (known as the "Anomalies" Bill) merely streamlined the insurance system by ending some abuses and depriving certain classes of the unemployed (married women, for instance) of benefit.[25] It did not make any major innovations in the system, such as extension of coverage to agriculture. Christopher Addison, who had taken on the ministry for the second Labour government after Noel Buxton's retirement to the House of Lords, did not have time to do more. Next month the government collapsed and

Ramsay MacDonald formed a national government to meet the financial and economic crisis.

Unemployment insurance for agricultural workers surfaced again in 1933 when the national government began to prepare for a major revision of the administration of unemployment relief.[26] In July 1933, French reported that the Ministry of Labour had finally come around to the view that agriculture should be included under unemployment insurance and recommended the wholehearted support of this proposal. The acceptance of the principle of inclusion did not resolve the questions of when and how it should be implemented. The next month representatives of Agriculture and Labour met to discuss the government's forthcoming comprehensive bill on unemployment. Agriculture officials reiterated that the government ought immediately to provide unemployment insurance for agricultural workers, but Labour officials were still skeptical about the feasibility of doing that. The Ministry of Labour regarded industrial workers as their own constituency and also had no wish to burden further the already insolvent system of unemployment insurance.[27] As a compromise, French suggested that the bill should allow for the inclusion of agriculture at some later date, but Ministry of Labour officials sought to weaken French's proposal by having the bill merely authorize a statutory commission to consider the practicability of a scheme for agriculture. They argued that the government must allow for the eventuality that such a plan might prove impossible to devise.[28]

Later in August French had to grapple with a setback within his own department. Walter Elliot, the national government's minister of agriculture, did not wish to divert department energies to deal with unemployment insurance because he thought the ministry was too busy preparing new marketing schemes.[29] Even so, Elliot authorized French to discuss the issue with the parliamentary secretary, Earl de la Warr. In reporting his own views to de la Warr, French warned that an adverse decision made for "temporary reasons" could have a "permanent effect." The parliamentary secretary saw the force of this argument and encouraged French to elaborate his views and present them to the minister.

French set out four options for the ministry: (1) continued exclusion, (2) immediate inclusion, (3) a statutory commission on practicability, and (4) delayed inclusion. French recommended the fourth option, but the minister recorded his preference for the third option. Charles Nathan, a principal in the Economics Division, wrote to P. Y. Blunden, an assistant secretary in the Unemployment Insurance Department (see appendix for both) at the Ministry of Labour, informing him of Elliot's opinions on the issues: "The Minister's very definite view is that the Government should not incur in the Bill a statutory commitment—even a conditional one—to introduce a scheme of unemployment insurance for agricultural workers." Nathan added that the minister did like Blunden's idea for a commission to consider the issue, but he expressed his own view that this policy "cannot of course be expected to satisfy the Agricultural Workers' Organizations."[30]

In September, the minister of labour, Henry Betterton, wrote to Walter Elliot urging that in the bill unemployment insurance be extended to include agriculture. Policy decisions taken at the Cabinet level explain this turnabout. Earlier in the year, Betterton had bowed to pressure led by Neville Chamberlain to centralize the administration of relief for the able-bodied unemployed.[31] Now he had to convince Elliot that if agricultural workers became eligible for assistance under the proposed reorganization of unemployment relief, then they should have an insurance scheme as well.[32] Nathan, who agreed with the fourth option listed by French, had predicted that the minister of labour would also press for that option.[33] Sir Francis Floud—who had served most of his official career at Agriculture but was then permanent secretary of the Ministry of Labour—also agreed with Nathan, although he observed:

> From the selfish point of view of the interest of agriculture, I feel that there is a great deal to be said in favour of the argument that agriculture should not under this Bill be brought within a contributory scheme of insurance since agriculture workers would get substantial benefits under the assistance scheme without payment.[34]

This would, of course, involve the very inconsistency that Betterton now sought to avoid.[35]

Within a week of this exchange the ministers of labour and agriculture, each accompanied by his parliamentary secretary and a senior official from his department, met and agreed to have the unemployment assistance bill provide for a statutory commission to bring into operation an unemployment insurance scheme that included agriculture. The work of the ministry's officials played a crucial role in this success by pressing their views in the face of the initial hostility of the Ministry of Labour and the indifference of their own minister. The Unemployment Insurance (Agriculture) Act of 1936 finally extended unemployment insurance to agricultural labor.

The successful passage of this act did not end the ministry's involvement in controversies about unemployment insurance for agricultural workers, however. Within two years the insurance fund for relieving unemployment among agricultural workers began to show a surplus. Disagreement inevitably arose about how best to utilize this bonus. Farmers naturally favored reducing contributions whereas workers pressed for an increase in benefits.

The Ministry of Agriculture consistently supported the position of the agricultural laborer in this issue. R. E. Stanley—who in 1937 at the age of fifty-three had finally been promoted to principal—cited both the preference of the workers for increasing the benefits and the inequity of the discrepancy between "the treatment of agriculture workers when unemployed and that accorded to industrial workers." Stanley also advocated raising the 30s upper limit on the benefit. Stanley concluded: "From the point of view solely of making agricultural employment more attractive there is a lot to be said for using the surplus entirely for improving the benefit rate for men." E. L. Mitchell, an assistant secretary in the Livestock and Labour Division (see appendix), strongly supported Stanley's analysis of the situation, arguing that improving the conditions of employment for agricultural workers would produce a "a more contented and more efficient labour force."[36]

Both the permanent secretary and the minister endorsed these recommendations, and the ministry continued to press for improved benefits for agricultural laborers to lessen the disparity between their benefits and those paid to industrial workers. In December 1938, the Ministry of Agriculture recommended to the Unemployment Insurance Statutory Committee that they use the surplus funds to increase benefits. The Statutory Committee followed the ministry's recommendations, raising the ceiling on benefits from 30s to 33s, increasing the adult dependent benefit from 7s to 9s, and increasing the adult benefit from 14s to 15s, although they also reduced contributions. At the end of 1939, officials again argued that the ceiling should be raised and that the benefit rates for agriculture should increase if those for industrial workers increased.[37] Officials thus closed the interwar decades as they began, endeavoring to protect and improve the situation of agricultural workers.

Here, and throughout negotiations taking place at different times and under the auspices of different governments, Agriculture civil servants demonstrated their concern for the position of agricultural laborers. The issue of unemployment insurance finally proved amenable to compromise, but the impetus to reach that compromise came from permanent officials rather than from political leaders or even the parties most directly involved, the farmers and farmworkers. Civil servants manifested this same concern for the plight of agricultural workers when they wrestled with the problem of tied cottages. However, with this issue, they did not enjoy the same degree of success.

Tied Cottages

Tied cottages, cottages controlled by the farmer and let to his employees at nominal rents, constituted an important element in the network of rural labor relations. Between one-third and one-half of agricultural workers lived in tied cottages, and the shortage of housing in rural areas gave farmers who could provide a cottage along with a job considerable leverage over their workers.[38] Late in 1929, after the Labour party returned to power and Noel

Buxton resumed the office of minister of agriculture, ministry officials took the opportunity to bring up the question of tied cottages.

R. E. Stanley began the interdepartmental discussion with an analysis of the role of the tied cottage in the rural economy. Stanley, who had served as secretary to the Agricultural Wages Board reconstituted by the first Labour government, admitted that the chief advantage of tied cottages lay in their convenience for both farmer and worker. Their disadvantage was that living in a tied cottage increased a worker's dependence upon the employer's goodwill. Agricultural workers resented this position and pressed for the outright abolition of tied cottages, a move opposed by the farmers. Stanley urged a "vigorous policy" to repair existing rural housing and to provide more housing. Because the low wages of agricultural labor prohibited economic rents, he argued that the state must provide subsidies for rural housing. Stanley thought that Health should administer such a program due to the "notorious apathy" of local authorities.[39]

A policy of subsidies would necessarily take some time to produce results, and Stanley therefore suggested that the government do something immediately "to ameliorate the unfair position in which the tied cottage often places the agricultural worker." To underline the urgency of the matter, Stanley cited cases of intimidation of workers paid less than the minimum wage, which had come to the ministry's attention in their administration of the Wages Act. To combat such abuses Stanley recommended legislation that would require one month's notice prior to eviction, during which time the worker could appeal to the local wages committee. The wages committee could be empowered to give a worker a certificate for continued occupation until he found another cottage, if they found that he had been fired "without fair cause."[40]

Stanley's view of the matter generated some controversy within the ministry. The permanent secretary, C.J.H. Thomas, wrote that he had "grave objections" to these proposals. He agreed that providing a one-month period of grace for the worker would alleviate many cases of hardship among agricultural workers, but he thought it could also easily cause hardship to farmers. In another analysis of Stanley's proposals, A. D. Stocks, the legal adviser of the ministry (see appendix), commented that although Stanley's suggestions were an application of the Rent Restriction Act, they also constituted "a somewhat drastic amendment of the general law of master and servant." He predicted that farmers would strenuously oppose what they would regard as interference. He also cautioned that controlling rural cottages might make their owners reluctant to rent to agricultural workers. Stocks recommended that, if such legislation were introduced, the county court would make a better tribunal than the wages committee since county court judges already had similar responsibilities under the Rent Restriction Act.

Principal assistant secretary H. L. French agreed with the criticisms made by Stocks. He also added that Stanley's notion of "without fair cause" remained too vague. French, like Stocks, believed that farmers would oppose legislation, but he did not address the problem because he regarded it as a political question, which therefore lay beyond the province of a civil servant. Despite French's criticisms, he remained sympathetic to Stanley's definition of the problem, agreeing that agricultural workers had a "perfectly justifiable grievance," a grievance that "is a source of constant irritation."[41]

In December 1929 the permanent secretary sent the record of this discussion to the minister, Noel Buxton. Thomas noted his own support of Mr. Stocks's proposal that county court judges would constitute the best tribunal, if the minister wished to take the matter further. Buxton decided to send a proposal to the Ministry of Health, which embodied the main features of Stanley's scheme with the modifications suggested by Stocks, French, and Thomas, the permanent secretary. The letter sent to Arthur Greenwood under Buxton's name put the case strongly (not too surprising since Stanley drafted the text): "Some steps ought to be taken to deprive farmers of their present arbitrary right to evict a worker from a cottage at will."[42]

The Ministry of Health did not embrace these suggestions with enthusiasm. French, in a memorandum written on New Year's Day, 1930, described an interview with E. R. Forber (see appendix) at the Ministry of Health. According to French, Forber, speaking for the ministry, had argued that Health should not have the responsibility of administering any such program and had pointed out difficulties inherent in comparing hardship in the case of the worker with hardship for the farmer. French reported:

> I further said that from our point of view, the essential thing was to give the labourer a feeling that he had some right of appeal from the arbitrary decision of some employer who found himself in a position to make things extremely difficult for a particular worker and his family. Mr Forber admitted that there were hard cases but said that he doubted if they were anything like so numerous as the Trade Unions were anxious to make the Government believe.

Stocks commented ruefully on this interchange: "The whole bristles with difficulties and is highly contentious." French reported to his colleagues that Buxton remained unimpressed by the Ministry of Health's reaction and suggested that tenants simply be allowed two months after leaving a farmer's employment to find another home. Stocks thought that this would be subject to the same objections as the earlier proposal but agreed that the matter certainly came under the purview of the Ministry of Health.[43]

A meeting between Buxton and Greenwood, each accompanied by his top official adviser, did not resolve the impasse between the two departments of state. Everyone agreed that a problem existed. The difficulties in solving it revolved around the complexities of weighing the hardship of farmer and worker, although most informed opinion agreed that in this case the tenant needed more protection.[44] Nothing substantive came of the discussion. Buxton's poor health led him to retire from the ministry to go to the House of Lords. Christopher Addison, Buxton's successor, concentrated on the creation of marketing boards; but he also had little more than a year in office before the Labour government collapsed in 1931.

Neither the Housing Bill of 1930 nor the Housing (Rural Authorities) Bill of 1931 affected the tied cottage system. An interdepartmental committee appointed in October 1930 to consider the question of tied cottages soon foundered in hopeless deadlock. Farmers and landowners insisted that tied cottages were required in order to carry on agricultural work efficiently. Representatives of farmworkers contended that tied cottages represented an intolerable weapon, which farmers could use to intimidate their workers. The committee produced two reports, each signed by three of its members. One report urged abolition of the tied cottage system; the other urged its continuance. Because of the controversial nature of this impasse the seventh member of the committee, H. H. George, the Ministry of Health's housing expert (see appendix), declined to sign either report. He explained: "It would be improper for me as a civil servant, to associate myself with either of the Reports or to make independent recommendations."[45]

Despite the initiatives of officials, the tied cottage system remained intact throughout the interwar period. Writing in 1939, Christopher Addison called for freeing "the farm worker from the thraldom which the tied cottage so commonly imposes," as a crucial element of what the agricultural worker expects from the Labour party's agricultural policy.[46] However, the tied cottage continued to be a feature of the English agricultural system and a continuing grievance for the National Union of Agricultural Workers into the postwar decades. In the mid-1960s as many as 48 percent of farmworkers still lived in tied cottages.[47] Political leaders, reluctant to grapple with such a contentious issue, made no move to remedy this grievance; and Ministry of Agriculture civil servants could not act on their own. The civil servants' impulse to ameliorate the living conditions of agricultural workers, although persistent, could not move the other interested parties to an agreement.

The Ministry and the Agricultural Community

A series of reports compiled by the Ministry of Agriculture at the end of the 1930s demonstrates the consistency of civil servants' attitudes toward agricultural workers. Agriculture officials monitored the position of labor in the countryside throughout the interwar period. In the 1930s, a shortage of labor rather than unemployment began to concern them. In 1936, assistant secretary R. R. Enfield (see appendix) observed that the conversion of arable land to pasturage and increasing mechanization "pushed" labor off the land, while the attraction of nonagricultural work "pulled" men to urban areas. Enfield believed that this phenomenon tended to keep wage levels up; a contention with which the acting second secretary, A. W. Street (see appendix), disagreed. Street argued that a good deal of underemployment still existed and that Enfield had "too rosy a picture of the wage situation from the worker's point of view." Street's objections to the contrary and concern for the shortage of skilled labor on the land and its ostensible causes (the inferior status and situation of agricultural labor compared to industrial labor, for instance) continued to grow during the five years preceding the outbreak of the Second World War.[48]

In 1937, and again in 1938, the ministry compiled extensive reports on the state of agriculture. Based on information gathered from questionnaires distributed to the ministry's staff of inspectors stationed throughout the country, these reports detailed conditions of agricultural employment. They did not paint an idyllic rural scene. On the employers' side, the inspectors noted that farmers' attitudes toward their workers remained essentially unchanged. Farmers persisted in firing workers who joined unions or who tried to obtain their rights under the Agricultural Wages Act. Such instances of victimization, in the view of Agriculture officials, suggested that "the attitudes of many farmers toward their employees had not advanced with the times and leaves much to be desired."[49]

If the farmers had not advanced sufficiently with the times, the observations of the inspectors implied, farmworkers had advanced too far. The reports linked changes in workers' attitudes to an improved standard of education and a greater knowledge of the world; and the inspectors did not regard this development as necessarily a positive one. In evaluating prevailing sentiment among workers, the inspector for the four northern counties remarked: "Some weight must be given to the modern spirit of discontent. The 'frivolous unrest of mass-produced minds' is no longer harboured in the town alone." Inspectors criticized the curriculum of county schools where, they alleged, rural children learned to be discontented.[50]

The tenor of these remarks, written just before the outbreak of the Second World War, helps define the limits of the officials' views of agricultural policy. Perceiving themselves as much more progressive than the average farmer, civil servants sought both to protect the farmworker from his employer and to preserve an agricultural community in England. Officials' concern with the plight of agricultural workers, although not entirely free of a paternalistic flavor, led them to work energetically, and with some moderate success, on the farmworkers' behalf. In the next stage of my analysis, I would like to examine more closely both the circumstances that enhanced civil servants' influence over the formulation of policy and those that limited their scope to act.

Agricultural Policy in the 1920s

Sir Daniel Hall Versus Sir Francis Floud

During the 1920s two distinct voices sounded in departmental discussions of agricultural policy, the voices of Sir Daniel Hall and Sir Francis Floud. Floud, a career civil servant who had entered the Ministry of Agriculture in 1894, became permanent secretary in 1920 and remained in that position until 1928. His promotion displaced Sir Daniel Hall, who moved over to take the position of chief scientific adviser. Their disagreements reveal the range of opinion within the department and point up the importance of political climate in determining the direction of government policy during the 1920s.

The repeal of the 1920 Agricultural Act left Ministry of Agriculture officials without a policy. Civil servants had to redefine the proper relationship between the state and the agricultural community in a time of oversupply and declining prices. The question of whether the state ought to intervene again to protect agriculture arose almost immediately. During the 1920s ministry staff argued that the government should undertake measures to ameliorate conditions in the agricultural community. In this discussion, only Sir Francis Floud supported the laissez-faire policy pursued by the Conservative governments of the period. Floud thus advanced advice that was congenial to his political superiors.

After the repeal of the 1920 act, civil servants anticipated (correctly, as it turned out) that farmers would react to the rapid fall in prices by taking arable land out of production and by cutting wages. Officials did not welcome either prospect. Assistant secretary Thompson suggested in 1922 that the government devise a way to provide credit to enable farmers to wait until prices stabilized before selling their crops. Sir Francis Floud found Thompson's suggestion impractical. Any credit scheme would require legislation and hence take too long to implement. In addition, he observed: "I should be afraid that the farmers would take the credit and still reduce the wages."[51]

Sir Daniel Hall supported Thompson rather than Floud, recommending that the government underwrite some kind of credit scheme for farmers. Hall predicted that as the price of wheat continued to fall farmers would convert their land from arable land to pasturage, reduce wages, and discharge their men. He thought that out of 869,000 men employed in agriculture, some 50,000 to 100,000 might be unemployed. Even though no program of unemployment benefits for agricultural workers existed, Hall believed that the government could not ignore unemployment on this scale. He argued that it would be cheaper to prevent unemployment—using a scheme of short-term credit for farmers—than to provide unemployment assistance for the workers. Thompson also reiterated this theme to Floud, warning that "failing assistance to farmers, it may be necessary to consider assistance to workers." These representations elicited a more considered response from Floud, who explained that he opposed government interference because of both its cost and its ineffectiveness. He also rejected Hall's dire predictions about unemployment. In elaborating his own view, Floud suggested:

> In the present political atmosphere I think the sound course is to allow agriculture to take the course that self-interest dictates without attempting to direct it into a different course, and if there should be substantial unemployment I should leave relief measures to the Guardians who in country districts have hitherto hardly felt the burdens that have fallen on the urban areas in consequence of prevailing unemployment.[52]

Later in 1922 he set out a point-by-point refutation of Hall's suggestions.

Floud saw only two areas in which the government could profitably act. Encouraging scientific research and education would, he argued, lower costs of production and thereby increase profits. (This represented the traditional role of the Ministry of Agriculture and Fisheries since its inception as a Board in 1889, only five years before Floud began his career there.) Floud also suggested that the government could reduce the tax burden on land imposed by rates and tithes. On the other hand, Floud did not believe in the effectiveness of any government-sponsored loan program and thought it politically impossible for the government to organize marketing. Floud's perspective prevailed at this stage, coinciding as it did with the government's. When the minister, Arthur Griffith-Boscawen, wrote to Lloyd George outlining his proposals for agriculture, his recommendations included the main features of Floud's ideas, such as the removal of tax burdens and the encouragement of cheaper costs of production.[53]

Floud's opinion suited the fiscal conservatism of government under the influence of the cost-cutting mandated by the Geddes Committee, but farmers could not be expected to welcome this bleak evaluation of the efficacy of government assistance. Floud was quite willing to defend it to their faces, however. He recommended a frank answer to the NFU's requests for government aid, arguing irritably, "We must try and get the farmers to abandon their habit of constantly looking to the Government for policy without contributing anything as to the elements of that policy themselves." In a draft reply to the NFU, Floud exhorted farmers to "make up their minds to face their difficulties without Government interference and without any expectation of subsidies from the taxpayer." An anonymous, but more tactful, hand excised these and other points from the letter actually sent in the minister's name to the NFU.[54]

When the Conservative party returned to power in 1925 after the brief interlude of the first Labour government, Floud took a more optimistic view of the agricultural situation, observing that the state of agriculture was then improving, with both prices and the proportion of land in arable production stable. He reiterated his belief that subsidies and protection were "outside the range of practical politics" and inadvisable if agriculture was ever to be conducted on an economic basis. He softened his stand on marketing schemes, which he now recommended that the government assist. Floud also urged that the government encourage both occupying ownership and small holdings by facilitating land purchases by tenants.[55]

Sir Daniel Hall's contribution to this discussion had a much less optimistic tone. Although Hall agreed that agriculture had recovered from the 1920–1921 fall in prices, he stressed that the present profitability of agriculture stemmed from a decline in production costs, in other words the fall in wages. Hall asserted that British agriculture neither produced enough food nor employed enough people, a situation that probably could not be changed without government intervention on a large (and expensive) scale. But Hall did not find the prospects for such intervention encouraging.

Protection, Hall observed, would not only involve administrative difficulties but also lead to increased food prices, the benefits of which would accrue to the landowner rather than the farmer. Hall concluded: "Protective duties in all probability are only politically defensible in countries where the great bulk of the land is farmed by its owners." Subsidies do not tax the consumer, but Hall believed it impossible to confine their effect to those sectors of agriculture that truly needed their assistance. Hall also rejected direct governmental control of agriculture, either through the nationalization of the land or through socialization of the market process whereby the government would become the sole buyer of produce. He believed that agriculture was not a suitable industry for experimentation in nationalization, and that the gains produced by the socialization of distribution did not warrant "such a fundamental disturbance of existing social methods."[56]

Hall was even more pessimistic in his belief that there was nothing the state could do either to ameliorate the difficulties farmers had obtaining credit or to rectify the inequities in existing land tenure arrangements: "The problem of credit may almost be regarded as insoluble under existing conditions of land tenure." He argued that it would be better for the state to assume the role of landlord—by nationalization—rather than indirectly encourage redistribution of the land only to have to do so again in two generations. But Hall had already rejected such a drastic course of action.[57]

Hall's bleak but thoughtful analysis and Floud's hardheaded appraisal of the situation of English agriculture had one thing in common: neither required the government to undertake any dramatic departure in policy. In September 1925 when Floud forwarded a memorandum to the minister—then E.F.L. Wood (later Lord Halifax)—with his recommendations on the proper government policy to pursue for agriculture, he observed that the "appropriate course for a Conservative Government that believes in private enterprise" was to do nothing spectacular. Floud argued that the Labour party's policies of control, nationalization, and stabilization were open to attack. He pointed out that the lack of agreement about agricultural policy could only lead to a political reversal should the government attempt to introduce some major change, and he concluded:

> I suggest therefore that the agricultural policy of the Government should be based on a belief in private enterprise without State interference or subsidies, coupled with provisions for assisted land purchase for those who wish to buy their farms, and a development of small holdings on wise lines.

Although Floud's exposition of these views elicited an enthusiastic endorsement from Lord Bledisloe, the ministry's new parliamentary secretary, Wood apparently expected something more positive. "But I thought that we had already reached common ground in that?" he asked.[58]

Wood, who soon left Agriculture to become viceroy of India, did not have time to formulate his own response to these recommendations. Walter Guiness replaced Wood, holding the position of minister of agriculture throughout the rest of the Conservative party's time in office. Guiness's leadership did not produce any innovation in agricultural policy, but he did support several small positive measures. In 1926 the Rural Workers' Housing Act provided for the reconditioning of existing cottages. In 1928 the Agricultural Credits Act provided for loans to purchase farms, and the government granted further rate relief to farmers in 1928 also.[59]

In 1928 Floud left the department where he had begun his career thirty-four years before, although his career as a government official was not over; in subsequent years he served as permanent head of the Board of Customs and Excise and the Labour Ministry. While permanent secretary of the Agriculture Ministry, Floud's views had coincided closely with the inclination of the Conservative party and had dominated the development of policy within the ministry, but he did not reflect the opinions of all his colleagues. Sir Daniel Hall represented an alternative point of view within the ministry, although it was one that had lost political favor with the dismantling of the 1920 Agriculture Act. Floud's promotion to the post of permanent secretary in 1920 and Hall's removal to the post of chief scientific adviser reflected the weight accorded their views not only by Lord Lee, the minister responsible for these changes, but also by successive Conservative governments. Although far readier than Floud to urge the government to intervene in the conduct of agriculture, Hall could not develop a persuasive alternative for government policy after his program had been rejected by the repeal of the 1920 Agricultural Act.

Despite their official differences of opinion, the personal relationship between Floud and Hall remained cordial. When Hall retired as full-time scientific adviser in 1927, Floud persuaded the Treasury to allow Agriculture to retain him on a part-time basis, an arrangement that remained in force until 1935.[60] Shortly after making these arrangements, Floud left Agriculture to take up his new duties at Customs and Excise. Thus, of the two voices that contended within the Ministry of Agriculture during the 1920s, Hall's voice enjoyed the more enduring influence. That influence rested not just on Hall's continued presence on the ministry's staff after Floud's departure, but also on Hall's closer identification with the spirit that animated Agriculture officials' approach to policy. Floud's authority, in contrast, derived from the convergence of his views with those of the prevailing political climate of the 1920s.

Ministerial Leadership in the Ministry of Agriculture

Despite the disasters of the years immediately following the First World War, Agriculture officials managed to place their stamp on government policy. Their influence over policy stemmed in part from the low political prestige of their ministry. The ministers who directed its activities often lacked any special interest in or knowledge of agricultural issues. Of the eleven men who served as ministers between 1919 and 1939, only four had any expertise in agricultural policy. The Agriculture Ministry also suffered from a rapid turnover in ministers during the interwar period. Seven men served as minister of agriculture between 1919 and 1925. Four held that office between 1929 and 1932. In only one instance did a minister and a civil servant forge a relationship anything like the one that grew up between H.A.L. Fisher and Selby-Bigge at the Board of Education. The 1917 Corn Production Act briefly stood as a monument to the partnership of R. E. Prothero and Daniel Hall.

The most knowledgeable minister to direct agricultural policy was Prothero, a universally respected scholar of British agriculture who became president of the Board of Agriculture during the First World War. Lloyd George appointed the author of the classic *English Farming Past and Present,* when he formed his war Cabinet in 1916.[61] Prothero brought the prestige and authority of scholarly expertise and scientific objectivity to agricultural policy. Prothero's appointment thus functioned for agriculture in the same way as H.A.L. Fisher's appointment to the presidency of the Board of Education functioned for educational policy. Daniel Hall was appointed permanent secretary at this time to support Prothero's efforts.

Both men, entering government service late in life, had difficulty adapting to their new careers. Prothero did not take to public life as Fisher had done; he found the conduct of politics particularly uncongenial. Once, while directing the debates on the 1917 Corn Production Act, Prothero accepted an opposition amendment against the advice of his officials simply because he was tired of doing what he was told. Although this existential assertion of his identity provided an appreciative House some diversion, the coalition government monitored his behavior more closely after that.

Prothero, created Lord Ernle, retired from office in 1919, and Lord Lee of Farnham took over the ministry. During the war Lord Lee had been head of the Food Production Department where the rather relentless, energetic quality of his leadership had contributed to the almost miraculous increases in food production achieved by British agriculture during the war.[62] Lee reorganized the ministry, promoted Floud, and moved Hall out of the mainstream of events. He oversaw the passage of the Agriculture Act of 1920, which sought to establish the innovations of the 1917 Corn Production Act on a more permanent basis. He left Agriculture to become First Lord of the Admiralty in 1921. His successor, Arthur Griffith-Boscawen, took office in a time of fiscal emergency and consequently had to preside over the dismantling of the policies of both Prothero and Lee.

The Labour party brought to office two aggressive and knowledgeable ministers of agriculture, but neither man had enough time in office to develop and implement a comprehensive policy for agriculture. Noel Buxton, although far more thoroughly versed in foreign affairs than domestic affairs when he took office in 1924, had held a seat in Norfolk for many years and had a long-standing relationship with George Edwards and the National Union of Agricultural Workers. Christopher Addison, better known for his work on housing and as the first minister of health, purposefully groomed himself for a niche in the Labour party by educating himself in agricultural issues. Addison served at Agriculture as Noel Buxton's parliamentary secretary during the second Labour government and succeeded him as minister when Buxton resigned to enter the House of Lords in 1930. Addison then had only one year in office to devise his own policies before the collapse of the second Labour government during the 1931 fiscal crisis.[63]

A combination of circumstances and the idiosyncracies of individual personalities thus allowed civil servants a great deal of leeway within the Ministry of Agriculture. Lack of vigorous leadership, except at brief intervals, left officials the opportunity to press their own views upon the government, and civil servants used that opportunity to urge the implementation of measures to make the agricultural community both more efficient and more humane. Their motivation to act stemmed from their view that the agricultural community, if left to its own devices, could not make such progress. Civil servants stood by, ready with their "best advice," willing if necessary to buttress that advice with the force of law.

Conclusion

Ministry of Agriculture officials tended to urge a cautiously progressive position on the various matters that came before them. Their support of government-funded land drainage to alleviate rural unemployment neatly illustrates this perspective. To support public works, as Agriculture officials did, automatically put them in opposition to the prevailing Treasury view of the efficacy of public works in the relief of unemployment (as we have seen, the Ministry of Labour also opposed aiding the farming community).[64] Yet, Agriculture was not an administrative backwater that harbored officials more radical than those in other departments of state.

The formation of marketing boards did not elicit similarly unqualified support, however, particularly in the 1920s. Civil servants thought that government-sponsored marketing constituted a more radical intervention in the marketplace than the situation warranted. They also believed that the English farmer was not inclined to participate in cooperative ventures.[65] The difficulties British agriculture was experiencing in competing with imported produce, combined with the failure of voluntary marketing schemes during the 1920s, began to persuade many of those interested in English agriculture's economic health of the necessity of mandatory marketing organizations.[66] Even so, the marketing boards created by the 1930 act came about largely through the efforts of Christopher Addison, who managed to generate support among Liberal ranks for this more controversial measure in spite of opposition among farmers and suspicion among some members of the Labour party. The subsequent success of the marketing boards—due in part to the energy with which Walter Elliot administered the act—came as somewhat of a surprise to all parties involved.[67]

The most striking element of the civil servants' view of agricultural policy must have been their stance toward rural labor relations. They consistently exhibited sympathy for the position of agricultural workers, their analyses of both wages boards and tied cottages revealing a concern to protect the worker from exploitation by the farmer. This concern had both a scientific and a paternalistic aspect. On the one hand, civil servants sometimes displayed toward farmers a hostility that stemmed from the resistance farmers, not unnaturally, put up against ministry efforts to inspire them to improve their farming methods.[68] The desire of farmers to protect themselves financially by cutting wages represented for Ministry of Agriculture officials another example of farmers' reluctance to modernize. On the other hand, the weakness of union organization among agricultural workers meant that workers could not protect themselves, leaving them vulnerable to farmers and their much stronger organization, the NFU. This analysis remained the official view through the 1960s.[69]

Recent discussions concerning the development of a "corporatist" approach to agricultural policy stress the central role of the NFU and the evolution of a close working relationship between the NFU and the Ministry of Agriculture in regulating agricultural production.[70] To focus on labor relations rather than production and marketing, however, casts a different light on the interaction between NFU and state. This perspective shows up the willingness of Agriculture officials to act as a countervailing influence directed against the power of the NFU within the rural community. Civil servants sought to redress this imbalance on behalf of agricultural labor, but they did not defend their stance in terms of social reform. Rather, they placed it in the context of their efforts to put the conduct of British agriculture on a more efficient, even scientific, and enlightened footing.

Ministry officials did have a measure of success translating their views into policy. The eventual inclusion of agricultural workers under a system of unemployment insurance owed much to the efforts of civil servants who worked strenuously to achieve this end, in the face of ministerial indifference and the opposition of the Ministry of Labour. The civil servants' vigorous defense of land drainage schemes helped preserve one modest public works program in the face of the cost-cutting rage that swept through English government in the early 1920s. On the other hand, Agriculture officials could do nothing to preserve the major reforms achieved under Prothero, which fell victim to the zeal for fiscal constraint generated by the rapid downturn of the British economy immediately following the war. And their ambivalence toward marketing boards did not appear to handicap Christopher Addison in carrying through that legislation.

In rewarding those with expert knowledge, the Ministry of Agriculture's recruitment and promotion practices selected a staff whose credentials differed markedly from those in other departments. Of the civil servants who participated in the discussions, only three had enjoyed the advantages of a public school and an Oxbridge education, the hallmarks of the typical open competition entrant to the civil service. Only two of these men, A.T.A. Dobson and Charles Nathan, spent their entire careers at Agriculture. The third, Donald Fergusson, had begun his career at the Treasury, coming to Agriculture as permanent secretary in 1937. Excluding Fergusson, only two, Nathan and French, had entered Agriculture via open competition. Stanley, whose voice was one of the most often heard in departmental counsels, spent almost his entire career in the Second Division.

The commitment of these men to encouraging the most up-to-date and scientific methods of agricultural practice often put them at cross purposes with both landowners and farmers. This same commitment led them to intercede on behalf of agricultural workers in order to impose a modicum of equity on rural labor relations. At Agriculture as at the Board of Education, the departmental recruitment and promotion practices and the departmental view of policy proved to be logical concomitants. The difference between the two departments lay in the nature of the vision that animated their respective staffs. The Board of Education strove to maintain the exclusive nature of an educational system that buttressed class hierarchies. The Ministry of Agriculture, in contrast, called upon the power of the state to enforce more equitable relations among the social groups in the agricultural community.

5 The Ministry of Labour: Accentuating the Negative

■ *It remains to profit by experience in order to fashion a wise policy for the future. . . . So long as the depression continues—and unhappily the horizon is still dark—it may not be possible to do more than meet current problems as they arise.*
—T. W. Phillips

Within three years of its formation in 1917, the Ministry of Labour began what turned out to be a protracted struggle with the crisis in unemployment that marked the interwar period. Cresting in 1921 and again in 1932, unemployment in Britain exceeded 10 percent of the insured workforce every year from 1921 until 1939 (with the exception of 1927 when the unemployment rate dipped to 9.7 percent).[1] Those who had advocated a Ministry of Labour could not have anticipated that it would almost immediately confront a problem of such magnitude. The intractable nature of interwar unemployment became increasingly apparent as the years passed, and the pessimistic prognosis of T. W. Phillips, who became the Ministry of Labour's permanent secretary in 1935 (see appendix), proved accurate. The Ministry of Labour did not produce any creative departures in policy to treat what became a national emergency in the early 1930s. Other ministries and government bodies did no better, however, and the inability "to do more than meet current problems," as Phillips had put it, remains the most distinctive feature of interwar domestic politics.

Ministry of Labour officials would seem to have come well prepared to meet the challenge posed by the prolonged depression of the interwar years. The Board of Trade departments that formed the basis for the Ministry of Labour had been associated with the forefront of innovations in social policy before the First World War. The Board of Trade had used unorthodox recruitment practices, so the men on its staff were drawn from a greater variety of backgrounds—including the trade union movement—than any other of the social service departments. The uniformity of recruitment imposed on the entire civil service in 1919 meant that new officials now came to the ministry via open competition examination. Nevertheless, promotion practices continued to show no preference for those educated at well-known public schools and Oxford (the "open competition" type favored by the other departments). Indeed, only at the Ministry of Labour does educational background provide no clue to an individual's promotion prospects. The products of prewar recruitment held senior positions in the ministry throughout the interwar period.

Innovative personnel practices apparently failed to produce innovative policy during the 1920s and 1930s, however. A Labour Ministry that did not formulate an effective response to unemployment could not command much respect, and the department's reputation remained low throughout the interwar period. When Ernest Bevin became minister of labour during the Second World War, he took up his duties with "considerable doubts" about the quality of his advisers there. Bevin, however, was pleasantly surprised by the ability of his officials, and after 1945 no fewer than ten Ministry of Labour civil servants eventually attained the rank of permanent secretary.[2]

Periods of departmental dynamism before 1914 and after 1939 thus bracketed the interwar decades of seeming failure in nerve and imagination. But to draw such a conclusion too hastily would neglect the extent to which the official arena permitted innovation. Two factors sharply limited the scope of the ministry's response to problems and issues. Examination of the role of Ministry of Labour civil servants in policy making during the 1920s and 1930s shows that the preconceptions officials brought to bear on the formulation of policy kept acceptable policy within narrow confines. In addition, officials often had little influence when policy touched hotly contested political issues.

The departmental understanding of the nature of the crisis afflicting England after the First World War constrained the kind of policy Labour Ministry officials would endorse. In their view, the state should not take sides in the struggle between labor and capital but should instead act judiciously to avert conflict and assist the smooth running of the economy. This stance did not stem from official indifference to the plight of the unemployed, or from hostility toward labor, or even from a reluctance to use the power of the state to direct the economy. Rather, contemporary economic thought buttressed the civil servants' opinion that radical departures on the part of the government to create employment would prove futile.

Political realities vitiated the power of the Ministry of Labour to such an extent that the views of its officials often had small effect on the development of policy. The volatile nature of issues of unemployment and industrial relations, which dominated the political as well as the social life of the nation during the interwar period, meant that major policy decisions did not always remain in the hands of Ministry of Labour officials or even in those of the minister of labour. Political leaders at the highest levels could, and did, ignore the most forceful official advice.

In the analysis below, after outlining the origins and organization of the Ministry of Labour, I first delineate the critical and skeptical attitude of ministry officials toward policy innovations to stimulate employment. I then contrast this stance, which in large measure earned the department its reputation for negativism, to the resistance mounted by the department to the Conservative party's attack on trade unionism in the aftermath of the General Strike. Finally, I consider the character and the fate of some positive suggestions put forward from within official ranks. Taken together these episodes show the moderate—but progressive—views of the ministry's officials. They also demonstrate that the civil servants at the Ministry of Labour had much less influence on the formulation of policy than their colleagues at the Board of Education and the Ministry of Agriculture.

Origins and Organization

The administrative apparatus of the Ministry of Labour actually predated the ministry itself. The creation of labour exchanges and trade boards in 1909 and the passage of the National Insurance Act of 1911 required an expansion of the state's bureaucratic machinery. The consequent growth took place largely under the auspices of the Board of Trade. Support for the creation of a separate Ministry of Labour already existed. Arguments for a new ministry drew upon both the sentiment in the labor movement that labor ought to have a voice to represent it in the Cabinet and the view that a single, central agency ought to direct government policy on employment. The classic statement of this idea (like the analogous arguments for a Ministry of Health) was associated with Sidney and Beatrice Webb and appeared in the *Minority Report of the Poor Law Commission*. After the First World War the Ministry of Labour failed to move beyond those measures that had given the ministry its original raison d'être. In addition, the ministry's oversight of these programs could not prevent their becoming tainted with the stigma of the dole.[3]

In 1917 the Ministry of Labour was assembled from the relevant sections of the Board of Trade. These included the Employment Department, which dealt with labour exchanges and unemployment insurance; the Chief Industrial Commissioner's Department, which had responsibility for industrial relations; the Office of Trade Boards; and the part of the Board of Trade's Statistical Department that treated labor. At the beginning of the interwar period the Ministry of Labour's organization also included additional departments formed to carry out newly implemented policies, such as the Joint Industrial Branch (which administered the formation of Whitley councils) and temporary departments charged with supervising programs necessitated by demobilization.[4] These included the Appointments Department, which provided employment for ex-service officers and men, and the Department of Civil Demobilization and Resettlement (see table 11).[5] The new ministry largely achieved the goal of housing a single, centralized government agency to administer all aspects of public policy on labor and employment; although it did not absorb the Industrial Division of the Home Office, which supervised working conditions in factories and mines, until after Ernest Bevin became minister of labour during the Second World War.[6]

However, the Ministry of Labour did not constitute a streamlined and efficient administrative unit at the close of the First World War. Rather, it represented an amalgam of departments, of a size to handicap efficiency. The duties of the new ministry required a large staff, not only in London but throughout the British Isles. In 1920 the total employed by the Ministry of Labour stood at almost twelve thousand.[7] In the home civil service, only the Post Office employed greater numbers. Labour not only had a large staff, but in 1920 nearly two-thirds (66 percent) was employed in a temporary capacity. The lack of a headquarters building in London further hampered the smooth operation of the new ministry.[8]

The administrative class staff of the Labour Ministry originally came largely from the Board of Trade. Many of these men had entered government service by appointment during the rapid expansion of the Board of Trade's duties between 1909 and 1912. As we have already seen, after the First World War, the Ministry of Labour drew upon open competition entrants for its administrative class recruits. Even though many of those who had directed the successes of the prewar Board of Trade did not remain part of the Ministry of Labour, the new department embarked on its career staffed with talented, experienced officials.[9] They found, unfortunately, that they could not duplicate earlier achievements in the hostile environment of the interwar decades.

Resisting Innovation and Experiment

The Ministry of Labour came under increasing pressure to develop measures to reduce the incidence of unemployment or at least to mitigate its effects, as the level of unemployment remained above 10 percent during the 1920s. Although no one knew how best to respond to the overriding social problem of the period, the department did not lack for suggestions of policies for the government to pursue. The evaluation of such suggestions constituted one of the duties of Ministry of Labour officials. The civil servants who fielded the various proposals brought to the attention of the government appraised them with critical eyes. Raising the school-leaving age, diverting unemployment insurance funds to aid industries, and mounting large-scale public works programs were among some of the policy options pressed upon the

TABLE 11. *Ministry of Labour, 1920*

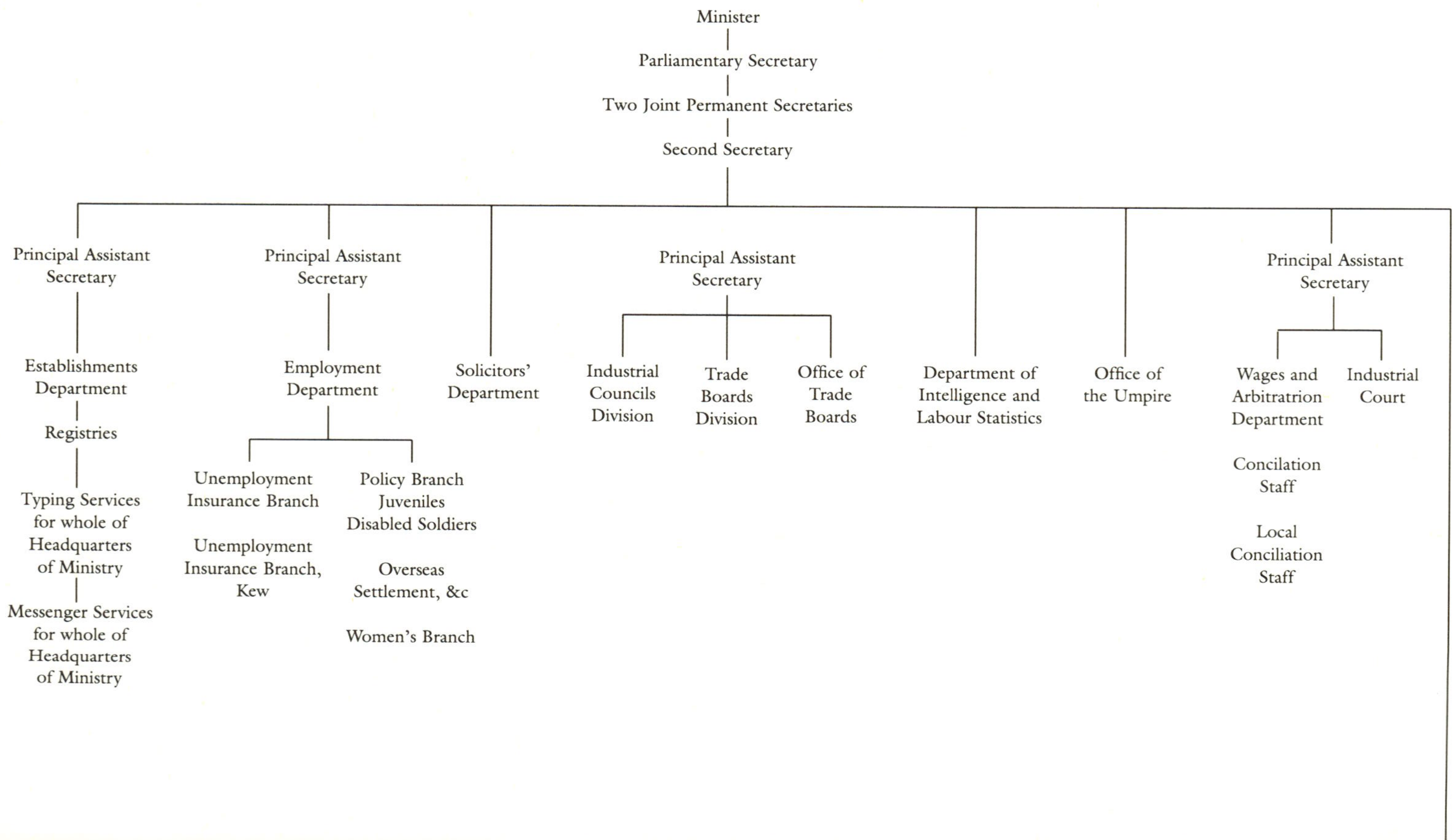

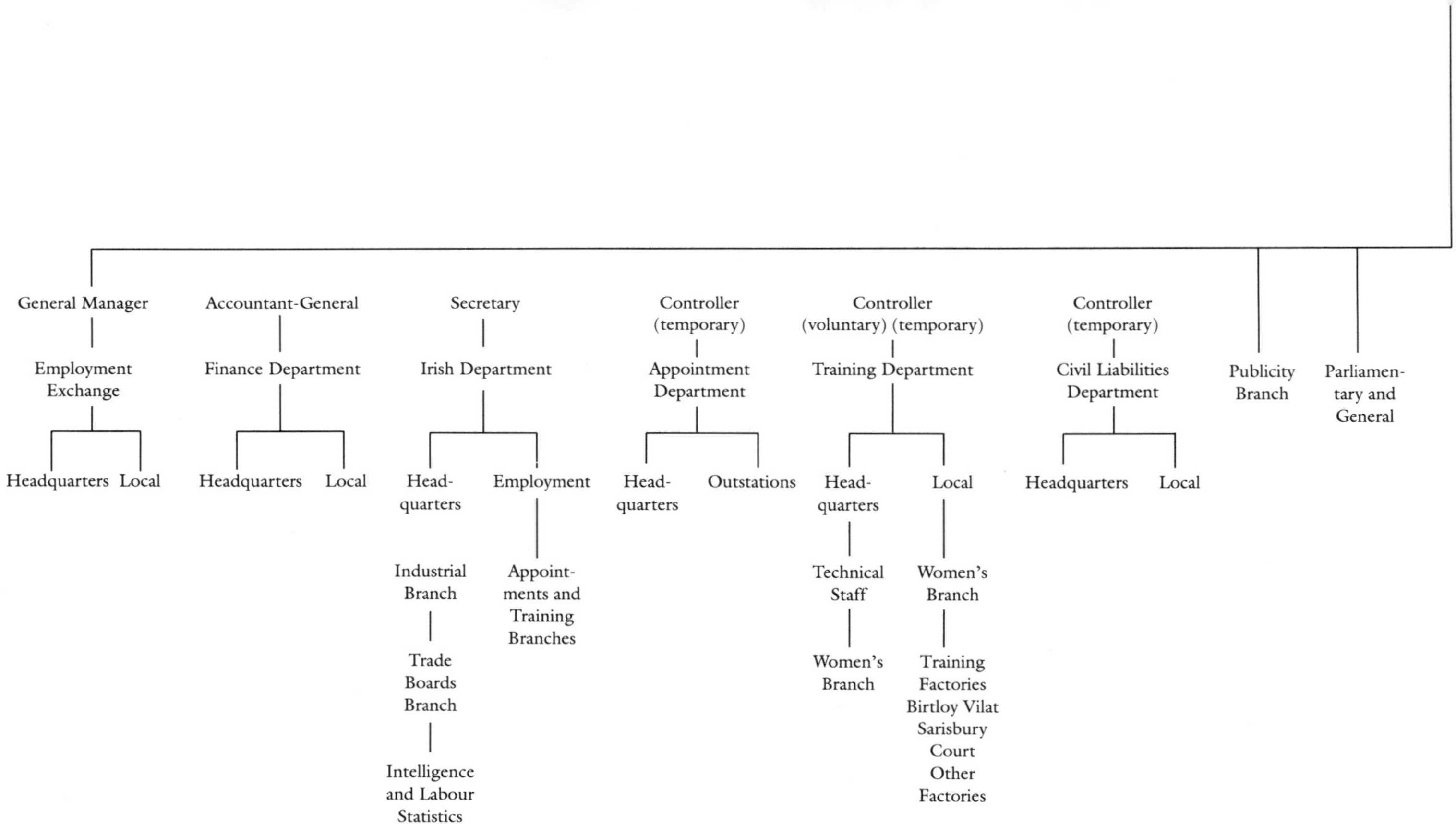

Source: Reports of the Committees appointed to investigate the staffing and methods of work of the Ministry of Labour, the Ministry of Agriculture and Fisheries, and the Royal Commission of Sugar Supplies, Appendix II. Cmd. 1069 (1920).

ministry during the interwar decades. All these received a cool reception from Labour officials.

Throughout the period, civil servants at the Ministry of Labour consistently maintained the view that such measures could not reduce unemployment. For example, in 1927 Eustace Percy, the president of the Board of Education, requested that Arthur Steel-Maitland, minister of labour during Stanley Baldwin's Conservative government, evaluate the impact a higher school-leaving age would have on unemployment. R. H. Tawney, in an essay entitled "The Possible Cost of Raising the School Leaving Age," contended that such action would save £9 million a year in unemployment insurance. Tawney assumed that removing fourteen-year-olds from the labor force would leave vacancies for older workers to fill.[10]

When asking for advice on Tawney's contentions, Percy expressed his own doubts that such a measure would have any impact on adult unemployment, and Ministry of Labour officials shared Percy's view. Older workers would not necessarily take the place of younger workers removed from the labor market because, one official argued: "The unskilled man could not (in most cases he would not be sufficiently dexterous and nimble), the skilled man in most cases would not, while more than a third of the unemployed woman labour consists of textile operatives, who are largely immobile." Ministry officials believed that "scarcity of juvenile labour has never yet resulted in a larger employment of adult labour and is never likely to." Even if adult workers did replace juvenile labor, this would tend to raise labor costs of production, which would lead to higher prices. Increased wages combined with increased prices would not lead to any increase in consumption and would make British industry less competitive. On the other hand, employers might replace juvenile labor with labor-saving devices, a tactic that would definitely not reduce adult unemployment.[11]

Ministry civil servants did not find Tawney's arguments convincing. Indeed, one official dismissed Tawney's suggestions as "too unreal for serious discussion." In response to this discussion within the department, Phillips—at that time deputy secretary of the Ministry of Labour—observed that the crux of the problem lay in Tawney's assumption that adult labour would replace juvenile labour. "This would be impracticable," Phillips wrote, "even if desirable." Steel-Maitland then sent Percy the memorandum that recorded this discussion.[12]

Many groups opposed raising the school-leaving age as a way to reduce unemployment. Employers feared the reduction of the pool of cheap, unskilled labor. The Board of Education insisted that such a measure must be advanced primarily on its merits as an educational reform. The Conservative party did not wish to exchange certain increased expenditure on education for a problematical saving for the unemployment insurance fund.[13] Ministry of Labour officials added their voice to this chorus by stressing the uncertainty of using such a measure as a means to an end. They even questioned the merits of the end itself, that is, withdrawal of young adolescents between the ages of fourteen and fifteen years from the labor market.

As the economic situation worsened during the second Labour government, Ministry of Labour officials had to evaluate an increasing volume of proposals to alleviate unemployment. Official receptivity to these suggestions did not increase. For instance, A. S. Comyns-Carr (see appendix) submitted a scheme to use the unemployment insurance fund to aid industry. P. Y. Blunden, assistant secretary in the Employment and Insurance Department (see appendix), advanced four main criticisms of this idea. The implementation of such a scheme would require legislation that Blunden thought would be difficult to carry through. Blunden believed the scheme to be basically inequitable because the unemployment insurance fund, which was contributed to by all, would be used for the benefit of a few. In addition, Blunden argued, the cost of administering such a scheme would be high, and employers would not agree to the conditions imposed upon them in order to qualify for aid.[14]

O. C. Allen, who also served in the Employment and Insurance Department as a principal, had a different criticism to make. Allen pointed out to W. W. Marsh, director of the Establishments Department (see appendix for both):

> In stipulating both for the employment of the full normal complement and for efficient and up-to-date equipment in the establishment receiving the subsidy, Mr Comyns-Carr seems to me to be a little inconsistent. The purpose of industry is not to employ labour but to meet a market at the smallest cost.[15]

Blunden and Allen had prepared their evaluation of Comyn-Carr's proposal at the request of a conference of the heads of the various departments of the ministry. The instruction to be "as constructive as possible" in their analysis apparently did not much restrain them in the composition of their critique. Phillips, after reviewing the initial response to this task sent an interim note to the minister, Margaret Bondfield, stressing the difficulties of administering such schemes and the objections to using public money to subsidize employment. Allen, Blunden, and Phillips then composed a more general memorandum on schemes to use the unemployment insurance fund, pointing out that since it was then in debt it could do little to provide help to industry. They concluded: "On the whole, we feel that it would be wrong in principle to use the Fund to any substantial extent for purposes other than its original one of providing benefit for insured contributors during periods of genuine unemployment." In short, they did not recommend an extension of the ministry's powers to use the unemployment insurance fund for any but its original purpose.[16]

Within a few months ministry officials had to grapple with another controversial issue raised by another prominent public figure. Ernest Bevin had submitted a memorandum to the Economic Advisory Council on the relationship between rationalization of industry and unemployment. Ernest Bevin, general secretary of the Transport and General Workers Union from 1921 until his appointment as minister of labour in 1940, had been one of the first appointed to the Economic Advisory Council when Ramsay MacDonald formed that body in 1930 to provide the government with expert advice on economic issues. Rationalization, one proposed solution to the declining competitiveness of Britain's export industries, involved the reduction of excess capacity and the reorganization of industry into larger and more effective units for production and marketing.[17] Bevin contended that men displaced by rationalization would not easily find work again, and that industry should bear the responsibility for the unemployment it generated.

Wilfred Eady (see appendix) had the responsibility of drafting the ministerial reply to Bevin. Eady stressed the seriousness with which Bevin's proposals should be treated. A credible answer to Bevin's arguments, Eady asserted, must challenge their economic premises. Eady explained that in order to do that, he had to go "rather outside departmental policy." Marshaling support early on for this excursion beyond departmental bounds, he noted that the views he expressed in the draft reply had already been accepted by J. H. Thomas and endorsed by Sir Otto Niemeyer of the Treasury and H. D. Henderson, the joint secretary of the Economic Advisory Council (see appendix for both).[18]

In his analysis of Bevin's arguments, Eady focused on the issue of rationalization. He explained that British industry must undergo rationalization not only because of a worldwide fall in prices, but also because of Britain's economic position as an exporter in the world market. To make those displaced by the rationalization process a prior charge on an industry wishing to reorganize itself would hamper a process believed to be crucial to the maintenance of Britain's position in world trade. Eady denied Bevin's assumption that the displacement of workers by rationalization would be permanent. This position underlay the government's case for rejecting Bevin's suggestions because, as Eady pointed out: "Unless that assumption is challenged the case for treating the unemployment that follows, by unemployment insurance, is very much weakened." Unemployment insurance, of course, provided a remedy only for temporary unemployment.[19]

Eady's views did not represent unanimous opinion within the Ministry of Labour. The accountant-general, F. G. Bowers (see appendix), thought Eady "unduly optimistic," but he also thought Bevin too pessimistic and described his proposals as "impracticable." Bowers agreed with Eady that industry could not make provision for men displaced by rationalization. If provision had to be made for them at all, the government must do so. But, Bowers asked, if the government did take that task upon itself, how would it distinguish those unemployed because of rationalization from other categories? He pointed to another weakness in Bevin's reasoning, noting that his memorandum "seems to be based on the idea that money is going freely to rationalized industries but that is a profound mistake."[20]

Many of these proposals turned up repeatedly throughout the interwar period. As late as February 1939 we find E. A. Hitchman, the minister's principal private secretary, writing G. H. Ince, principal assistant secretary of the Employment Department (see appendix for both), to tell him that the minister wanted a note prepared to comment on various suggestions to combat unemployment put forward in a recent debate in the House of Commons. Hitchman listed fifteen headings to be considered, including raising the school-leaving age, restricting the hours of work, and public works. Ministry officials had seen all these suggestions before. The analyses they prepared in 1939 remained as critical as ever. Civil servants cited expense (old-age pensions) and the lack of efficacy (raising school-leaving age) or both (public works) as reasons to reject all these courses of action.[21]

Later that spring the Trade Union Congress (TUC) sent a memorandum on unemployment to the prime minister and requested a meeting to discuss their proposals.[22] R. M. Gould of the Ministry of Labour (see appendix) devised the response to this memorandum, which had been drawn up by the TUC Economic Committee on Unemployment. The TUC document compared the period between 1881 and 1914 to the period since 1921 and pointed out the persistence of a high level of unemployment; the particularly bad situation of certain industries, such as cotton, coal, iron, steel, and shipbuilding; and the recurring slumps that characterized the latter period. The TUC rejected both the notion of a single cause and the notion of a single remedy for these economic ills. Instead they contended: "The unemployment figures are sufficient proof that the remedies so far attempted have failed lamentably to meet the situation," and so the government stood accused of lacking any positive policy to meet the present slump. The government's ostensible "desire to 'restore confidence,' " the TUC explained, "implies the reluctance to take any action on the grounds that it *might* worsen the situation rather than make a determination to take any action designed to improve it." This attitude combined with "the influence of Treasury considerations" precluded the possibility of public works schemes or any other "measures designed to alleviate the effects, or shorten the period of . . . a slump." The TUC's memorandum concluded by recommending the formation of a special body to investigate unemployment and to make practical suggestions.[23]

Gould, in his reply to the TUC's analysis, used several different strategies. He pointed out that unemployment was already in decline, and he made assurances that the government would not further reduce social services. He disassociated present policy from earlier widely held but erroneous explanations for unemployment by declaring that the government did not view the present unemployment as caused either by the character of the unemployed or by temporary industrial setbacks. Gould criticized the TUC's statistics on unemployment before and after the First World War, arguing that the figures for the two periods were not comparable because they did not pertain to the same groups of people. He asserted that the different elements of government policy had been coordinated and had not been implemented piecemeal. The government had not used public works, Gould explained, because public works did not reduce unemployment. Gould rejected the TUC's proposal for a special body to study unemployment as administratively inefficient: "What the Trade Union Congress wants is greater and more extensive planning of industry by the State. If this were thought desirable it could be carried out through the existing machinery or an extension of it." F. W. Leggett forwarded Gould's analysis to T. W. Phillips, now permanent secretary, without comment except a remark that it had "an air of finality which may be open to criticism." Leggett also added that he assumed any additional proposals from the TUC would be welcome. The secretary then forwarded the entire brief to the minister as approved.[24]

The firmness and consistency with which Ministry of Labour officials responded to the many proposals for alleviating unemployment during this period of stress belied the frustrating burden such work must have entailed. Allen, for instance, once declared that he did not know what to do about projects submitted to him "when these involved grants from Public Funds or raised technical issues with which neither I nor my assistants were competent to deal." He complained: "It was not the duty of the Ministry of Labour to make itself responsible for fathering any and every proposal that was put to it because of the supposed responsibility of the Minister of Labour for creating unemployment."[25]

The Ministry of Labour's permanent secretary, Francis Floud (who had just been transferred from the Ministry of Agriculture to replace H. J. Wilson, who had become chief industrial adviser) replied to this outburst by reminding Allen that it was indeed the responsibility and the duty of the ministry "to consider the employment aspects of any such proposals." Floud reminded Allen that this should be done by the appropriate department, within the bounds of approved policy. Projects "worthy" of government support should be sent on to the minister. Civil servants continued to evaluate suggestions about the proper policy to ameliorate unemployment right up until the outbreak of the war, but they did not find much "worthy" enough to merit their support.[26]

TUC proposals to reduce unemployment that were entertained by the Ministry of Labour in 1939—and the civil servants' response to them—can stand for the whole period between the wars. Although there is some evidence that Treasury officials became more flexible and more receptive in the 1930s, Ministry of Labour officials rejected such suggestions consistently for twenty years.[27] But their negativism did not express simple malaise, timidity, or failure of nerve. Neither did it reflect Treasury constraints. Rather, it stemmed from the belief that the root cause of unemployment was the inability of English industry to compete on the world market. Attempts to treat unemployment that increased the costs of production would, in this view, merely prolong a difficult period of readjustment. This stance did not necessarily preclude the possibility of a positive role for the state in facilitating this transition, however. As we shall see, Ministry of Labour officials did have their own ideas as to which lines of action the state could most profitably pursue.

The various replies from Labour civil servants to the different suggestions showered upon them exhibit certain similarities. On the most obvious level, their analyses reflect the deeply held belief that such expedients simply would not make any significant reduction in unemployment. The pursuit of such chimeras could only result in disappointment. On another level, Ministry of Labour officials believed that all these suggestions, if implemented, would interfere in one way or another with the adjustment of British industry to the postwar conditions of world trade. At a time when British goods could not compete on the world market, to restrict the labor market, provide subsidies, or burden industry with their own unemployed all would obstruct the painful reorganization and streamlining of British industry that was necessary in order to reduce production costs and return to prosperity.

Resisting Reaction

The consistency with which Ministry of Labour officials rejected suggestions that the state take action to alleviate unemployment gives some grounds for the suspicion with which civil servants were viewed by those outside government. But Labour officials also resisted more conservative policy initiatives. They successfully deflected a Treasury attempt to stop funding the Unemployment Grants Committee (UGC) in the 1920s, for example. Their efforts to moderate the legislative attack on trade unionism in the aftermath of the General Strike enjoyed less success. In the 1930s the Ministry of Labour also forced Neville Chamberlain to make substantial modifications in his plan to set up an extra-parliamentary body to administer unemployment assistance. The first episode demonstrates that Ministry of Labour officials did not invariably suffer defeat in confrontations with the Treasury. This provides a useful qualification to the sometimes exaggerated influence of the "Treasury view."[28] The second episode illuminates the limits to official influence over policy. The last episode shows energetic ministerial leadership to be a vital prerequisite for departmental success.

The Political Necessity of the Unemployment Grants Committee

In 1926 disagreement arose between the Treasury and the Ministry of Labour about the future of the UGC. Established in 1920, this body helped fund public works projects launched by local authorities to relieve unemployment.[29] In July 1926 the minister of labour, Sir Arthur Steel-Maitland, asked Winston Churchill, then Chancellor of the Exchequer, for the authority to continue operating the UGC. In response to this request, P. J. Grigg of the Treasury (see appendix) detailed for F. N. Tribe, the minister's private secretary (see appendix), the Treasury's view that unemployment at that time was due to the stoppage in the coal industry. Nothing could be done about reconsidering the continuation of the UGC until the coal strike ended, Grigg explained, at which time the matter could be taken up again.[30]

Ministry of Labour officials regarded with dismay the prospect of dismantling the UGC. Tribe believed that to close down the scheme completely would result in a great critical reaction on the part of the public. Eady pointed out that the public would demand an alternative policy, and that such a policy would be difficult to devise. He warned:

> Administratively, both our position in regard to unemployment benefit, and the position of the Ministry of Health in regard to the control of poor law expenditure, will undoubtedly be made more difficult if it can be represented that the Government is indifferent, or unsympathetic to the condition of many of these areas.

At the end of the month Tribe asked the minister if he was going to accept the chancellor's view on the UGC, and if so, whether this change in policy would be announced publicly. Tribe, in his minute, called Steel-Maitland's attention to the fact that "the Chancellor of the Exchequer bases his arguments on certain quite false hypotheses. Unemployment is not at present entirely due to the coal strike." He reiterated the view of Ministry of Labour officials that to shut down the UGC would cause political trouble for the minister. Tribe evenhandedly conceded that the Treasury's position had some merit:

> On the other hand, something may be said for deliberately refusing all assistance to necessitous areas so as to drive men to more profitable occupations in other districts, and on general financial grounds it is arguable that the

less is spent on relieving unemployment the quicker will unemployment be cured.

Economic theory did not, however, address political realities.[31]

At the behest of his advisers, Steel-Maitland continued his struggle with Churchill to preserve the UGC. Although the public works projects it supported never bulked large in any government's strategy to deal with unemployment, the UGC continued to fund and to supervise a modest public works program. The second Labour government even expanded its operations, although it finally fell victim to the general economy drive following the crisis of 1931. In 1926, the energy to defend the program came from Ministry of Labour officials rather than from the minister of labour. They advanced primarily political reasons for preserving the UGC, and Steel-Maitland found them persuasive. Steel-Maitland, with the support of his civil servants, for once faced down his more flamboyant colleague.[32]

The 1927 Trade Disputes Act

The Ministry of Labour could upon occasion hold its own in the discussions of policy that took place in official circles. But in the highly charged atmosphere of the interwar period, controversies over policies under the purview of the Ministry of Labour took on such political significance that the ministry could lose control of the direction those policies were taking. The passage of the Trade Disputes Act the year after the defeat of the 1926 General Strike vividly illustrates the relative powerlessness of Steel-Maitland and the Ministry of Labour during the 1920s over the formulation of government policy on labor relations.

Pressure to change the statute regarding the powers of trade unions came from prominent business leaders and from the right wing of the Conservative party. Baldwin's Conservative government formed a Cabinet Legislative Committee to consider possible legislation shortly after the collapse of the General Strike. The Lord Chancellor, Lord Cave, had suggested the formation of this committee, and he became its chairman. Steel-Maitland was an important member, as was his rival Winston Churchill. Steel-Maitland tried to preserve some semblance of equity in the proposals the committee entertained, and his officials fielded the suggestions brought to the Ministry of Labour.[33]

In July 1926, Sir John Corcoran (see appendix) of the National Union of Manufacturers (NUM) wrote to Steel-Maitland asking for an interview and enclosing a statement of NUM's views on the amendments needed by the trade union law. These proposals included a secret ballot for strikes; the replacement of "contracting out" by "contracting in" for union political funds; the separation of benefit and strike funds; the registration of unions and their rules; and the repeal of the clauses of the 1906 Trade Disputes Act that granted unions immunity from tort and that established the legality of "peaceful persuasion." The second item on this list threatened to restrict the trade unions' financing of the Labour party by requiring individual trade union members to agree to the payment of dues for political purposes ("contract in") instead of allowing those not wishing to pay dues to seek an exception ("contract out"). H. B. Betterton, Steel-Maitland's parliamentary secretary, accompanied by J.A.N. Barlow, principal assistant secretary of the ministry's Industrial Relations Department (see appendix), gave the deputation from the NUM a warm reception at a meeting that took place the following October.[34]

Business leaders such as Corcoran focused their hostility toward trade unions on the 1906 Trade Disputes Act. They saw a relationship between the change in statute and the increasing incidence of labor unrest since that time. Ministry of Labour officials did not believe that such a relationship existed and attempted, without much success, to refute this popular notion. In a letter to J. Forbes Watson of the National Confederation of Employers' Organizations (see appendix), H. J. Wilson detailed the results of the ministry's investigation of this hypothesis.[35]

M. A. Bevan, a Ministry of Labour official, prepared an analysis of the officially recorded strikes and lockouts between 1898 and 1913, to test two theses: that fewer strikes occurred after the Taff Vale decision in 1900 (which held unions responsible for damages caused by their members during strikes) and that more strikes occurred after the passage of the 1906 Trade Disputes Act (which reversed this decision). Bevan observed that the least working days lost due to industrial disputes were in 1904 and 1907. He found that the general trend between 1898 and 1909 was comparatively peaceful and that the number of disputes increased after 1910. Bevan isolated several factors to account for this pattern, which included the rise of the Labour party, the development of mechanisms for conciliation, the growth of trade union membership, and the popularity of syndicalism. He noted that labor leaders tended to be more peaceful than their followers and that "acts of employers were in many cases the starting point of disputes." Bevan concluded:

> Taking all these factors into consideration it is impossible to assign any definite share of the industrial disturbances of the years preceding the war to the Trade Disputes Act of 1906 and it would be incorrect to assert that the Trade Unions deliberately took advantage of their immunity under the Act to foster disturbances.[36]

Horace Wilson, the permanent secretary, followed Bevan's analysis in his letter informing Forbes Watson that "the fluctuations in the amount of unrest must have been due to a variety of factors and that on no construction of the evidence is it possible to assign more than a slight share of responsibility to the position in law of trade unions during the period." Wilson singled out 1910 as a turning point, noting that the cost of living was increasing at that time and wages would not have kept up without disputes. He also pointed out the inverse relationship between unemployment and the number of disputes.[37] Representations of this sort, however, did not have any effect on opinion among business leaders or inside the Conservative party.

In addition to this report, Ministry of Labour officials gathered information on industrial action and its legal status throughout the Western world. Wilson also requested the ministry's chief conciliation officers to report on the state of opinion among trade unions in their areas. From Birmingham came the warning that restrictive legislation would strengthen trade unions because it would be regarded as further evidence of a coalition between owners and government. Birmingham employers apparently had been making little or no effort to achieve industrial peace. In Scotland unions remained both strong and politicized, although the workers were "not revolutionary, all they want is a decent standard of life and security in this." There had been some reaction against trade union leaders, but not against trade unionism as such in the northwest area. Furthermore, the Ministry of Labour's officer in the northwest predicted that "so long as the Trade Unions are threatened with legislation restricting their powers so long will the problem of cooperation on the existing conditions remain impossible of achievement."[38] All these reports tended to support the case that the ministry attempted to build against the proposed legislation.

The most famous clause of the 1927 Trade Disputes Act required that trade unions alter their ways of assessing dues for political purposes by substituting "contracting in" for "contracting out." The Ministry of Labour argued against using statute to mandate such a change. Ministry of Labour civil servants thought the legislation not only unnecessary but useless. The bill, if passed, could not prevent cases of intimidation that already existed (and ministry officials thought them uncommon) because "It is just as easy to pillory a member who has not declared himself willing." Ministry officials believed that abuses of political funds by unions could only be effectively controlled by the union membership. They predicted (accurately, as it turned out) that the bill would have a serious, but only temporary, impact on Labour party funds. Civil servants judged this "politically and industrially inopportune" bill to be "the first piece of legislation definitely aimed against the Labour Party since the political and legal existence of the party was recognized." Passing it would undermine moderates in the party.[39]

Civil servants at the Ministry of Labour regarded the proposed legislation as essentially punitive. This critical view of such an alteration in the law on trade unions was not confined to the Labour Ministry. In May 1926 Warren

Fisher, permanent secretary and official head of the civil service, warned Neville Chamberlain that civil servants opposed emergency legislation against trade unions. Steel-Maitland supported his official advisers, consistently arguing against the form the bill was taking. In a memorandum circulated before the Cabinet Legislative Committee, Steel-Maitland observed: "I am quite convinced that if, in fact, we set out to attack trade unions, we may delude ourselves into the belief that we are really only acting for their own good and are in fact their best friends, but we shall not delude others." Steel-Maitland warned that such an approach would "consolidate the trade unions and the Labour party and play directly into the hands of the extremists."[40]

Despite the forceful arguments marshaled by Steel-Maitland's advisers and his dogged opposition to the measure, the Trade Disputes Act passed into law after several days of acrimonious debate in 1927. Although some of the more extreme measures proposed (such as the repeal of the protections provided by the 1906 act) did not find a place in the statute, the act still contained the two clauses opposed most strenuously by the Ministry of Labour: the provision to prevent victimization of trade union members by their own unions, and the provisions requiring the "contracting in" method for assessing dues for trade unions' political funds.

Consonant with their opposition to the 1927 Trade Disputes Act, officials recommended moderation on other issues raised by the General Strike. When the question arose of how to implement the prime minister's promise that there would be no victimization following the collapse of the General Strike, for instance, they argued that trade unions ought to be left to govern themselves. At the end of October 1926, Steel-Maitland was presented with two different views on the government's responsibility for those who had worked during the strike. One view was that the department was not doing enough to help victims of trade unions, that the issues involved the prime minister's personal honor, and that the government should consider legislation to correct the situation. This minute argued: "If we give the impression that we are dependent upon the good will of the executives of the unions and upon their construction of their own rules, it will give a most unfortunate impression." An alternative view of the matter was given by Ince, a principal in the Industrial Relations Department, who noted that one hundred cases of such victimization had been reported to the department. Forty-one of these had already been disposed of, the rest were in the process of appeal. The policy of the department had been to encourage the men to utilize the appeal process in their union. Ince concluded: "On the whole, the Executives of the Unions have taken a very reasonable attitude." Steel-Maitland's memorandum to the Cabinet on victimization by trade unions followed the same lines as Ince's and recommended against legislation.[41]

Ministry of Labour officials urged the government to take an enlightened view of the trade union movement after the General Strike. Yet neither Steel-Maitland nor his official advisers displayed the consistent sympathy for the trade union point of view that Agriculture officials evinced toward agricultural workers. Churchill, rather than Steel-Maitland, was the one to support the coal miners in their efforts to achieve a national agreement with mine owners after the collapse of the General Strike.[42] Steel-Maitland, in contrast, initiated a test case before the Industrial Court on the question of whether miners that were unemployed as a direct result of the strike's causing a mine to close remained eligible for unemployment benefits. In this action, Steel-Maitland had the full support of his officials. The umpire ruled in favor of the miners, however. Blunden, an assistant secretary in the Employment and Insurance Department, concluded: "The matter seems settled against us." Settled at some political cost, however, as the Miners Federation protested bitterly what they saw as obstruction by the government to prevent their members from obtaining benefits they deserved.[43]

Civil servants' professional assessment of events as they arose could lead them to oppose the overtly political aims of the 1927 Trade Disputes Act. This stance also could well lead them, as here, to oppose the state's provision of undue aid to the trade union movement. Although skeptical of innovation, Ministry of Labour negativism does not evidence a self-conscious class partisanship. Rather, the limitations imposed upon civil servants by their own theoretical presuppositions in combination with inescapable political realities virtually eclipsed their scope to initiate positive action.

Defending Unemployment Assistance from Poor Law Principles

In 1933 Wilfred Eady, then principal assistant secretary of the Transitional Payments Department, undertook the task of formulating a general view of the problems facing the government and the policies it should consider in order to deal with those problems. In his view, the prospects for employment remained generally bad. If the situation worsened, he warned, both the government and the Ministry of Labour would be open to criticism. He then turned his attention to the means test and the Ministry of Health's proposed bill to create a national system of means-tested relief for the able-bodied poor administered by an independent National Assistance Commission.[44]

This bill, as originally conceived, would have implemented Neville Chamberlain's proposal to centralize the administration of all kinds of relief in the hands of an extra-parliamentary body. Chamberlain's attempt to reform the provision of relief in this way set off a full-scale struggle between the Ministry of Labour on one side and the Ministry of Health and the Treasury on the other, a struggle that had to be resolved at the Cabinet level. Labour eventually had to concede the principle of a centralized body to administer unemployment assistance but had more success in preserving the distinction between the able-bodied unemployed and other categories of those in need, as well as the distinction between those provided for by unemployment insurance and those dependent upon relief provided by the state. The energetic leadership of the department's minister, Henry Betterton (enthusiastically supported and astutely advised by his officials), accounts for the degree of success achieved by the Ministry of Labour in this political struggle.[45]

Eady's observations in the early stages of the controversy focused on how a proposal ostensibly intended to reform the Poor Law in fact combined the stringency of relief characteristic of the Poor Law in an administrative apparatus removed from the democratic influence of the political process. Eady pronounced the bill "hopeless," both "politically and in practice," and "Poor Law in its conception." The bill did not even offer a reformed Poor Law, because "where it differs from the existing Poor Law it introduces greater harshness." The bill "purports to repeal the Poor Law but continues the Poor Law and extends it to cover four times as many people." Eady pointed out bluntly: "The elected Authorities disappear and the officials remain. The Authorities and the officials may like this, but the people will not." He believed the bill in that form would transform those merely critical into actively hostile opponents. He conceded that the bill would help to tidy the Poor Law and it would certainly "relieve local Authorities of an unwelcome administrative burden," but it would also expose "the greater part of those who will come under it to worse conditions and less security" than they already enjoyed. To relieve the local authorities necessarily meant a greater burden for the Exchequer. Under those circumstances, if the Exchequer wished to reduce expenditure, it could only do so "at the expense of the applicants and their families."[46]

Eady's analysis again illustrates the positive side of the Ministry of Labour's negativism. In this instance the department's view had more effect on policy than it had under Steel-Maitland's leadership in the aftermath of the General Strike. Eady's minister, H. B. Betterton, successfully opposed this version of Neville Chamberlain's scheme to create an independent national body to administer relief to the able-bodied poor—a scheme that finally took concrete form in the Unemployment Assistance Board created in 1934.[47] It is ironic that this development opened up career opportunities for Eady himself, who took on an important position in the administration of the newly formed Unemployment Assistance Board.

The Theoretical and Practical Basis for a Positive Policy

These episodes show that Ministry of Labour officials' resistance to policy initiatives did not necessarily constitute official negativism toward progressive innovation. If Ministry of Labour civil servants thwarted Liberal and Labour proposals calling for the state's intervention in the economy in order to stimulate employment, they also opposed Treasury and Conservative pressure to withdraw from responsibilities already undertaken by the state. Ministry opinion, bracketed on the left and the right, suggests the attempt to adhere to a middle way. Buffeted by the push of economic realities and the pull of political realities, civil servants found that such a middle way remained elusive throughout the interwar period.

An examination of the civil servants' treatment of the various policy options suggested to them may leave an exaggerated impression of official negativism and obstructionism. But the Ministry of Labour did not limit itself to preparing responses to suggestions brought to its attention. During these years Wilfred Eady prepared several lengthy memoranda in which he attempted to formulate a more comprehensive response to the economic difficulties England faced.

Wilfred Griffin Eady, one of the most brilliant civil servants produced by the Ministry of Labour, had an extremely successful career. He had attended Clifton and Jesus College, Cambridge, before sitting for the open competition examination held in 1913. After serving briefly in several departments, he entered the Ministry of Labour when it was formed in 1917. Rising to the rank of principal assistant secretary at the Ministry of Labour in less than fifteen years, Eady also served as secretary of the Unemployment Assistance Board and chairman of the Board of Customs and Excise before becoming joint second secretary of the Treasury in 1942. The views he expressed in some speculative essays composed during his tenure at the Ministry of Labour represent the cutting edge of progressive thinking within official circles. They did not always evoke a sympathetic response from Eady's colleagues, but they do reveal the principles that formed the foundations for and the limitations of such thought.

Eady's efforts show the Ministry of Labour capable of developing an original and comprehensive analysis of the failings of the interwar economy. The department could also propose concrete and practical courses of action to soften the impact of unemployment. In 1919, for example, Labour Ministry officials suggested that the award of government contracts be based in part on employment considerations. The opposition sparked by Ministry of Labour attempts to construct a positive policy demonstrates the formidable obstacles that undermined departmental influence.[48]

Wilfred Eady: "Systematic Guidance" Provided by the State

In August 1926 Eady, at that time assistant secretary in the Employment and Insurance Department, outlined a proposal to make more use of the money in the unemployment insurance fund. Eady noted that a common criticism of the fund was that to pay men to be idle constituted a poor use of money. He first enumerated the difficulties that would arise in any effort to use its moneys for any purpose other than the payment of benefits. Any such scheme would require legislation. Payments to contributors were a contract liability of the fund, a liability so heavy that any experimentation with it could prove dangerous. Eady conceded that many suggested schemes would indeed be inappropriate uses of the fund. (Officials later rejected Comyns-Carr's idea to subsidize industry using the unemployment insurance fund.) Eady suggested instead that 1 percent of the fund's annual income could be used to finance the training and transportation of workers out of depressed areas of the country. He predicted (accurately, as it turned out) that even if trade revived, certain depressed areas would remain. The fund would benefit from the reduction in unemployment, Eady argued, but the Exchequer would probably continue to be unwilling to approve adequate funding for such a program for the training and transfer of labor.[49]

Eady coupled this rather modest proposal with a bolder one. He suggested that 2 percent of the annual income of the fund should be set aside for relieving unemployment whenever unemployment reached serious proportions. The creation of such a fund would give the Ministry of Labour the resources to carry out an active policy to combat unemployment:

> Although the Minister of Labour through his administration of the Insurance Fund and the work of the Employment Exchanges has by far the most detailed knowledge of the unemployment problem, he has had no responsibility for any financial expenditure for the relief of unemployment, and has had no control over such expenditure.

Eady thought that his proposal would go some way to remedy that unsatisfactory situation.[50]

Eady's colleagues did not treat his proposal any more sympathetically than they treated similar ones pressed upon them from outside the department. Among the criticisms leveled against Eady's plan was the contention that trade unions might object to it and that training was the responsibility of industry. In the end the minister himself, Arthur Steel-Maitland, decided against pursuing Eady's suggestion. Eady had failed to convince him that the scheme could work. The minister thought such action would set a dangerous precedent and, even if successful, could benefit only a small number of people.[51]

Later in 1926 Eady advanced other, even more speculative, proposals. First, he identified two sharply opposed views of the current problem. One saw unemployment as differing in degree but not in kind from previous slumps and thus predicted a slow but even recovery. The other regarded the current situation represented something new and different, which consequently required different solutions. The first view had been the more popular one and had so far resulted in the policy of "tide over" that underlay the reliance on unemployment relief. Eady offered his own detailed analysis of the economic situation based on the second proposition.[52]

Eady believed that the war had dislocated the relationship between trade and the labor force. Wartime industries had created an abnormal distribution of population that turned regions into impoverished areas after war industries disbanded. Since the war, according to Eady, trade unions had both modified the action of competition on prices and checked the fluidity of labor. The munitions industry had created a pool of highly paid unskilled workers. The solution to these difficulties lay in securing the fluidity of the labor supply, which (Eady asserted) must be as flexible as the supply of capital.[53]

The question remained, How was the country to achieve this end? Eady argued that the situation required what he called "systematic guidance." He contended that previous experience (that is, the Road Fund, the Electricity Bill, the Housing Acts, and the Trade Facilities Acts—none of which were the responsibility of the Ministry of Labour) "all point to the necessity for some novel and difficult relation between Government and the capital expenditure that will be required to ensure a proper industrial development." But both the Poor Law and unemployment insurance tended to tie men to a particular district, hindering the free flow of labor. Government and trade unions must cooperate "if the change-over to the post-war distribution of trade is not to be unnecessarily checked." Because of this need, trade unions must be seen in perspective, not simply in terms of their recent militant policy. Industry must gain a new equilibrium, but "the effort of industry may be haphazard and even short-sighted." The problem, according to Eady, was "to bring to bear upon industry the additional and wider knowledge that Government, and only Government, can obtain and possess."[54]

Eady's views could not have been popular among his colleagues. He is here outlining a vision of the role of government in economic planning that was not widely accepted in England until the 1960s. Revealing an awareness of the controversial nature of his views, Eady wrote H. D. Hancock, the permanent secretary's private secretary (see apppendix), early in 1927: "While support of Mr Keynes is nowadays officially a dubious reference, the Nation for 12th February also suggests . . . some kind of deflection of the channels of investment." In a minute to the permanent secretary in July 1927, he said that his memorandum of the previous autumn had been too speculative to be revised after only six months. Nevertheless he took the opportunity to reiterate his view that the prewar industrial equilibrium could not be restored and that "to reduce the effects of the transition towards a new industrial balance, organized intervention is necessary, most suitably through the government."[55] Eady did not receive any official support for these views within the Ministry of Labour during the 1920s.

Eady continued to believe that a solution to the problem of unemployment in England had to await improvement in international trade. Although he did concede that what he termed "artificial employment" could be generated by public works, he remained critical of that strategy: "Nothing has been so damaging to the proper study of our competitive position over recent years," he contended, "as the amount of distraction that has been introduced by successive annual schemes of public works expenditure." He termed it "deplorable" and "dangerous" that the *Times* should encourage Keynes "to state the case for a loan policy on public works at its most extreme and its most fallacious."[56] Eady suggested that job training and land settlement were more useful lines for the government to pursue.

Eady then turned his attention back to an analysis of the government's policy, which in his opinion was based upon an expectation of a revival of trade and rising prices. Eady did not believe that this would occur. He conceded that it was "theoretically possible" to create a rise in prices "either on the lines suggested by Mr Keynes or in other ways," such as inflation. He argued, however, that such an approach would also mean a rise in both the cost of production and the cost of living. "Mr Keynes seems to think that a rise in prices can be so engineered as to affect only the prices of primary products," Eady observed, "leaving all other prices, including wages, as they are." He pronounced this "nonsense." On the contrary, he argued, secondary costs would have to be adjusted to the fall in primary prices. The truth of this proposition must be acknowledged, Eady warned, or unemployment would grow, the cost of unemployment would increase, the condition of the depressed areas would worsen, and the mood of the unemployed could change.[57]

After thus dismissing Keynes, Eady suggested two possible policies for the government. The first he termed a national treaty, following the lines of the MacMillan Report.[58] This would consist of a general, enforced agreement to reduce costs that would cover wages, rents, transportation, and interest. Eady commented that to adopt this policy "would need courage, but if it were done and succeeded, there is little doubt that our competitive position would be improved and, what is more important, the mood of the country would be much healthier."[59]

On the other hand, Eady suggested, the government could pursue what he called a policy of reconstruction. This policy had several components. The government would have to undertake to supply housing to the working class at rents that they could afford to pay. This would require, according to Eady, "translating the supply of working-class houses into a public utility or social service comparable with the supply of water, gas or electricity." Eady admitted the existence of powerful interests—builders and landlords—with which the government would have to contend if it chose to pursue this option.

Eady also recommended the compulsory reorganization of not only coal mining, but also the iron and steel industries, the mercantile marine, and agriculture. Here again powerful interests would oppose this strategy. Eady realized that a "problem of compensation arises, and this would have to be dealt with as ruthlessly as a private amalgamation would deal with the values of a redundant plant." In addition, local authorities in depressed areas would have to be reorganized.[60]

Eady did not argue that these steps would be practicable at that time. He acknowledged that their undoubted unpopularity would make their implementation possible only in an emergency atmosphere. He contended that some such steps might well become necessary and that the government should be prepared to undertake them. In his conclusion, he underlined the authority conferred on civil servants by virtue of their expert knowledge:

> We at the Ministry of Labour have a special responsibility to the Government in that we alone of the Departments have a living contact with very large numbers of the working people. We are bound to call attention to the fact that if working people believe that the Government's main interest in the unemployed is to operate the means test under sharper conditions a political situation will arise in which more than the electoral existence of the present government will be at stake.[61]

Nothing came of the various suggestions Eady put forward in 1926 and 1933. He could not muster strong support for his ideas even among his colleagues, much less persuade any of the ministers he served of their worth. Even if he had been able to accomplish both these feats, no interwar minister of labour commanded sufficient political strength, strength comparable to Neville Chamberlain's, to convince a skeptical Cabinet of the need to attempt any of these schemes. However, Eady's continued success as a civil servant during this period indicates that the Ministry of Labour apparently did not demand that Eady sacrifice his career to express his relatively advanced opinions.

Eady's view rested on the same premises that led civil servants to reject many of the measures proposed by those outside government. Ministry of Labour officials believed that the solution to the problems plaguing the English economy lay in the ability of industry to reorganize, in order to increase productivity, and in the development of mechanisms to make the labor supply match more closely the changing needs of industry. From this perspective, both unemployment relief and public works represented only temporary palliatives and were actually counterproductive in the long term. Officials thus assumed a position neither radical nor reactionary. They did not seek to preserve laissez-faire capitalism at all costs, or to replace the market mechanism with state direction. Rather, they believed that a judicious application of the power of the state could make capitalism work more smoothly with a lower social cost. Eady's contributions to the often heated but largely futile debates about how the government should treat the continuing high levels of unemployment demonstrate that one did not have to be a follower of Keynes to devise a constructive and progressive policy.

As Eady's writings amply illustrate, the officials of the Ministry of Labour did not meet postwar difficulties entirely bereft of ideas. Yet even when Ministry of Labour civil servants agreed among themselves on a course of action, they could seldom impose their view beyond their department. Throughout the interwar period, Ministry of Labour civil servants failed to make any significant impact on government policy. Their suggestions invariably had to run the gauntlet of hostile scrutiny, both internal and external. The government's effortless disregard of official advice about the 1927 Trade Disputes Act demonstrates how civil servants found themselves helpless in the face of powerful political interests. In contrast, Ministry of Labour officials' staunch and moderately successful defense of the Unemployment Grants Committee shows them to be more than mere functionaries.

Conclusion

Between the First and Second World Wars, the Ministry of Labour administered unemployment relief and collected the most detailed and comprehensive information available about the incidence of unemployment. Yet the Ministry of Labour found itself virtually excluded from the formulation of policy on unemployment. At no time during these two decades did the Ministry of Labour have a political leader who could impose a departmental stamp on policy made at the Cabinet level. The vagaries of the ministry's political leadership account for much of the department's ineffectiveness.

Immediately after the First World War the Ministry of Labour had four ministers in five years. Sir Arthur Steel-Maitland then held the office for four years during Baldwin's Conservative government. But Steel-Maitland—although everyone agreed he worked hard and meant well—could never do more than hold his own in conflicts with his stronger-minded colleagues, especially Winston Churchill.[62] The second Labour government, rather than depend upon the Ministry of Labour, formed extra-departmental groups such as the Unemployment Committee (chaired by the Lord Privy Seal J. H. Thomas) and the Economic Advisory Council to develop a policy to deal with unemployment.[63] Henry Betterton, who served at the Ministry of Labour from 1931 to 1934 during Ramsay MacDonald's national government, did have a measure of success in forcing modifications in Neville Chamberlain's pet scheme for the able-bodied unemployed. But Betterton engaged in this conflict more to uphold the principle of ministerial responsibility than to construct a positive policy to provide unemployment relief in a more equitable way.[64]

No matter how much civil servants might dominate a department's policy, they must have an effective advocate in the Cabinet to shepherd their view through the political process. However, Ministry of Labour officials staffed the department that Ramsay MacDonald dubbed the "Cinderella" of Whitehall. They had to wait twenty-three years until Ernest Bevin acted as their "Prince Charming," rather surprisingly taking the form of an aggressive and abrasive trade union organizer with no previous ministerial experience.

The advice Ministry of Labour officials gave did not challenge any fundamental elements of the economic and political system, but they did not necessarily cling to the principal of laissez-faire. They consistently opposed any large-scale programs of public works financed through deficit spending. But in this, Ministry of Labour civil servants did not succumb to pressure to follow the "Treasury view."[65] Rather, they adhered to the logic of contemporary economic thought. The theoretical rationale for public works and deficit spending as an appropriate response to depression rests on the multiplier effect, a concept not elaborated until 1931 and not incorporated into Keynes's work until the middle of the 1930s.[66] Labour Ministry civil servants instead emphasized the active role government should play in encouraging the free movement of labor, from one region to another (by not subsidizing those who wished to remain in their homes) and from one industry to another (by subsidizing training programs). The government's duty, in their view, lay in encouraging the mobility of labor so that the supply of labor could be as fluid as the supply of capital.

Labour exchanges, the Ministry of Labour's original foundation, had been formed in part to carry out just this mission. A policy premised on such an understanding of the government's role in economic processes could have two components, one positive and one negative. Training and transfer programs could "pull" labor to more prosperous regions and industries. Simultaneously, administering unemployment benefits according to the principles of "less eligibility" and "genuinely seeking work" could "push" labor out of depressed areas. Ministry of Labour civil servants saw only the latter of these two principles implemented effectively during the interwar years, and that only because those who dominated the Conservative party shared this view.[67]

The prospect of war finally brought different kinds of problems to the attention of ministry officials. During the spring and summer of 1939 the Ministry of Labour held conversations with both the general council of the TUC and the National Confederation of Employers' Organizations. Late in March the minister made a statement to these interested parties on the emergency labor provisions embodied in the Control of Employment Bill. In April

Walter Citrine, representing the TUC, met with the minister of labour. In June he submitted to the minister a scheme treating these matters prepared by the TUC's general council, and W. H. Hardman, a principal in the Employment Department (see appendix), prepared an analysis of the TUC view. Hardman noted that the Confederation of Employers' Organizations had not yet submitted a formal proposal but that they had, when consulted, tended "to advocate full-blooded industrial conscription immediately on the outbreak of war." Hardman wanted to preserve as much scope as possible for voluntary action, but he admitted that some measures for compulsion must be foreseen. He warned: "It is axiomatic that a discontented workman is inefficient and that stoppages of work owing to industrial disputes would be even more unfortunate." Therefore, he argued, "It was essential . . . that arrangements for controlling employment should be made as acceptable as possible without at the same time rendering the control ineffective or misdirected."[68]

Turning to the TUC's proposals, Hardman pointed out that these tended to "secure the maximum rate of wages" at the same time as they guaranteed workers no rise in the cost of living. Hardman argued that if England were forced to adopt monetary depreciation the consequent rise in the cost of living would be, under the TUC plan, necessarily accompanied by increased wages. This would involve the country in a vicious circle that would lead inexorably to financial collapse. In another meeting with TUC representatives, the Ministry of Labour discussed the ministry's reservations about their proposals and asked the TUC to make further recommendations. Ministry officials had another meeting with Citrine in July at which the distance between the views of the TUC and the government were sufficiently narrowed to allow the government to proceed with drawing up and submitting a bill.[69]

In this round of negotiations we can see Ministry of Labour officials fulfilling a role they strongly identified with. Acting as intermediaries between capital and labor, they maintained their own vision of the best interests of the state, and in light of this, they strove to achieve a workable compromise. In this instance their efforts met with a measure of success they seldom experienced. In the following year the department's fortunes improved even more with the appointment of a new minister, Ernest Bevin, whose energetic leadership engaged their professional commitment. His position of power in the Cabinet guaranteed that their efforts would no longer go for naught, as they had done so often during the years between the wars.

This late episode also demonstrates the vitality of the Ministry of Labour. Hardman, who had been at the ministry only since 1934, here spoke with the departmental voice. This voice, developed during the heady days of the Labour Department's expansion under the auspices of the Board of Trade, survived the vicissitudes of the interwar period and the Treasury's growing power over both departmental finances and personnel.

The Ministry of Labour thus managed to retain a departmental identity fostered in part by its own personnel practices. These tended to sever the link between career success and elite educational institutions found in other departments like the Board of Education and the Ministry of Health, at least insofar as was possible within the context of a recruitment process that, with its generalist bias, worked in the opposite direction. The Ministry of Labour thus could provide a vehicle for an individual of really obscure social origins to attain high rank (as is evidenced by the career of Horace Wilson).[70] It also created a setting that fostered innovative thought among those who were products of conventional recruiting methods (such as Wilfred Eady). The distancing of the professional ethos of Ministry of Labour officials from their social origins lent their views the authority of objectivity and neutrality.

In their formulation of policy, Ministry of Labour civil servants did not perceive themselves to be class agents. They resisted pressure to use the state's power to further class interest at the expense of national interests when they perceived such a process at work. Their understanding of their role helped to build a state apparatus that could institutionalize class relations and, in so doing, blunt the energy of class antagonisms.

6 The Ministry of Health: Fiscal Versus Social Responsibility

■ *There were giants in those days who kept expenditure so low . . .*

—William A. Ross

The Ministry of Health constituted one of the few concrete and long-lasting accomplishments of the postwar Reconstruction program promised by Lloyd George's coalition.[1] The new ministry proved a disappointment, however. Its potential both as an administrative reform and as a social reform remained unfulfilled during the interwar years. The abrupt reduction of spending with which the government responded to the downturn in the economy in 1920 crippled the ambitious housing program launched by the first minister of health, Christopher Addison. The fiscal constraints insisted upon by the Treasury after that episode limited the other policy options the ministry could pursue. Yet, "Treasury control" does not provide a sufficient explanation for the implacable consistency with which Ministry of Health officials upheld principles of fiscal stringency during these years.

The civil servants who staffed the upper levels of the Ministry of Health—lacking any grounding in social policy as such—took the restraint of spending to be paramount among their duties. This orientation toward policy questions drew sustenance from recruitment and promotion practices at the Ministry of Health. The department's preference for the open competition aspirant virtually guaranteed that the Ministry of Health would be staffed by men who brought to their duties no special knowledge of or experience with social policy or social problems. This distinguishes the Ministry of Health from the three other departments considered above, all of which looked for some evidence of expertise, however defined, or interest in the department's arena of responsibility. The theory behind the "generalist" civil servant favored by the MacDonnell Commission and by Warren Fisher, permanent secretary at the Treasury and head of the civil service from 1919 until 1939, presumed that the well educated and intelligent would bring with them the intellectual resources and flexibility necessary to deal with whatever task they took on. As a consequence, officials at the Ministry of Health had no alternative point of view to counter the tradition of Poor Law "less eligibility" inherited from Health's administrative progenitor, the Local Government Board (LGB).[2]

The Ministry of Health differed in another important way from the other social service ministries we have examined. Health enjoyed the advantage of aggressive and dynamic ministerial leadership provided by a politician of stature and authority, Neville Chamberlain, who dominated policy making at the ministry for most of the interwar period and who concerned himself chiefly with matters of finance and administrative efficiency. Ministry officials found in Chamberlain a kindred spirit, and an astute politician who enjoyed considerable leverage in the Cabinet.

In the analysis below I will examine the creation of the Ministry of Health in order to establish the institutional context within which Health officials worked. Then, a survey of the departmental view of a number of policy questions will demonstrate the consistency with which officials placed a high priority on fiscal considerations. The chapter concludes with an assessment of the influence of Neville Chamberlain's leadership on the department's approach to policy.

Origins and Organization

The creation of the Ministry of Health at the end of the First World War seemingly represents a final, unequivocal acceptance of the principle that the state has an interest in and a responsibility for the health of its citizenry. The passage of the Ministry of Health Act in June 1919 formed an important element in the reconstruction of English society promised by the Lloyd George coalition following the war.[3] The long and ultimately successful struggle for a Ministry of Health had gone on intermittently since the first half of the nineteenth century. The first attempt, dominated by the figure of Edward Chadwick, had resulted in the formation of the General Board of Health in 1848. In 1858 this Board was dissolved and its functions divided between the Home Office and the Privy Council. This arrangement did not prove satisfactory, however, and the report of the 1869 Royal Sanitary Commission issued a second call for a central authority to administer both public health measures and the Poor Law. Following the Commission's recommendations, the government then created the Local Government Board to carry out these duties.[4]

The establishment of the Ministry of Health in 1919 culminated a third effort to form a central governmental body to take responsibility for public health. The performance of its predecessor, the LGB, had disappointed so many that a movement arose to create a new central government agency to oversee the health of the populace. This campaign had gone on for at least a decade prior to the passage of the 1919 Ministry of Health Act, although those who championed the cause did not fully recognize the contradictions among the different ends they sought to achieve through this administrative change.[5]

The twentieth-century movement for a Ministry of Health encompassed at least three distinct goals. The first was the desire to increase efficiency in government. Administrative efficiency, according to this view, required that public services be supervised by centralized governmental agencies defined by the services they provided. Health services thus should be grouped together under a Ministry of Health. These arguments had been enunciated by Sidney and Beatrice Webb in the *Minority Report* of the 1909 Royal Commission on the Poor Law, and again in the 1918 *Report of the Machinery of Government Committee* chaired by Lord Haldane, an ally of the Webbs. (Analogous arguments had justified the earlier creation of the Ministry of Labour.) The state's interest in a Health Ministry, according to efficiency enthusiasts, stemmed from the need to secure the maximum health standards for the populace. Thus benefits assigned to individuals actually accrued to society and did not belong to the individual by right.[6]

A second component of the drive for a Ministry of Health, in contrast, derived from belief in the moral duty to relieve suffering. This tended therefore to emphasize the cost of health problems to the individual. During the First World War, many followed Lord Rhondda—president of the LGB from December 1916 until June 1917 and a key figure among those urging the establishment of a Ministry of Health—who came to support this position because of Britain's high rate of infant mortality (infant deaths exceeded deaths on the battlefield by a factor of one-third).[7] Those who agitated against the high infant and maternal mortality rates sought the establishment of a Health Ministry to alleviate the conditions responsible. Enhancing governmental efficiency, while not unimportant, thus represented a means to an end, not an end in itself.

A third element motivating the drive for a Ministry of Health was the antipathy toward the Poor Law and the government department charged with its administration (the Local Government Board), which translated into a demand for a totally new ministry. The 1834 Poor Law Amendment Act had inspired virulent hostility from the time of its inception. By the twentieth century this hostility had hardened into an implacable opposition that encompassed the LGB as well. The LGB's reputation suffered also from its lack of participation in the innovations in social policy that were sponsored by the Liberal party between 1906 and 1914. Lloyd George had to create a new government department, the National Health Insurance Commission (NHIC), to administer his insurance scheme, in part because of the opposition of the LGB and its president, John Burns, to this innovation.[8] The Board of Education claimed jurisdiction over the health of school-age children and proceeded to expand the school medical service. The Board of Trade took charge of labour exchanges although the LGB had previously been responsible for legislation treating unemployment.[9] This piecemeal implementation of social programs not only vitiated the LGB as an administrative unit but also alarmed those interested in increasing government efficiency.

In 1919 those who had worked for a Ministry of Health appeared victorious. Two of the leaders of the campaign for the new ministry played key roles in the early stages of its organization: Dr. Christopher Addison became the first minister of health and Robert Morant (see appendix) became its first permanent secretary. Morant entered the new ministry with ambitious plans for the reform of maternity care and the treatment of the mentally ill. He looked forward to a public medical service and wished to encourage research, both for its own sake and as a remunerative career.[10] None of this came to pass, however, and the auspicious beginning led instead to disappointment. Morant died in harness the next year with his work unfinished. Addison's much vaunted housing policy rapidly became so expensive that Lloyd George succumbed to pressure and removed him from his post.

Addison subsequently broke with Lloyd George completely and resigned from the government in 1923. However, in a few years his political fortunes recovered, and he went on to have a long and distinguished career in the Labour party where he developed a special expertise in agricultural policy. It is ironic that Addison's career culminated after he entered the House of Lords, where he supervised the passage of the Beveridge Report into law during the postwar Labour government. His many later accomplishments, however, never entirely erased the shadow of his early failure.[11]

The Ministry of Health could not have lived up to the high expectations so many had for it. The new department as actually constituted did not embody the goals of those who had worked so hard to bring it into being. It did not even have a monopoly on the health services provided by the state, as those interested in efficiency thought necessary. The Home Office continued to administer the various factory acts, which regulated conditions in the workplace. The Board of Education also retained important responsibilities for monitoring the health of school-age children. (The practice of appointing the same person to hold the position of chief medical officer in both the Ministry of Health and the Board of Education mitigated somewhat the division of responsibilities between these two departments.) More important, the creation of a Ministry of Health failed to accomplish a thorough overhaul of the LGB. Sir Arthur Newsholme, the last medical officer who served the LGB, characterized the event with some accuracy when he described it as a "change of name for the Local Government Board, with added functions."[12]

The great majority of the officials who staffed the Ministry of Health had spent their previous career in the LGB, which had recruited its higher-level civil servants through open competition examination. The lower salaries paid by the LGB failed to attract large numbers of top-flight recruits, however.[13] These men had no special expertise in social problems, and their subsequent behavior indicates they did not perceive the poor as being their special constituency. Rather, they regarded it as their duty to protect the government from the demands made upon it by the vagaries of local officials in whose hands lay the machinery to relieve the less fortunate. When faced with the social problems generated by mass unemployment and widespread wage reductions caused by the interwar depression, ministry officials interpreted their role in light of their duty to control expenditure rather than relieve suffering. The failure of the Ministry of Health to live up to its promise thus stemmed from the contradictory goals set for the department. The difficult circumstances the ministry had to cope with during the interwar period exposed these contradictions in an uncompromising way.

The Administrative Impetus for Economy in Social Services

The two basic goals of the campaign for a Ministry of Health—government intervention to improve public health and the increased efficiency of that intervention—did not appear incompatible to those who had advocated them or to those who had framed the 1919 Ministry of Health Act. The agreement among the various groups so vigorously seeking a Health Ministry rested upon the ambiguity that surrounded the notion of efficiency, however. The question of whether efficiency is understood in terms of the level of well-being enjoyed by the populace or in terms of the cost to the Exchequer incurred by ministry programs did not arise in those more prosperous days. But the depression that gripped England by 1922 created social and fiscal problems that apparently could not be remedied simultaneously. The fiscal responsibility demanded by one of the ministry's goals, as understood by its officials, came into conflict with the social responsibility enjoined by the other goal. Forced to choose between these two goals, ministry officials almost invariably choose to reduce or to limit expenditure. The memoranda they composed in support of departmental policy involving a broad range of issues reveal a consistency of attitude that suggests they found this choice a congenial one.

The Ministry of Health inherited from the LGB the responsibility for the supervision of local Boards of Guardians in their administration of poor relief. Such a task, even under the best of circumstances, necessarily involved a certain measure of friction. The widespread unemployment and the fall in wages caused by the postwar slump placed unprecedented strain on the relationship between local and national authorities. Boards of Guardians in particularly hard-hit areas tried various expedients to meet the incidence of suffering in their communities. When these expedients included what the Ministry of Health regarded as excess or unauthorized expenditure, ministry officials would intervene. The most famous of several such episodes involved the London borough of Poplar.

The danger of unrest among the unemployed became so great in 1920 that the Ministry of Health authorized Boards of Guardians to grant out-relief (that is, allowing the payment of relief to those who continued to live outside a workhouse). H.W.S. Francis (see appendix), assistant secretary at the Ministry of Health and the ministry's Poor Law expert, pointed out that by allowing such a departure from normal procedure "the Ministry have disclaimed responsibility for supervising the conditions of relief." Ministry officials subsequently found themselves unable to take effective action to restrain expenditure of Boards of Guardians such as the one in the borough of Poplar who were determined to spend beyond their means to relieve the unemployed. Civil servants supported the idea of using rate equalization to help Poplar meet its particularly heavy rate burden, but other, more prosperous London boroughs opposed this approach. Instead, Poplar was allowed to borrow from the Metropolitan Common Poor Fund, despite Francis's warnings that the government could not control Poplar's spending from that source either. Events proved Francis's prediction accurate.[14]

The Ministry of Health made these concessions under duress. Both the threat of open unrest in Poplar and the fear of an adverse public reaction to any steps they might take to restrict the Poplar Board in a time of mass unemployment moved the ministry to permit departures from the stringent management of public funds. Such latitude, so grudgingly granted, could not continue, however. Under Neville Chamberlain's leadership, later in the 1920s, the Ministry of Health began to reclaim control of too generous Boards of Guardians. Legislation passed at his behest put an end to such anomalies: the Board of Guardians' (Default) Act gave the minister the power to suspend Boards of Guardians; the Local Authorities (Emergency Provisions) Act of 1928 put the Common Poor Fund under the authority of the Metropolitan Asylums Board, whose staff included eighteen Ministry of Health nominees. This allowed the ministry to assume virtual control of the Fund. Although Chamberlain's legislation did not deny the franchise to those receiving poor relief (as his civil servants had urged), officials acted promptly and vigorously to reassert their authority over the granting of poor relief. When the Boards of Guardians were abolished in 1930, aggressive supervision and inspection combined with the threat of suspension had greatly reduced the number of those on poor relief, even in previously defiant Poplar.

Rural Boards of Guardians, representing much smaller constituencies than their urban counterparts, had less leverage with the Health Ministry. In

1922, when wages of agricultural workers had fallen so low that men with large families had difficulty keeping food on the table, some Boards of Guardians in Norfolk began to supplement the wages of men who headed large households. The Ministry of Health soon put a stop to what they regarded as a dangerous practice. G. H. Hervey, a ministry inspector, reported that he had visited the offending Boards to point out to them "the error of their ways." Hervey told the Boards that they must not resort to an allowance system because it amounted to a subsidy of wages and therefore of employers. Sir Arthur Lowry, the Ministry of Health's chief inspector (see appendix), observed in a memorandum to Francis: "I don't think I need to enlarge upon the dangers of the reintroduction of a system of subsidising by Poor Law relief the wages of agricultural labourers." Francis had the ministry's inspectors investigate the extent of this twentieth-century revival of the Speenhamland system. He subsequently recommended that the ministry deny such relief, except in cases of illness, and that the ministry send a representative to a conference of Norfolk Boards of Guardians to explain the ministry's view. Sir Aubrey Symonds, the ministry's second secretary (see appendix), readily agreed to these measures. Hervey, after attending this conference, reassured Francis that a firm stand by the ministry should put a stop to the rebellion.[15]

Generous Boards of Guardians did not represent the only challenge to departmental policy on poor relief. Early in 1929 Ministry of Health officials had to meet what they perceived as another threat to the ministry's efforts to administer relief on efficient lines. This one came from one of Neville Chamberlain's Cabinet colleagues. In response to an inquiry from Eustace Percy (who in addition to serving as president of the Board of Education was active in a charitable organization known as the Lord Mayor's Fund), ministry officials had to determine how Boards of Guardians ought to evaluate the Fund's practice of issuing food vouchers to adults.

Francis pointed out to his permanent secretary that Chamberlain's policy rested on the principle of "prevention of the duplication of relief." Francis thought the ministry would find it difficult to modify this principle, even in the distressed coal areas. The ministry's inspectors had already been told, Francis reported, to inform Guardians that assistance through the Lord Mayor's Fund "is given in respect of a need which is not covered by the present scale of relief." Francis said he could not recommend that more than this be done, but he obviously did not feel very comfortable about the situation.[16]

At the time these instructions were issued, relief provided by the Lord Mayor's Fund was confined to "in kind"—such as, clothes and food for children and mothers. The Lord Mayor's Fund now proposed to issue food vouchers to adults. These vouchers, Francis argued, thus became a form of cash. He commented: "To extend the suggestion I have already made to the inspectors to the virtual ignoring by the Guardians of these vouchers is obviously a serious matter." Francis also raised the question whether it was equitable to allow this in some areas but not in others. Francis concluded: "We shall have to make the best excuse we can in maintaining our policy in the areas outside the coal areas on the ground that the exception made is temporary and due to the extreme distress."[17]

Francis did not display much confidence in taking this tack, as he thought that neither contention was certain. He also worried about the misapplication of the funds represented by the vouchers, pointing out that one major difficulty was to ensure they were used for food.[18] The official most directly concerned in setting policy on these matters, Francis focused his energies largely on the fiscal integrity of poor relief rather than on its efficacy in maintaining a minimum standard of living for a population hard-hit by depression.

The response of Health Ministry officials to attempts by some local authorities to mitigate the impact of wage reductions upon the families of farmworkers or the impact of long-term unemployment upon the families of urban workers do not represent isolated incidents. The inclination of civil servants to regard even charitable relief as income illustrates the zeal with which they carried out Chamberlain's policy. This zeal fueled a drive to reduce expenditure that pervaded all aspects of policy at the Ministry of Health during the interwar period.[19]

The Health Ministry required economy of expenditure from Guardians for indoor relief as well as for outdoor relief. The weekly cost per inmate in Poor Law institutions actually fell during the early 1920s, partly because of the fall in prices, but partly also because of the reduction in new building occasioned by the ministry's practice of discouraging such capital outlays. Chamberlain's 1929 Local Government Act transferred control of institutions built under the auspices of the Poor Law from the Boards of Guardians to county councils. This act did offer those councils an incentive to spend through a system of block grants. The aim here was to make the administration of relief more efficient, and ultimately less expensive, by providing specialized institutions to replace the old general workhouse, although the return Chamberlain expected from these "economies of scale" never materialized. The act was also meant to provide a larger local base to sustain the expenditure necessary to create this more professional system of relief. At that time, however, county government was no more willing than national government was to incur capital expenditure, so these changes came about very slowly.[20]

Except for the administrative reorganization introduced by Neville Chamberlain, successive ministers of health remained uninterested in the problems posed by vagrants and by the provision of indoor relief. Policy in such matters fell to the officials who staffed the Poor Law Department. M. A. Crowther, in a study of the workhouse system, concluded that these civil servants—many of whom had long careers in the LGB prior to the formation of the Ministry of Health—continued to believe in "the principle of deterrence set up in 1881."[21] Chamberlain's preoccupation with administrative efficiency thus neatly jibed with his civil servants' preoccupation with keeping down expenditure.

The desire for economy of expenditure also shaped the officials' changing definition of the family. The legal responsibility of family members to provide for one another's sustenance had been a part of English law since the Elizabethan Poor Law introduced it in 1601. Although the Ministry of Health administered a family means test, which assumed the legal obligations of family members to support one another, ministry officials avoided formulating a precise definition of the family. To define the family broadly when assessing its financial resources, and narrowly when calculating benefits, enabled officials to limit the responsibility of the state and thereby check the tendency for expenditure to increase. The Ministry of Health could thus shift part of the task of sustaining the unemployed onto the family.[22]

Many families did not have the resources to shoulder their burdens easily. Groups such as Eleanor Rathbone's Children's Minimum Council (CMC), concerned about the increasing incidence of malnutrition, demanded that the Ministry of Health investigate the relationship between family income and diet and establish minimum standards of nutrition. Ministry of Health officials rapidly became hostile toward the CMC campaign, however, preferring to deny the existence of any problem. Sir George Newman, the ministry's chief medical officer from 1919 until 1935 (see appendix), insisted that unemployment had no effect on nutrition. In 1934, Sir Ernest Strohmenger (see appendix), an undersecretary at the Treasury who had served as the Ministry of Health's accountant-general from 1919 until 1930, argued that malnutrition, if it existed, "might well prove to be a matter not so much of inadequate allowances (for relief) as of bad use of income." Arthur Robinson (see appendix), who served as Health's permanent secretary from 1920 until 1935, also believed that malnutrition was due to ignorance.[23]

Assessing the impact of unemployment on health in general and defining the contribution of malnutrition to ill-health both pose formidable methodological and analytical difficulties, and these issues remain contentious.[24] The ambiguity of the evidence available to policy-makers allowed civil servants to continue to voice their concern about maintaining the differential between rates of relief and wage rates that underlay their reluctance to admit the existence of widespread malnutrition among the families of the unemployed. When serving on the Anderson Committee in 1923, Arthur Robinson and Horace Wilson pointed out that, with the addition of dependents' allowances, relief could sometimes exceed wages. Thus, a man with a large family could be better off on relief than working. Both Robinson and Wilson found this prospect undesirable, to say the least.[25] Their stance represented nothing less than a twentieth-century restatement of the principle of "less eligibility" embodied by the 1834 Poor Law. Later in the 1930s, Sir Wilfred Eady, who had come from the Ministry of Labour to become secretary of the Unemployment Assistance Board (UAB), frankly asserted that the UAB lacked a "scientific standard for the calculation of all needs to be covered by the Board; the matter was one of social convention and expediency. The Office [UAB] had therefore proceeded on the principle of less eligibility." The refusal of Ministry of Health officials to set such a standard stemmed from their own allegiance to this principle.[26]

Despite their staunch adherence to this position, Health Ministry officials could not always, without qualms, hold the line on expenditure. In October 1928, a deputation of MPs and officials of the South Wales Miners Federation met with the ministers of Health and Labour. Neville Chamberlain explained his view of the issue of aid to Boards of Guardians, saying, "he had no wish to encourage inhumanity but it was his duty to avoid a landslide." He admitted the existence of "much actual hardship" but said his investigation of individual cases (the town of Pontypridd, for instance) had not found any cases of actual starvation. This meeting disturbed Arthur Robinson, Chamberlain's permanent secretary at the Ministry of Health. His concern about the plight of unemployed miners and their families led him to question

> whether the screws may not have been turned too tight in some of the bad South Wales areas, as a result of our attempts at once to secure the administration of relief on sound lines and to induce local authorities in South Wales to cut their financial coat according to their available cloth.[27]

Robinson worried that a bad winter could increase distress to the point that disturbances could break out. If such a sequence of events did transpire, the ministry would be blamed and unsound measures—the product of panic—might be undertaken. Robinson pointed out: "Short of this, there might be a condition of affairs among some of the people which on grounds of humanity or of public health we should not suffer to continue without some attempt to alleviate it." Robinson saw three problems in any attempt to take action. To increase relief might encourage Boards of Guardians in their extravagance; it might work counter to the policy of transfer; and it would require Treasury approval for the necessary funds. Robinson suggested that Sir Arthur Lowry make a careful inquiry into the deputation's allegations.[28]

Lowry, in a memorandum to the permanent secretary on conditions in South Wales, reported that he could find little evidence of actual sickness caused by malnutrition, although the amount of food consumed by many often fell below the theoretical necessary minimum. According to Lowry, the miners were physically unfit to work, but he did not know whether this was due to malnutrition or to a lack of exercise. Lowry, like many other observers, was especially struck by "the appearance of depression and lack of liveliness among the men one sees standing in groups at corners or walking along the roads."[29]

Lowry's report on South Wales was only one of several made by Ministry of Health officials during 1928. All these reports advanced the view that further relief measures would be counterproductive. In January 1928, a Health official evaluated a description of conditions in South Wales by Board of Education inspectors. This official did not deny the bleakness of the situation reported, but he could not approve of any additional remedies for the situation there. He argued: "The only hope for the South Wales area is in a redistribution of population which can be effected only by economic pressure." Since both unemployment benefit and Poor Law relief mitigated against this economic pressure, he continued, "It would . . . in my view be fatal to introduce other special measures for the relief of distress in the area." In February, ministry officials prepared two reports on conditions in South Wales and a report on Durham. In March, the Special Committee on Distress in South Wales issued a report that called for a transfer of excess population but also recommended measures to relieve the distress of the population and to reduce the burden of debt that local authorities had incurred.[30] These opinions placed social policy at the service of economic policy, by "pushing" excess labor from one region to another. Health officials here propounded a view that they shared with their colleagues at Labour.

Ministry of Health officials did not regard expenditure by the state on programs to reduce unemployment any more favorably than they regarded expenditure on relief. Civil servants had an opportunity to express these views because Health was one of the departments included in the discussions on unemployment policy during the second Labour government. At a conference of heads of departments held in July 1930 to elicit suggestions on possible large-scale projects for the relief of unemployment, Sir Arthur Robinson argued against the use of housing construction as a suitable vehicle for reducing unemployment. Robinson said he was satisfied with the progress of current housing programs, which were (he thought) meeting the demand for housing and reducing the arrears in the housing stock. Robinson feared that a massive new program would not only raise prices but also undercut the current programs of local authorities. Robinson instead recommended a policy that would stimulate local authorities to make greater efforts on their own behalf.[31]

The most comprehensive and innovative suggestions for public projects to provide work came from Lloyd George and the Liberal party, but both Labour ministers and their officials reacted to these in a uniformly hostile way. Housing policy, one of the responsibilities of the Ministry of Health, formed an important component of the Lloyd George program. A memorandum on proposals for regional planning prepared by Robinson and I. G. Gibbon (see appendix) for their minister, Arthur Greenwood, rejected the concept of Garden Cities, citing lack of evidence that they worked. Robinson and Gibbon opposed Special Central Planning machinery because that would undercut local authorities, and they deprecated the concept of regional planning as being only in its infancy. Records of subsequent conversations between Greenwood, Robinson, Gibbon (principal assistant secretary at the Ministry of Health), and William Robert Davidge (an architect and town planning consultant who represented Lloyd George) show that both Greenwood and his officials opposed the Liberal proposals, in principle and in particular. Robinson and Gibbon remained unsympathetic to the development of the centralized governmental machinery required, and they thought that the particular projects suggested were too expensive and impractical. Gibbon, for instance, rejected a proposal to build reservoirs in Berkshire to store water and enhance flood control of the Thames, arguing that there was little demand for such water and that flooding areas for the Thames already existed. Gibbon also disapproved of land reclamation projects because their cost exceeded the value of the land reclaimed.[32]

The Labour government's failure to implement this program did not stem the tide of suggestions pressed upon the government during this period. In 1933 the minister of health for the national government, Sir Edward Hilton-Young (a former Liberal who had joined the Conservative party upon the breakup of the Liberal party), asked officials of the Ministry of Health to evaluate Ernest Bevin's proposals for the alleviation of unemployment. Bevin's suggestions, set out in a pamphlet entitled "Plan for 2,000,000 Workless," included raising the school-leaving age to sixteen, optional retirement at sixty, and a shorter workweek. "I do not want a serious examination of this," Hilton-Young instructed, "but it would be of interest to have any obvious comments on the financial statement." Ministry of Health officials' response gave these suggestions short shrift. Bevin's schemes would be expensive to implement. Even if successful, they would merely substitute one group of workers for another, rather than expand employment, and in any case would not be successful in removing men from the labor market. Robinson noted that similar proposals had been considered by a committee of departments during the previous Labour government. This committee had found the cost so staggering "that nothing more was heard about it."[33]

Fiscal constraints imposed upon the Ministry of Health from above would have represented a formidable obstacle to the development of a more positive policy by that department's officials. Yet, as we have seen, Health officials needed no coercive pressure from the Treasury to control their department's expenditure. Ministry officials capably defended themselves when

Treasury efforts displayed no proper regard for the effect that reductions would have on programs they supported. E. J. Strohmenger, for instance, vigorously argued for the ministry's housing policy when it was under threat from spending cuts recommended by the May Committee. Strohmenger first informed the Treasury that to revise the housing subsidies could not be done "without a complete reversal of Government policy." He then suggested to Greenwood that economies in housing could be obtained by suspending the Housing (Rural Authorities) Act—"an extreme Measure," Strohmenger commented—or by curtailing building under the 1924 act. Strohmenger also recommended that more saving could be obtained by refusing to subsidize houses above a certain size, and by requiring that they not be let to those who could afford to make their own arrangements. Greenwood himself wrote Snowden, rejecting the possibility of carrying out the housing economies recommended.[34]

Strohmenger, in a letter to Alfred Hurst (see appendix) at the Treasury, explained the rationale for subsidizing housing at low rents. He pointed out that the rental rate maintained by the subsidy was a standard working-class rent, according to research by the Ministry of Labour. Strohmenger argued:

> the object of the Wheatley Act, namely the provision of sufficient houses to let at rents within the means of the poorer workers has notoriously not yet been achieved . . . and it is generally agreed that the present function of Local Authorities in the housing business is to endeavor to meet this need. There is no case for giving Exchequer subsidy to build houses at rents which can only be paid by the classes whose needs can already be met through private enterprise or the Building Societies, and that, so far as I can see, is what your suggestion really amounts to.

Strohmenger continued to press for the limitation of subsidy to houses of a certain size and cost, but he suggested to Greenwood that the department could simply "go slow" without actually suspending the operations of the housing acts.[35] The position Strohmenger espoused at this time might have surprised those better acquainted with his later career: he later transferred to the Treasury and then became the first chairman of the UAB. In that capacity he was regarded as an advocate of the Treasury view on social expenditure.

In opposing the gutting of the Ministry of Health's housing policy, Strohmenger defended one of the few positive achievements in social policy undertaken by the department since its inception. This policy had been the product of a series of energetic ministers who had interested themselves in housing—Christopher Addison, John Wheatley, and Neville Chamberlain.[36] The belated attempt to forge a new administrative apparatus to dispense relief to the unemployed who had exhausted their insurance benefits was also inspired by an active minister. Neville Chamberlain in the 1930s provided the same vital leadership to the Ministry of Health that he had in the 1920s. Civil servants played a subsidiary role, although in doing so they acted upon the basis of a distinctive departmental view.

Providing relief to the able-bodied unemployed posed especially acute problems of fiscal responsibility and administrative control. Local authorities, staggering under the financial burden of rendering such relief, looked to the government for additional funds. For their part, Ministry of Health officials remained acutely aware of their duty to prevent extravagance. During the 1920s local authorities had become obstacles to the officials' ability to carry out that duty. Civil servants demonstrated both their tenacity and the length of their memories in March 1933 when a deputation of representatives from local authorities in Lancashire, Yorkshire, and on the northeast coast met with the health minister and the labour minister, each supported by their officials. The deputation came to ask that relief for able-bodied unemployed be made a national charge because the cost had become too great for local government to finance. During the conference, the minister of health, Hilton-Young, stressed the need for local responsibility in expenditure. Sir Arthur Robinson recommended telling the deputation that the situation was being investigated, but that equalization of relief burden could not proceed without the consent of all local authorities involved.[37]

The noncommittal tone of this essentially negative reply did not accurately reflect the views of ministry officials. An internal memorandum on the subject stressed that economy of local administration grew out of the "fear of the local rate-payers." The removal of this inhibition, the note warned, would result in extravagance, as it had in the case of transitional payments and the London Metropolitan Common Poor Fund, which the infamous Poplar Guardians had drawn upon. To administer relief locally from a centralized fund could lead to the disassociation of the rate of relief from local conditions. To separate relief from the assessment of need would increase pressures to increase rates of relief. As a consequence the demand for "work or maintenance" would become very difficult to resist. The memorandum argued also that the centralization of relief would require uniform scales and rules for applying them, which would become so complex as to be practically unworkable.[38]

Even before Robinson forwarded these recommendations to Hilton Young, Neville Chamberlain had begun work on a plan for just such a centralized agency. In October 1932, Chamberlain wrote to his sister Hilda describing to her a "bold plan" he had devised that would entail "taking the whole relief of the able-bodied away from the local authorities and Ministers and putting it outside Party politics." Subsequently Hilton-Young, who acted as Chamberlain's surrogate when he served as minister of health, sent Chamberlain "the scheme which I have worked out to incorporate your ideas on the subject of the administration of public assistance and transitional payments." At this stage of development, Hilton-Young explained to Chamberlain, the scheme for a national agency had been discussed in a series of conferences he had held at the Ministry of Health attended by officials of the Treasury, Ministry of Labour, and the Scottish Office. The comments and criticisms of officials had been accommodated by the plan, but the ministers of these departments had not as yet committed themselves to support the scheme. The next question to be considered was how far administration should be recast by legislation.[39]

At the end of 1932, the Ministry of Labour disrupted the development of these plans by expressing its opposition to the creation of a statutory commission to administer unemployment relief. Minister of Labour Harold Betterton argued that so large a function of government should not be taken out of the hands of Parliament.[40] During 1933 the Ministry of Health struggled to reconcile the principle of ministerial responsibility to Parliament with the principle of an independent statutory commission. Making a minister an ex-officio member of the commission or giving a minister power to dismiss members or approve regulations would, civil servants believed, destroy the independence of the commission. Ministry officials also discussed the value of a nonindependent commission. Lowry preferred even a statutory commission with limited powers, but Robinson preferred public assistance administered by the Labour Ministry. In Robinson's view, opposition to the establishment of a commission was sufficiently strong to make the struggle to create one worthwhile only if it would constitute a distinct improvement in the administration of public assistance. Still, Robinson "strenuously" opposed the continued administration of public assistance through the public assistance committees that had replaced the Boards of Guardians in the 1929 reform of local government. Lowry also expressed a concern that administration by the Ministry of Labour "would mean inevitably that the family allowance doctrine would disappear."[41] This struggle reached Cabinet level as Betterton strove to maintain the principle of ministerial responsibility and Chamberlain, with Hilton-Young's support, worked to preserve the innovation of an independent body to administer relief.[42]

In 1933 the Unemployment Assistance Bill was drafted in the Ministry of Labour. The Health Ministry naturally took a great interest in the bill's provisions and upon request sent lengthy comments on the draft clauses. Officials of the Ministry of Health reacted to early drafts of the bill with "shock," because they feared the proposed Unemployment Assistance Board would be just as repressive as the Poor Law Guardians had been. A Health official observed:

> The openings given for an attack on these lines are so obvious that, remembering the Ministry of Labour's tactics in the past, there is room for wonder

> whether the object of the draft is not so to repel Ministers, or at any rate the House of Commons, as to require the withdrawal of the present draft, and the substitution of something which is to be appreciably milder in substance and may approach perilously near an admitted practice of work or maintenance.

The bill did not contribute to the breakup of the Poor Law but, rather, compounded its vices with some of its own.[43]

This sounds remarkably like Eady's criticisms of the original proposals from the Ministry of Health, although the two ministries perceived different weaknesses in the Poor Law.[44] Ministry of Labour officials sought to protect their special constituency, the industrial worker, from the taint of pauperism. The Ministry of Health strove to ensure economy of administration by removing from the hands of local officials the power to set relief levels. Despite these differences of perspective, the Ministry of Labour seems to have been receptive to the comments and criticisms of the Ministry of Health. In the fall of 1933, an official at Health observed that the redraft of part 2 of the bill went "a long way to meet the difficulties which we saw in the earlier clauses."[45]

The passage of the 1934 act that established the UAB represented a compromise between the Ministry of Health and the Ministry of Labour. The act also embodied Neville Chamberlain's hopes for a thoroughgoing reform of the administration of relief. The furor that immediately arose at the reduction in benefit effected by the UAB demonstrates beyond a shadow of a doubt that Chamberlain's dream of removing the issue of relief rates from the political arena represented a political impossibility.[46] The controversy also demonstrates that, in the economic context of the interwar period, the attempt of Ministry of Health officials to control and to reduce relief expenditure was ultimately a political act, not just an administrative one.

As at the Ministry of Labour, the crisis of depression and unemployment represented the primary challenge for the Ministry of Health during the interwar years. Ministry of Health civil servants met this challenge in a way that provides a telling contrast to the situation at Labour. They relentlessly insisted upon economy in expenditure and efficiency in administration above all other considerations, as if these in themselves constituted a coherent social policy. These two broad principles certainly did not represent a unique contribution to the debate on the state's proper role in the provision of social services. Neville Chamberlain arrived at the same conclusions independently of official advice. Such a stance, rooted in the Poor Law tradition of the LGB, would meet no challenge from the generalist bias that governed departmental recruitment and promotion practices.[47] Health officials, without their own positive vision of social services and with no stake in the amelioration of poverty, came to regard the state as their primary client. They thus sought to protect the state's resources against what they regarded as misappropriation, rather than to deploy those resources to meet the needs of the poor and unemployed.

Ministerial Leadership

Two men, Neville Chamberlain and William Arthur Robinson, dominated the Health Ministry during the interwar years. Sir Arthur Robinson became permanent secretary in 1920 upon the death of Robert Morant. He held that office until 1935, fifteen years in all. Neville Chamberlain first entered the Cabinet in 1923, as minister of health during the brief Conservative government formed by Baldwin following the collapse of the coalition. He found the department a congenial place to work, one that allowed the free play of his talents. He took on the job again, by choice, during Baldwin's 1924–1929 government.[48] When Ramsay MacDonald formed a national government in 1931 Neville Chamberlain returned to this post, but became Chancellor of the Exchequer when the national government was reorganized at the end of the year. He continued to take a strong interest in the development of policy at the Ministry of Health from his vantage at the Treasury. Chamberlain worked closely with both Hilton-Young, who was minister of health from 1932 until 1935, and Kingsley Wood. Wood had served as Chamberlain's parliamentary secretary at the Health Ministry between 1924 and 1929. He returned to the department as minister in 1935, remaining there until 1938.

Arthur Robinson began his career as an official in the Colonial Office, having placed first in the 1897 civil service examination. He served in several different departments advancing rapidly through the ranks. He became an assistant secretary in the Office of Works in 1912 and permanent secretary at the Air Ministry in 1917. After Robert Morant's sudden death in 1920, Christopher Addison had to find a replacement for the dynamic and powerful administrator. In Addison's judgment Robinson was the best man available at the time, although he did not believe him to be nearly so good as Morant. Addison wrote Winston Churchill, then secretary of state for War and Air, asking his approval for Robinson's transfer to the Ministry of Health. Churchill agreed to this move, observing that he had found Robinson "a very able man." With this endorsement, Robinson became permanent secretary at the Health Ministry in the spring of 1920.[49]

Robinson's approach to administration provided a marked contrast to Morant's. Morant undertook to understand even the technical details of the policies that came within his purview. He had also spent the whole of his official career dealing with either education or insurance, serving at the Board of Education, the NHIC, and finally the Ministry of Health. Robinson, on the other hand, personified the all-around or generalist tradition in the civil service. His work in social policy constituted only one stage in his career. He came to the Ministry of Health having three years before attained the rank of permanent secretary at the Air Ministry. He left the Health Ministry for the Committee of Imperial Defense, where he served as chairman of the Supply Board, finally ending his career as permanent secretary of the Ministry of Supply in 1939 and 1940. Robinson's varied career puts into perspective the advice he once gave one of his junior assistant secretaries: "Stick to general principles, don't bother much about detail."[50] At the Ministry of Health, control of expenditure constituted the most important of these general principles.

Both Morant and Robinson had enjoyed the advantages of a public school and Oxford education. Of the two, Morant (a Winchester–New College man) had the more prestigious educational credentials. The relationship between their educational experience and their subsequent careers differed significantly, however. Morant entered public service later in life, taking a position in the Board of Education after considerable experience in the field of education. Robinson, in contrast, took the open competition examination as a young man in his early twenties. Placing first, he entered the civil service and spent his entire adult life in Whitehall.

Neville Chamberlain's unfortunate adventures in foreign policy at the end of the 1930s, his identification with the disaster of appeasement, and his failure as a war leader have tended to overshadow his accomplishments in domestic policy earlier in the interwar period. During those years Neville Chamberlain held positions that enabled him to participate in most of the major developments in social policy. He used these opportunities to construct a positive policy that gave English social programs many of their distinctive qualities. Bentley Gilbert's generous evaluation of Chamberlain as "the most successful social reformer in the 17 years between 1922 and 1939" rests upon Chamberlain's ability to devise and implement politically feasible responses to the difficulties he tackled.[51] The nature of these reforms appealed to the predilections of the civil servants who served Chamberlain at the Ministry of Health.

During the 1920s and 1930s Chamberlain and Robinson developed a close relationship that was both professional and personal. Chamberlain helped Robinson obtain his GCB in 1928. When the Conservative party left office in 1929, Robinson wrote a wistful but prophetic farewell note to Chamberlain: "Someday I shall always hope we may work together again." In 1934 Robinson informed Chamberlain, then Chancellor of the Exchequer, about the development of housing policy saying: "The evolution is what you discussed with me many a time in the old good and great days."[52]

Chamberlain personally arranged for Robinson's transfer to the Supply

Board, and Robinson undertook the organization of a Ministry of Supply in 1939 at the behest of Chamberlain. When Chamberlain expressed his appreciation and relief that Robinson had agreed to become secretary of the new Ministry, Robinson responded:

> It is the simple truth that only your wish would have induced me to undertake the Ministry of Supply. Your letter touched me so deeply that I can but say that admiration of you increases every day, as does the very strong feeling of affection for you which was formed in our days at the Ministry of Health.[53]

Chamberlain made a deep impression on his officials at the Ministry of Health. Douglas Veale, who served as Chamberlain's private secretary during the Baldwin government, continued to keep in touch with his former superior throughout the 1930s, explaining in one letter: "I like to make the most of any opportunity of reviving the memory of what remains the happiest years of my life."[54] Veale's wholesale regard for Chamberlain, which only increased through the years, might be suspect if it had not been shared by his successor as private secretary, Arthur Rucker. Chamberlain, according to his permanent secretary, served as an inspiration to the department. And Chamberlain, in turn, valued their esteem. When one of the ministry's assistant secretaries, F. L. Turner, retired in 1926 Chamberlain recorded proudly: "He said I was the finest Minister they had had since Herbert Samuel."[55]

In the 1930s Neville Chamberlain continued to influence policy development at the Ministry of Health, through subordinate Cabinet colleagues. Hilton-Young worked especially closely with him. With the Ministries of Health and Labour locked in their struggle over the proper administrative structure for unemployment relief, Hilton-Young called upon Chamberlain's help in developing a housing policy. In letters to his wife, Hilton-Young reported various conversations with Neville Chamberlain on the subject of housing, explaining: "I much prefer to have any causes of difference out with him before we get to the cabinet." Chamberlain did not hesitate to proffer his views. In response to Hilton-Young's request for his thoughts about housing, Chamberlain sent him a memorandum detailing his views on slum housing. In his covering letter Chamberlain had the grace to include the proviso "I don't want to be barging into your territory."[56]

When the national government reorganized itself in 1935, Hilton-Young left the Ministry of Health. Upon his departure he wrote a letter to Chamberlain, thanking him for his advice and encouragement and reminding him that he had agreed with Chamberlain's policies and had tried to carry them out. In reply, Chamberlain extended his sympathy at Hilton-Young's having to leave the ministry, observing that he had entered the Ministry of Health with two handicaps, a lack of familiarity with the subject and a natural reserve.

Overcoming these, Hilton-Young had mastered his subject, seen his bill through, and had turned into an asset for the government. Chamberlain concluded with satisfaction: "I shall always look back on our association with unalloyed pleasure, and shall remember with pride that I suggested your name as the man best fitted to carry on in my old post."[57] This sentiment could easily have been genuine, as Chamberlain did not need to remain in his old post when he could depend upon Hilton-Young to carry out his policies.

Chamberlain's career at the Ministry of Health and the successes he enjoyed there recall the successes of other ministerial teams we have encountered, H.A.L. Fisher and L. A. Selby-Bigge at the Board of Education, and Lord Ernle and A. D. Hall at Agriculture. Chamberlain's partnership with Robinson contrasts starkly with the lack of effective ministerial leadership at the Ministry of Labour and with the conflict between Eustace Percy and his advisers during his tenure at the Board of Education. Officials could exert their greatest influence when they worked in tandem with an able and energetic minister. Such partnerships could translate the departmental view of policy into political reality.

Conclusion

Christopher Addison's hopes for the Ministry of Health he had worked so hard to establish did not materialize. He never had an opportunity even to begin to dismantle the Poor Law before he was forced to leave the ministry. The operation of the Poor Law remained intact until the passage of Neville Chamberlain's Local Government Act in 1929. That reform, when it finally came, reorganized the bodies of local government dispensing the various forms of poor relief but did not necessarily lead those bodies to provide relief with greater generosity or sensitivity. Indeed, Chamberlain devoted much of his energy to controlling the improvident expenditure of a few Labour-dominated local governments in areas especially hard-hit by the depression. The Ministry of Health did not even actively support the continuing fight against infant and maternal mortality, an issue that had played a prominent role in the agitation leading to the department's creation. Ministry officials instead concentrated their efforts on refuting the contention that malnutrition caused by unemployment and underemployment was a contributing cause of infant and maternal mortality.

The ways that Ministry of Health officials defined their duty led them to focus their energies on the supervision of expenditure. This emphasis on fiscal matters was not imposed upon them by the Treasury. Rather, it derived from both the philosophical legacy of the Poor Law and the ways that officials understood one of the chief rationales—efficiency—for the formation of the Ministry of Health. To Ministry of Health civil servants, a group selected by recruitment and promotion practices placing a premium on generalist rather than expert knowledge, "efficiency" meant cost management. Such an emphasis tended to strengthen the inclination to regard the department's chief client as the central government, rather than the poor. Budget accountability after all represents one rather obvious "general" principle that can be applied to any situation—a principle easily derived from the Poor Law legacy of the LGB.

To privilege fiscal responsibility over social responsibility, as Health officials did, was not an overtly class-conscious assertion of power springing directly from their educational experience. Rather, the career success of Health officials was predicated on educational credentials, which in turn nourished and sustained an approach to policy that inevitably worked in a class-biased way. In this, Health officials differed from civil servants at Education, Agriculture, and Labour, who worked in departments that in different ways placed a higher value on "expert" knowledge.

Officials at Health—unlike officials at Agriculture, Education, and Labour—never developed a positive policy of their own. It is ironic that Ministry of Health civil servants, benefiting from the leadership of a powerful and effective minister, perhaps enjoyed the greatest success among the four departments in seeing their policies actually implemented. Neville Chamberlain's domination of policy making at the Ministry of Health during the interwar years in turn partly depended upon the coincidence of sympathy and philosophy that underlay the close relationship he developed with his officials. Civil servants did not remain totally oblivious to the social costs of the policies they supported, but they continued to believe that protecting the financial integrity of social expenditure was in itself a social service.

CONCLUSION

The Influence of the Civil Service

■ *Power cannot be understood simply as a generalized means regardless of the end to which it is applied.*

—John Rex

This study began with a large problem posed in a straightforward way: How can we understand the relationship between social class and the exercise of power in England?[1] Of course, to put the question so simply belies the difficulties inherent in formulating an answer both general enough to sustain a measure of theoretical consistency and flexible enough to accommodate the specificity and variety of the past. The interwar period and the civil servants of four social service ministries provided the characters and the setting for our consideration of this issue. The subsequent analysis necessarily took up a wide range of topics, but now we must return to our starting point in order to pick out the patterns that emerge from the welter of events. The empirical investigation occupying the bulk of this work makes it possible to draw more general conclusions about the character of the English civil service as an elite group and to assess the nature and extent of the power that civil servants could actually command.

The Civil Service Elite

English government officials came, by and large, from the upper levels of English society. Given the biases of the English educational system and the professional status of the civil service, such a finding by itself presents no surprise. The educational experience of government officials did not simply reflect the university-educated population, however. A majority of all higher-level civil servants had attended the most prestigious universities and schools—Oxford, Cambridge, and the Headmasters' Conference schools. Products of Oxford and the Clarendon schools, moreover, enjoyed a success far out of proportion to their share of the pool of university-educated. Such a pattern suggests the existence of distinctive paths to different professions among the university-educated.[2] Furthermore, these paths developed through the intervention of the recruitment process and did not merely represent boundaries defined by the structure of English education.

A variety of factors taken together produced this pattern. The most obvious (obvious even at the time) was the bias favoring the curriculum of these universities that was built into the open competition examination. Not quite so obvious, but perhaps even more important, was the way that Oxford and Cambridge graduates, and especially those from Oxford, dominated the field of candidates for government positions. Informal but recognizable signposts marked out the appropriate career paths for those with the proper credentials. Those without those credentials apparently knew enough not to trespass. The criteria used in the promotion process in Education and Health also favored those who had been to Clarendon schools and Oxford. The strength and exact nature of the relationship between promotion and education varied enough from department to department to indicate self-conscious behavior on the part of those making personnel decisions.

The personnel practices of the pre-First World War Board of Education and Board of Agriculture define the latitude allowed government departments in creating their own identity before the reforms of 1919 imposed a common recruitment process. The Board of Education showed the strongest preference for Oxford graduates, to the virtual exclusion of men from other universities—even Cambridge graduates. Their practice illustrates how much educational experience could influence career opportunities and reveals a highly refined division of labor among the university-educated, which remains unexplored. The prestige of Oxford and Cambridge so overshadows other British universities that the widespread inclination to blur the distinction between them (symbolized by the conflation "Oxbridge") seems logical, although it obscures the different contribution each one made to different elite groups.

In contrast to the Board of Education, Agriculture officials so emphasized their need for practical expertise that they eschewed the usual civil service candidate. Agriculture resorted to promotion from the lower ranks so often that it became the most egalitarian of government departments, although the very highest positions remained in the hands of men more typical of the civil service as a whole. The idiosyncratic way that Education and Agriculture recruited their staffs prior to the First World War underlines the extent to which decisions made by individuals acting upon discernible principles governed the staffing of the civil service.

Studies of elite groups have traditionally focused on social background to define the identity of those composing the groups. Such an approach often assumes a reductionist relationship between social origin and adult behavior, however, an approach that is vulnerable to the refutation of counterexample.

The gap between social origin or educational experience and actions taken by individuals years afterward looms too large to accept such an inference without supporting evidence. The demonstration of such a relationship must depend upon the delineation of some ongoing process to connect social identity with behavior.

In the case of the higher levels of the English civil service, recruitment and promotion practices served as such a bridge. These practices not only functioned in terms of the social background of those who entered the civil service, they also manifested a frame for the different departments' views of policy. Recruitment and promotion mediated between social background and official behavior, establishing material but contingent links between the two. Social background by itself did not automatically bias officials' acts. Civil servants actively defined the limits of acceptable official behavior, revealing a highly self-conscious vision of their professional responsibilities. That vision often had a social significance, however, which was overlooked both by civil servants themselves and by those inclined to take their word at face value only.

The views of Charles Douie, a minor official at the Board of Education during the 1920s, show that the mere fact of attending a public school did not guarantee that an individual would internalize the experience as an educational ideal. A graduate of Rugby and Queen's College, Oxford, Douie regarded his privileged education with a gratitude mixed with shame. In an article on public schools that appeared in the July 1939 issue of the *Journal of Education* during 1939 Douie asserted: "The public schools have profited me and mine, whether they have profited England is another matter." In his essay, Douie detailed what he saw as the pernicious effect of the public school cult on English society. To counteract this effect Douie advocated throwing open the public schools to "the sons of workers in offices and factories" by a generous program of scholarships. These views differed sharply from those originally voiced by his Board of Education colleagues, but in 1939 Charles Douie no longer held a position there. One of four Oxford men who entered the Board by competitive examination in 1919, Douie recorded in his autobiography that "in time they all cut their losses and sought their fortunes elsewhere." Douie left the Board in 1927 to become secretary of University College, London.[3]

The Ministry of Labour, although more open to variety among its new recruits than the Board of Education, also set definite limits to the views it found acceptable for its officers. The career of C.E.M. Joad illustrates how the ministry could do this. Joad, who entered the Labour Exchanges Department of the Board of Trade by competitive examination in 1914, like Douie came from an unexceptional background. He had attended a less prestigious public school (Blundell's, Tiverton) but had obtained a scholarship to a more prestigious college (Balliol College, Oxford). At Oxford Joad had become what he termed a revolutionary socialist, "convinced that our social arrangements were contemptible, that they were not so of necessity but could be improved, but that nothing short of a change in the economic structure of society would improve them." Joad passed the open competition examination, placing twenty-second, and elected to enter the Board of Trade, "in the erroneous belief that Labour Exchanges and Unemployment Insurance might have something to do with Socialism."[4]

Joad spent the next sixteen years in the civil service, where he found himself "a square peg in a round hole and miserable in consequence." He made no secret of his political opinions, and his superiors expressed their disapproval by declining to grant him any promotions. Joad remained an assistant principal for his entire civil service career. The promotion panel that considered Joad's case in 1927 recorded their opinion that "Mr. Joad is an officer who had interests outside the Department which may be taken to reduce the effectiveness of his candidature for a Principal post." In his disappointment Joad did ever less work and finally left the Ministry of Labour in 1930. As a professor of philosophy at the University of London, Joad eventually became a well-known public figure. He was the principal speaker in support of the famous pacifist resolution passed by the Oxford Union in 1933, and his BBC broadcasts during the Second World War made his name a household word.[5] Even so, his old superiors at the Ministry of Labour probably did not regret their failing to utilize his talents.

Civil service departments could not rely upon the operation of some sort of social determinism to produce dependable officials, but then, they did not have to do so. Using the tools available they could not only sift out the incompetent but could also put a departmental stamp upon their officers. Those who had acceptable credentials but unacceptable views faced the barrenness of an unsuccessful, uncongenial working life. Sooner or later they would, like Douie and Joad, cut their losses and look for fortune elsewhere. Even so, departments did not enforce a rigid unanimity among their senior officials. W. C. Eady's views and their reception by his colleagues at the Labour Ministry and the discussions between Francis Floud and Daniel Hall at the Ministry of Agriculture amply illustrate the narrow, but real, possibilities for disagreement within a particular departmental setting.[6]

The English civil service has always been considered a homogeneous group, and in this analysis I do not challenge that widely held view. In theory, homogeneity constitutes an important aspect of the character of an elite group.[7] Shared social and cultural experiences certainly contribute to professional solidarity. Yet homogeneity, like beauty, to a great extent lies in the eye of the beholder. To an outside observer using all of English society as a point of departure, the variations among civil servants appear small. They might not have appeared so small to the civil servants themselves. Although officials certainly had more in common with one another than with the masses composing society at large, they did not compare themselves to the population at large but to one another. The variations in their educational experience helped form distinctive departmental identities, which in turn reinforced the development of identifiable departmental views of policy. This process underwent substantial modification during the period under study.

The adoption of uniform recruitment by competitive examination in 1919 severed the links between individual departments and recruitment. Civil servants as a group became increasingly homogeneous, although the group did not become increasingly representative either of the population as a whole or of the university-educated population. The view that the "all-rounder" rather than the expert made the most efficient civil servant justified this change. The higher-level official represented an expensive investment for the government. If officials could be readily moved from office to office in response to changing needs, the government could achieve a substantial saving.[8]

A perhaps unforeseen consequence of this approach to staffing was a change in the network of loyalties that officials worked within. If they could not call upon deep and intimate knowledge of a particular subject to guide their policy making, civil servants had to fall back upon general principles of administration (as the Ministry of Health's permanent secretary, Sir Arthur Robinson, had recommended to W. A. Ross).[9] These general principles would be more likely to reflect the interests of the state than the interests of those most affected by government policy. The unshakable resolve of the ministry to control expenditure provides the clearest example of this tendency. Ministry of Health officials were experts in administration rather than experts in ameliorating social conditions. Defining an acceptable level of government expenditure proved a more congenial task for them than establishing an acceptable level of well-being for the population.

Power

Civil servants found the power at their command limited in two ways. Civil servants, in their official capacity, could pass judgment only on a limited range of issues, the issues defined as being within the purview of their department. In addition, their power to translate judgments into action depended upon their having a sympathetic, and active, minister to press the department's views upon the Cabinet. Lacking such a minister, the power of civil servants could only be negative. They could perhaps block the introduction of policies they opposed, or they could put their stamp on the administration of policies already in place. They could not independently implement any new departures in policy. In his memoirs, C. K. Monro, who enjoyed a long and successful career at the Ministry of Labour, described the consequences of weak leadership at the top: "The broad effect of a minister who is not quite up to his job is a lack of any definite policy and a tendency to continue in old ways when those should be changed."[10]

To define the nature of the power of the civil servants as entirely negative does not mean that civil servants had only a negligible impact on the course of events. Civil servants had considerable influence on the development of social policy. But the extent of their influence in any particular instance depended in part on the strength of their minister and in part on the political significance of the issue at stake. Both these variables remained outside their control.

Civil servants did enjoy the tactical advantage of continuity in office, and rapid ministerial turnover could generate the illusion that the servants of state were actually in command. Sometimes, even civil servants themselves fell victim to this illusion. George Newman, who served as chief medical officer of the Board of Education and the Ministry of Health for many years, found himself answering to yet another minister in 1921 when Sir Alfred Mond replaced Christopher Addison. Newman wrote to a friend that he was "once more at work instructing a new Minister in the functions of a Ministry of Health—I am getting an old bird at this sort of thing—MacKenna, Runciman, Pease, Henderson, Lord Crewe, Fisher, Addison, Lurgh, Trevelyan, Lewis and Lord Astor."[11]

Despite the veiled implication here, this rapid succession of ministers did not strengthen the position of civil servants as much as it weakened the position of the department. Any substantial departure in policy must necessarily entail funding and perhaps legislation—only a strong minister could deliver these goods for his department. Consequently it was through the partnerships between civil servants and strong ministers that officials could make the greatest impact on government policy. Fisher and Selby-Bigge at Education, Chamberlain and Robinson at Health, and Prothero and Hall at Agriculture all formed teams that could accomplish far more than any one individual—whether minister or civil servant—could have done alone.

Officials depended upon their ministers to transform policy into reality, but ministers in their turn found themselves hemmed in by considerations of a political nature. Different issues evoked different responses from the various constituencies ministers had to answer to. Even if civil servants could carry their minister, their minister had to be able to carry the Cabinet and the party, and the government in turn had to carry the country. These political realities largely explain both the successes of civil servants at Agriculture and the failures of civil servants at Labour. Saddled with a series of weak ministers and faced with the most explosive of all the social issues of the interwar period—unemployment—Labour officials could do little to alter the government's course, a course they often disagreed with. In contrast Agriculture officials could work relatively quietly behind the scenes. Even if occasionally controversial, the policies promulgated by the Agriculture Ministry affected a relatively small number of people who, because of their small numbers, could not count on impressing their view on the government even when they were well organized and vocal.

If civil servants could only treat those matters within the competence of their department, their influence on the direction of the state could only be piecemeal, unless the work at separate ministries fit together into a coherent whole, either by some coincidence of purpose or by some sort of central direction. The changes in recruitment after 1919, by creating a more homogeneous body, would have enhanced the likelihood that civil servants in different departments would work toward common goals. In addition, the designation in 1919 of the permanent secretary of the Treasury as head of the civil service gave that important department the leverage to enforce a measure of discipline throughout the civil service. The often repeated phrases "Treasury control" and "Treasury view" imply a central role for the Treasury in the policy-making process. Although linked, the two phrases actually refer to two quite distinguishable propositions. "Treasury control" signifies the control the Treasury could exert on other departments; the "Treasury view," during the interwar period, was the Treasury's opinion of the proper course for the government to follow during the interwar depression. This consisted of a restrictive monetary policy, reduced public expenditure, and the rejection of large-scale government-financed projects meant to remedy unemployment. The evidence of this study advances important qualifications to both commonly held views.

The Treasury was no doubt the most prestigious and powerful of government departments. Because the control of expenditure represented one of its chief responsibilities and because virtually every government program and policy must involve some expenditure, the relationship between the Treasury and other government departments must have been of necessity adversarial. Once general levels of expenditure had been set (and this was a highly political process in which Treasury officials may well have played a critical role), then the Treasury had to see that other departments toed the line with their spending. Since the Treasury held the purse strings, Treasury officials had a distinct advantage in the resolution of any disagreements with other departments. But spending departments could, and often did, make successful defenses of their policies and were indeed expected to do so. After all, a policy that could not be defended probably should not be funded.

In the 1920s, the Ministry of Agriculture managed to preserve its drainage program, and the Ministry of Labour thwarted Treasury efforts to wind up the Unemployment Grants Committee. Board of Education civil servants acted vigorously to salvage Fisher's policies in the early years of the interwar period. The Ministry of Health's eagerness to restrict expenditure on poor relief represented the views of that department and were not the result of Treasury pressure. Officials at the Health Ministry proved they were capable of resisting Treasury moves to restrict their housing policy.

Most officials opposed Keynsian-style proposals that the government should take a more active role in the economy. They took this position because they believed the measures would not work, not because in principle they opposed intervention by the state in economic processes. The reluctance of civil servants to embrace Keynesian views in the 1930s and the readiness of their conversion later thus do not represent a puzzling philosophical about-face.

The pervasiveness of the "Treasury view" provides a convenient explanation for the interwar failures to treat mass unemployment with aggressive government action. Presumably the companion concept of "Treasury control" enabled the Treasury to impose its view on other government departments. But the pervasiveness of the "Treasury view" did not just reflect the power of the Treasury, it enjoyed the authority of the most respectable opinion of contemporary economists. When Keynesian ideas developed an increasingly sophisticated theoretical justification in the 1930s, they began to win over converts, even within the Treasury. Prior to that time an aggressive program of government spending had only the slenderest of speculative justifications. Civil servants at the Ministry of Labour, as well as at the Treasury, might be excused if they declined to gamble with the state's assets. "Treasury control" represented an important reality for civil servants but remained indirect, by no means complete and automatic.[12]

Class and Administrative Ethos

The day-to-day activity of civil servants both expressed and enacted class relations. In their official lives civil servants enjoyed a position predicated upon social inequality, at the same time as their direction of events coming under their influence reproduced social inequality. This is not to accuse them of engaging in a class-conscious conspiracy but rather to give full weight to the ways their careers reflected their own efforts as knowledgeable agents.

The relationship between educational experience and career success evidences decisions both deliberate and self-conscious, guided by definitions of the nature of the expertise regarded as the most appropriate for each department. Any such definition could not be innocent of social significance, given the structural inequality built into the English educational system that produced all potential candidates for the civil service. Government departments, insofar as they could shape their own official identity, developed a vision of government policy that in turn, necessarily, had enormous social significance. These visions differed from department to department and did not constitute a coherent and overarching consensus. The varying postures toward policy questions that were adopted by officials in different departments demonstrate the richness and complexity of the processes at work.

In the case of the Board of Education a kind of education associated with a social group, and crucial to the self-identity of that group, came to represent the ideal educational system. An important element of policy during this period was the preservation of this educational system, although civil servants accommodated limited changes in educational recruitment. The narrow educational ladder built by official policy protected the educational system and thus in turn protected a social order that was increasingly dependent on educational institutions to define social identity.[13] Middle-class and upper-class families fostered those qualities of character that enhanced a child's propensity to succeed in the educational system; the educational system in turn fostered an identifiable character and provided as well the social patina required for success in later life. Outstanding success in this system marked one as an expert in education for the Board of Education. Thus, at the Board of Education, educational values also constituted class values, although many civil servants would have strenuously denied this.

A very different situation obtained at the Ministry of Health and the Ministry of Labour. Although the Labour Ministry's staff was far more heterogeneous (comparatively speaking) than the staff at the Health Ministry, both departments shared a policy that treated labor as a commodity. Officials believed that the state's responsibility included ensuring the fluidity of the labor supply necessary for the smooth functioning of the economy. Labour's emphasis on job training and relocation on the one hand and insistence on "less eligibility" in unemployment relief on the other simply represented the carrot and the stick necessary to produce a mobile labor supply. Ministry of Labour officials had no qualms about employing the power of the state toward such an end. They opposed public works, not as an illegitimate use of state power but as an inefficient deployment of state resources. Health, too, embraced "less eligibility" and opposed public works. Officials there could also justify their approach to policy in terms of the fiscal requirements of the state.

The Ministry of Labour did not represent the same kind of class bias in the choosing of their personnel as the Board of Education and the Health Ministry. At Labour men drawn from a relatively greater variety of social backgrounds and experiences often shared an interest in and knowledge of social conditions not found elsewhere in the civil service (at the Ministry of Health, for instance). Their theoretical orientation, commanding the respect accorded to disinterested expertise, had, comparatively speaking, a progressive orientation insofar as they understood their role to be to enhance the efficiency of the economy. Obstacles to that end could be found among capitalists (mine owners, for instance) as well as trade unionists and in the ranks of the Conservative party as well as in the ranks of the Labour party.

Officials at the Ministry of Health regarded their duty in a similar way. The principle of "less eligibility" not only conserved the resources of the state but also protected the wage structure of industry and encouraged a flow of individuals into the workforce at the low end of the wage scale. The Health Ministry had responsibility for those sectors of the population that made relatively little "productive" contribution to society. Many of those who had campaigned for a Ministry of Health wished the new department to champion the well-being of the population. Officials, to the dismay of many, did not take on that task. Instead, the old LGB philosophy of "less eligibility" found reinforcement in twentieth-century notions of efficiency and the civil servants' definition of their professional identity, leaving no room for the vision of society as a community in which the strong could succor the weak through the mediation of the state.

At the Ministry of Health the generalist bias that marked both recruitment and promotion meant that officials did not develop a vested interest in social policy as such. Instead, they allied themselves to the interests of the state defined in the most obvious and straightforward way—fiscally. Such a stance worked to sustain a hierarchial class structure as it stood, but the impetus for the formation of policy at Health (and Labour) stemmed from the logic of officials' professional situation. This had the effect of cloaking the social implications of Health policy with the ostensibly neutral authority of the state.

A very different situation developed at the Ministry of Agriculture. There a predilection for a scientific approach to the conduct of agriculture combined with an abiding vision of the agricultural community and its importance for English society produced a very different kind of policy. The spirit of expertise that pervaded official life at Agriculture led civil servants to understand their duty in terms of the interest of agriculture, their responsibility in terms of improving the practice of agriculture. This led them to treat the apparatus of the state as a means to those ends, rather than as an end in itself. Even though the assumption that the agricultural community could not interpret its own needs constitutes a species of paternalism, the agricultural policy favored by civil servants envisioned both farmers and agricultural workers as partners in an important endeavor. Officials believed that the ministry regulation of the relationship between the two groups according to principles of equity represented the best interests of the whole. Agriculture's understanding of its role led its officials to recruit and promote on criteria very different from those of other ministries. Agriculture's policies built up a staff that had the broadest social base of all the social service departments, at some cost to the department's standing in the civil service.

Agriculture officials could not have adhered strictly to the economic principles espoused at Health and Labour because, in the twentieth century, English agriculture was not strictly speaking an economic enterprise. Cheap transportation made English agriculture uncompetitive on the world market. The most up-to-date agricultural methods and cooperative marketing boards could only mitigate the impact of this reality. Yet officials believed that English agriculture had to be preserved and encouraged, not only for security reasons (reasons vividly illustrated by both world wars), but because rural England represented a community worth preserving for itself and for its role in defining the character of English society at large. Sir Daniel Hall, when asked by the 1919 Royal Commission on Agriculture to envision a state of affairs where peace in the world had finally been secured, insisted that even under those circumstances, the state needed to secure the position of the agricultural community. Hall declared:

> I do not think the kind of countryside which has been adumbrated, where you have the towns carrying on manufactures, and the countryside entirely laid down to grass and to sporting estates, is a desirable state of the community; and I would say that it is worth some labour and expense on the part of the State to avoid that state of things coming about.[14]

The sentiments articulated here by Sir Daniel animated the view of policy taken by most Agriculture officials, which contrasts sharply to the antagonistic and mechanistic vision of society characterizing the other social service ministries. The normative basis for social policy at the Ministry of Agriculture and the way that vision differed from the views that predominated in other departments point up the pivotal significance of the development of distinctive systems of values within government ministries.[15] Such a value-laden departmental ethos would form a contingent and reciprocal link between the social and the professional identity of civil servants in turn acted upon by them in carrying out their duties.

Conclusion

Civil servants employed the power and resources of the state to achieve limited ends, to solve particular problems, to avert or mitigate crisis. In doing this, officials (especially those in departments where professional ethos subsumed class identity, such as Labour, Health, and Agriculture) began to build a state apparatus that could uphold a hierarchial social order by gathering more power in public hands—power to direct the economy, to mediate conflict, to distribute scarce goods. The objective and professional stance of civil servants, as the state took on these tasks, thus tended to defuse the antagonism inherent in class relations. The varying postures toward policy questions adopted by officials, combined with the varying degree of success met by the strategies they employed, underline the problematic nature of the intersection between social and political processes. That problematic provided an arena where individual agency could work itself out. Such agency, nevertheless, did not and could not command a space without bounds.[16] The work and careers of civil servants both drew upon and sustained larger systems of social relations.

In this study, with its close analysis of the way officials carried out their duties within a self-created professional setting, I have endeavored to give concrete particularity to the large-scale theoretical implications of claims about the extent and nature of the power enjoyed by the civil service. The voices of L. A. Selby-Bigge, W. C. Eady, Arthur Robinson, and Daniel Hall (to name only a few of the civil servants encountered in these pages) sounded out with individual personality, even within the severe constraints on self-expression imposed by the composition of official memoranda. The significance of what they said and did resonates with meanings lent by context—social, political, institutional.

In this intersection between the particular and the general—an intersection that history as a discipline seems especially suited to investigate—we can see civil servants deliberately constructing an identity by formulating goals and endeavoring to achieve them. And, as the foregoing pages have shown, what they said and did could, in a variety of ways, make a difference in the outcome of events. Those who have regarded government officials with suspicion often had reason to do so. Civil servants enjoyed a measure of power, which they necessarily deployed in carrying out their work. Such suspicions, however, tend to make simplistic assumptions about the dynamic of the elements put into play—conflating individual agency with social agency. This study, in its focus on the articulation between these two aspects of human behavior, has attempted to show the complexity and nuance of the ways in which individuals acting on their own behalf could also enact larger-scale processes of social domination.

Appendix

Notes

Index

APPENDIX

Biographical Notes

This listing of brief biographical summaries includes the careers of the civil servants and a few other individuals involved in the policy discussions described in the body of the text. It does not include ministers, since biographical information about them is readily available. The entries have been compiled from a wide range of sources, including the standard biographical dictionaries *(Who's Who, Who Was Who, Debrette's, Kelly's Handbook),* school and university registers, as well as official publications and government documents *(Imperial Calendar and Civil Service List,* the Civil Service Commission's *Annual Reports).*

ABBREVIATIONS OF BRITISH HONORS

CB	Companion of the [Order of the] Bath
CBE	Commander Order of the British Empire
CIE	Companion of the [Order of the] Indian Empire
CMG	Companion of the Order of St Michael and St George
CVO	Commander of the Royal Victorian Order
FBA	Fellow of the British Academy
GBE	Knight Grand Cross of the [Order of the] British Empire
GCB	Knight Grand Cross of the [Order of the] Bath
KBE	Knight Commander of the [Order of the] British Empire
KC	King's Counsel
KCB	Knight Commander of the [Order of the] Bath
KCMG	Knight Commander of St Michael and St George
KCSI	Knight Commander of the [Order of the] Star of India
Kt	Knight
LL.B.	Legum Baccalaureus (Bachelor of Laws)
LL.D.	Legum Doctor (Doctor of Laws)
MBE	Member of the [Order of the] British Empire
MC	Military Cross
OBE	Order of the British Empire
PC	Privy Councillor
RA	Royal Artillary

J. B. Adams. A graduate of Aberdeen Grammar School, he later rose to the position of principal assistant secretary in the Ministry of Labour. He then served as the controller of the ministry's Northeast Division. In 1935 he became secretary of King George's Jubilee Fund.

Oswald Coleman Allen, CBE (1920). Born 1887. Allen was appointed an assistant insurance officer at the Board of Trade in 1912 after serving as a civil servant at the Local Government Board. Allen was promoted to assistant secretary in the Ministry of Labour in 1930. He ultimately rose to the position of principal assistant secretary in the Civil Defense Department of the Home Office in 1945 and served as a representative of the United Kingdom on the Social Commission of the United Nations from 1947.

James Alan Noel Barlow, CBE (1918), CB (1928), KBE (1938), KCB (1942). Born 1881, the son of Dr. Thomas Barlow, physician to Queen Victoria. Barlow attended Marlborough and Corpus Christi College, Oxford. Appointed as a junior examiner at the Board of Education in 1907, Barlow later transferred to the Ministry of Labour, where he served as a principal assistant secretary from 1925 until 1934. He then transferred to the Treasury as an undersecretary and rose to the position of joint second secretary in 1938.

Percy Young Blunden. Born 1883. Blunden attended Christ's Hospital and Hertford College, Oxford. Blunden entered Internal Revenue in 1907 after placing forty-fourth on the Class 1 examination. In 1912 he was appointed assistant chief of section in the newly formed Central Office for Labour Exchanges and Unemployment Insurance at the Board of Trade. In the Ministry of Labour, Blunden reached the rank of assistant secretary in 1925, and the rank of acting principal assistant secretary in 1939.

N. D. Bosworth-Smith, CB (1946). Born 1886, the son of R. Bosworth Smith, author. Bosworth-Smith attended Harrow and Pembroke College, Cambridge. He taught briefly at Gresham's School in Holt, Norfolk, and entered the Board of Education as an inspector in 1911. He moved to the administrative side of the office in 1912. He served as director of Establishments from 1936 to 1939, principal assistant secretary from 1940 to 1945, and undersecretary from 1946 until his retirement in 1947.

Frederick Gatus Bowers, CB (1929), OBE. Born 1882. Bowers attended Bancroft's School and the London School of Economics. Bowers became a chartered accountant in 1907. In 1912 he was appointed auditor of the National Health Insurance by the Treasury. He became accountant-general of the Ministry of Labour in 1919, a position he held until 1933.

Edmund K. Chambers, CB (1912), KBE (1925), FBA. Born 1866, the son of Reverend William Chambers, Fellow and Tutor at Worcester College, Oxford. Chambers attended Marlborough and Corpus Christi College, Oxford, and entered the Board in 1892, rising to the rank of second secretary in 1922. A respected Shakespearean scholar, Chambers published various scholarly works including *The Medieval Stage* (1903), *The Elizabethan Stage* (1923), and *William Shakespeare* (1930).

Thomas Sidney Chegwidden, CB (1943). Born 1895. Chegwidden attended Maidstone Grammar School, Royal Military Academy, Woolwich, and Worcester College, Oxford. After passing the 1919 Reconstruction examination, Chegwidden entered the Ministry of Labour where he rose to the rank of assistant secretary in 1938. Chegwidden served as undersecretary of the Ministry of Production from 1942 until 1946. After that time he held a variety of appointments to various boards and commissions, finally serving as chairman of the Interim Federal Public Services Commission in South Rhodesia from 1953 until 1955.

Arthur Strettrell Comyns-Carr, Kt. (1949). Born 1882. Comyns-Carr attended Winchester and Trinity College, Oxford. A Liberal MP from 1923 until 1924, Comyns-Carr wrote a series of books on the economic situation during the early 1930s, including *Escape from the Dole* (1930).

John Corcoran, CB (1919), KBE (1924). Born 1862. Corcoran attended University College, Dublin, and the Royal University, Ireland. He entered the War Office by appointment in 1886. He rose to the rank of assistant undersecretary in the War Office before his retirement in 1925 to become director of the National Union of Manufacturers, a position he held until his death in 1932.

Douglas du B. Davidson. Born 1883, the son of Sir Walter Edward Davidson, KC, MC. Davidson attended Winchester and Balliol College, Oxford. He entered the Board of Education in 1904. Davidson rose to the rank of assistant secretary in 1931 and became the Board's accountant-general in 1937.

William Robert Davies, CB (1909). Born 1870. Davies attended Manchester Grammar School and Balliol College, Oxford. Davies entered the Board of Education in 1899. He rose to the rank of principal assistant secretary in 1920 and retired in 1930.

Ronald C. Davison Kt. (1938). Born 1884, Davison worked at Toynbee Hall from 1908 until 1910 and became a civil servant in the Labour Exchanges Department of the Board of Trade in 1912. He spent ten years as a principal in the Ministry of Labour until 1927. He then became a lecturer at London University. His works on unemployment, including *The Unemployed: Old Policies and New* (1929), *What's Wrong with Unemployment Insurance* (1930), *The New Unemployment Act* (1934), and *British Unemployment Policy* (1924), are still regularly cited in scholarly literature on the subject.

Allen Tabor Austin Dobson, CBE (1930), CVO (1932), CB (1939). Born 1885, the son of Austin Dobson, LL.D. Dobson attended Clifton College and Emmanuel College, Cambridge. He entered the Board of Agriculture by open competition examination in 1908 and reached the rank of assistant secretary in 1920, principal assistant secretary in 1935, and undersecretary in 1946.

Francis R. G. Duckworth, CBE (1942). Born 1881. Duckworth attended Rossall and Trinity College, Oxford. He taught at Dover School (1904–1905), Cheltenham (1905–1908), and Eton (1908–1915, 1920) before entering the Board of Education's inspectorate in 1920, rising to the position of senior chief inspector.

Wilfred Griffin Eady, CMG (1932), CB (1934), KBE (1939), KCB (1942). Born 1890. Eady attended Clifton College and Jesus College, Cambridge. After placing thirty-sixth on the 1913 Class 1 examination, Eady entered the India Office. After serving briefly in the India Office, the Home Office, and the Foreign Trade Department, Eady entered the Ministry of Labour in 1917. There he rose to the rank of assistant secretary in 1922 and principal assistant secretary in 1929. He then served as secretary of the Unemployment Assistance Board (1934–1938), deputy undersecretary at the Home Office (1938–1940) and as chairman at the Board of Customs and Excise before becoming a joint second secretary at the Treasury in 1942.

Ralph Roscoe Enfield, CB (1944), Kt. (1947). Born 1885. Enfield attended the High School, Nottingham, Bedales and Christ Church, Oxford. He entered the civil service in 1913, serving on the Board of Trade and the Ministry of Munitions before entering the Ministry of Agriculture in 1919. Enfield reached the rank of principal assistant secretary in 1942 and served as the Ministry of Agriculture's chief economic adviser from 1945 until 1952. Enfield published *The Agricultural Crisis, 1920–23* in 1924.

Francis Lewis Castle Floud, CB (1918), KCB (1921), KCSI (1941), KCMG (1938). Born 1875, the son of Reverend H. Castle Floud. Floud attended Cranleigh School and King's College, London. He entered the Board of Agriculture in 1894, where he rose to the rank of permanent secretary in 1920. He served as chairman of the Board of Customs and Excise from 1927 until 1930 and as permanent secretary of the Ministry of Labour from 1930 until 1934. He left Labour in 1934 to become high commissioner in Canada. Floud held a variety of other governmental positions from 1938 until 1943 when he became chairman of the Agricultural Wages Board.

Edward Rodolph Forber, CBE (1918), CB (1924), KCB (1932). Born 1878. Forber attended Liverpool College, then University College, Liverpool, and Trinity College, Cambridge. He entered the Local Government Board in 1901 placing twenty-seventh in the Class 1 examination. Forber served the Ministry of Health as a principal assistant secretary from 1922 until 1925 and as deputy secretary from 1925 until 1930. He left the Ministry of Health in 1930 to become chairman of the Board of Customs and Excise. Forber held that position until 1934 when he became chairman of the Board of Inland Revenue where he served until 1938.

Herbert William Sidney Francis, CB (1938), OBE. Born 1880. Francis attended Blundell's School and Balliol College, Oxford. Francis entered the Local Government Board in 1903 after placing fortieth on the Class 1 examination. He became an assistant secretary in 1919 and attained the rank of principal assistant secretary in 1930. Francis left the Ministry of Health in 1938 to become secretary and comptroller general of the National Debt Office, a position he held until 1946.

Henry Leon French, OBE (1918), CB (1920), KBE (1938), KCB (1942), GBE (1946). Born 1883. French was educated privately before attending King's College, London. French entered the civil service by open competition in 1901 and was promoted to the First Division in 1909. He served first the Board and then the Ministry of Agriculture throughout most of his career. French attained the rank of assistant secretary in 1920, principal assistant secretary in 1930, and second secretary in 1937. French served as permanent secretary of the Ministry of Food from 1939 until his retirement in 1946.

Herbert Horace George, CB (1944), MC. Born 1890. George attended Westminster City School and Trinity College, Cambridge. He rose to the rank of undersecretary for Finance and accountant-general at the Ministry of Health, retiring in 1950.

Ioan Gwilym Gibbon, CBE (1918), CB (1931), Kt. (1936). Born 1874, the son of David Gibbon, mining engineer. Gibbon attended Oswestry High School and the London School of Economics. He entered the Local Government Board after placing ninth on the 1902 Class 1 examination. In the Ministry of Health, he served as assistant secretary from 1919 until 1926 and as principal assistant secretary until his retirement in 1936.

Robert MacDonald Gould, CB (1946), Kt. (1948). Gould served in the administrative class of the Ministry of Labour from 1926. He rose to the rank of assistant secretary in 1939 and chief industrial commissioner in 1952.

Percy James Grigg, KCSI (1936), KCB (1932), PC (1942). Born 1890. Grigg attended Bournemouth School and St. John's College, Cambridge. He was appointed to the Treasury in 1913 where he served as principal private secretary to Chancellors of the Exchequer from 1921 until 1930. He became chairman of the Board of Customs and Excise in 1930 and then of the Board of Inland Revenue. He was permanent undersecretary of state for War from 1939 until 1942, when he entered Parliament as a National Conservative and became secretary of state for War, serving in that capacity until 1945.

A. Daniel Hall, KCB (1918). Born 1864. Hall attended Manchester Grammar School and Balliol College, Oxford. Hall was director of the Rothansted Experimental Station of the Lawes Agricultural Trust before becoming permanent secretary of the Board of Agriculture in 1917. He became chief scientific adviser of the Ministry of Agriculture in 1920, a position he held until 1935.

Henry Drummond Hancock, CMG (1942). Born 1895. Hancock attended Haileybury and Exeter College, Oxford. After passing the 1920 Reconstruction examination, Hancock entered the Ministry of Labour where he was promoted to principal in 1929. Hancock left Labour for the Unemployment Assistance Board in 1934. Hancock rose to the position of permanent secretary of first the Ministry of National Insurance in 1949 and then the Ministry of Food in 1951.

Wilfred Henry Hardman, MC, CBE. Born 1894. Hardman attended Christ's Hospital and St. John's College, Cambridge. After passing the 1920 Reconstruction examination he entered the Ministry of Transportation. In 1934 Hardman became a principal at the Ministry of Labour, where he rose to the rank of assistant secretary after the Second World War.

Edward Lindsey Heath. Born 1878, the son of Reverend Edward Heath, Catholic Apostolic Church. Heath attended Merchant Taylors' School and St. John's

College, Oxford. Heath was an LEA official from 1903 until 1907. He entered the Board of Education as an inspector in 1908, then transferred to the administrative side in 1908. He was promoted to principal in 1921 and remained at that rank throughout the rest of the interwar period.

Hubert Douglas Henderson, Kt. (1942). A distinguished academic economist, Henderson was joint secretary of the Economic Advisory Council from 1930 until 1934.

E. A. Hitchman, CB (1948), KCB (1952). Born 1903. Hitchman attended St. Bartholomew's Grammar School, Newbury, and Downing College, Cambridge. After passing the 1926 Class 1 examination, Hitchman entered the Ministry of Labour. He rose to the rank of undersecretary in 1946 and went to the Treasury in 1947. Ultimately Hitchman served as permanent secretary of the Ministry of Agriculture from 1952 until 1959.

Maurice Gerald Holmes, OBE (1919), CB (1929), KCB (1938), GBE (1949). Born 1885. Holmes attended Wellington and Balliol College, Oxford. He entered the Board of Education in 1909 as a barrister, becoming a Board examiner in 1911. He served as director of Establishments in 1924 and 1925 and became the principal assistant secretary of the Secondary Branch in 1926. Holmes was promoted to deputy secretary in 1932 and to permanent secretary in 1937, serving until his retirement in 1945. He was a governor of Wellington from 1939 until 1960. He died in 1964.

Alfred William Hurst, CB (1926), KBE (1929). Born 1884. Hurst attended Market Bosworth School and Emmanuel College, Cambridge. He entered the Treasury in 1907 after taking first place on the Class 1 examination. Hurst rose to the rank of undersecretary at the Treasury in 1936.

Godfrey Herbert Ince, CB (1941), KBE (1943). Born 1891. Ince attended Reigate Grammar School and University College, London. He entered the Ministry of Labour in 1920, after passing the 1919 Reconstruction examination. Ince spent his entire career in the Ministry of Labour where he served as permanent secretary from 1944 until 1956.

Spencer Leeson. Born 1892, the son of Dr. J. R. Lesson, M. D. Leeson attended Winchester and New College, Oxford. He held the position of assistant principal at the Board of Education from 1919 until 1924. In 1924, Leeson left the board for a teaching career. He took a post as an assistant master at Winchester in 1935. In 1939 Leeson became Chairman of the Headmasters' Conference. He was the author of numerous publications on religious and educational subjects.

Frederick William Leggett, CB (1933), KT (1941). Born 1884. Leggett attended City of London School, Strand School, and King's College, London. Leggett entered the civil service in 1904 and became private secretary of the parliamentary secretary of Ministry of Labour in 1917. He attained the rank of assistant secretary in 1919, principal assistant secretary in 1930, undersecretary in 1939, and deputy secretary in 1942.

Sir Arthur B. Lowry, CB (1918), Kt. (1928). Born 1868, the son of Reverend C. H. Lowry. Lowry attended Eton and Trinity College, Oxford. He was appointed to the position of assistant general inspector at the Local Government Board in 1903. Lowry served first the LGB and then the Ministry of Health as chief inspector from 1913 until 1933. Lowry then rose to the rank of deputy secretary in the Ministry of Health, a position he held in 1933 and 1934.

H. E. Mann. Born 1877. Mann attended Bedford Grammar School and Lincoln College, Oxford. He was secretary to the registrar of the University of London before entering the Board of Education in 1904. Mann attained the rank of assistant secretary in 1930.

William Walker Marsh, CBE (1935). Born 1877. Marsh attended Twyford Village School and King's College, London. He entered the Board of Trade in 1893 where he served as Llewellyn Smith's private secretary. Marsh became director of Establishments at the Ministry of Labour in 1926; he headed the Trade Boards Division from 1931 to 1937 and served as chairman of the Court of Referees from 1937 until 1939. Marsh also distinguished himself in amateur fencing. He was Amateur Champion Sabre in 1908 and 1909 and represented Great Britain in the Olympic Games in 1908, 1912, 1920, and 1924.

Arthur Maxwell-Lyte. Born 1881, the son of Sir Henry Churchill Maxwell-Lyte, deputy keeper of public records. Maxwell-Lyte attended Eton and Magdalen College, Oxford. He entered the Board of Education in 1905. He was promoted to principal in 1921 and to assistant secretary in 1936.

Edwin Lawrence Mitchell, OBE (1929), CBE (1933), CB (1942). Born 1883. Mitchell attended King's College, London, after having been educated privately. He entered the Board of Agriculture by appointment in 1903 where he rose to the rank of assistant secretary in 1930 and served as a principal assistant secretary from 1939 until 1945.

Robert Morant, CB (1902), KCB (1907). Born 1863. Morant was educated at Winchester and New College, Oxford. After doing educational work of various kinds (he served as tutor to the royal family of Siam), Morant entered the Education Department in 1895. Morant served as permanent secretary of the Board of Education from 1903 until 1911, as chairman of the Insurance Commission from 1912 until 1919, and as permanent secretary of the Ministry of Health from 1919 until his death on March 13, 1920.

Charles Nathan, CB (1944). Born 1891. Nathan attended Rossall School and Brasenose College, Oxford. He entered the Board of Agriculture in 1915 after taking the 1914 open competition examination. Nathan rose to the rank of assistant secretary in 1937 and served the Ministry of Agriculture as deputy secretary from 1945 until 1947.

George Newman, Kt. (1911), KCB (1918), GBE (1935). Born 1870. Newman attended Sidcot School, the University of Edinburgh, and King's College, London. Newman served both the Ministry of Health (1919–1935) and the Board of Education (1907–1935) as chief medical officer. Newman was a prolific author of works on public health and his professional memoir, *The Building of a*

Nation's Health (1939), is an important source for developments during this period.

Otto Ernest Niemeyer, CB (1921), KCB (1924), GBE (1927). Born 1883. Niemeyer attended St. Paul's School and Balliol College, Oxford. In 1906, after placing first in the Class 1 examination (John Maynard Keynes placed second on the examination list that year), Niemeyer entered the Treasury where he had a long and distinguished career. He then served as Director of the Bank of England.

Hugh William Orange, CIE (1906), CB (1914), Kt. (1919), KBE (1928). Born 1866, the son of Dr. William Orange, CB, MD. Orange attended Winchester and New College, Oxford. Orange was director-general of education in India from 1906 until 1911. He entered the Board of Education in 1911 as accountant-general and served in that position until 1928.

Edward Henry Pelham, CB (1921), KCB (1933). Born 1876, the son of Prof. Henry F. Pelham of Trinity College, Oxford. Pelham attended Harrow and Balliol College, Oxford. He entered the Board of Education in 1900. He became principal assistant secretary of secondary education in 1920, and then of elementary education in 1926. He served as deputy secretary to the Board from 1930 until 1932, and as permanent secretary from 1932 until 1936.

Thomas William Phillips, CBE (1918), CB (1922), KBE (1934), KCB (1936). Born 1883. Phillips attended Machynlleth County School and Jesus College, Oxford. He entered the Board of Trade in 1906 after placing ninth on the Class 1 examination. Phillips rose to the position of deputy secretary of the Ministry of Labour in 1925 and served as Labour's permanent secretary from 1935 until 1944.

Edmund B. Phipps, CB (1916), KT (1917). Born 1869, the son of Colonel Ramsay Weston Phipps, RA. Phipps attended Winchester and New College, Oxford. Phipps held a variety of teaching posts before he began his career in the Board of Education. He was a tutor to the children of HRH the Duke of Connaught from 1893 until 1896. He taught at Clifton in 1896 and then served as assistant secretary for the Girls' Public Day School Company from 1897 until 1901. He entered the Board of Education in 1901 where he served as private secretary to Permanent Secretary Robert Morant. He became a principal assistant secretary in the Elementary Branch in 1912 and became deputy secretary of the Board in 1926. Phipps retired in 1929.

Henry Maunsell Richards, CB (1920), Kt. (1930). Born 1869, the son of Reverend J. Richards, Senior Chaplain, Bengal Establishment. Richards attended Merchant Taylors' School and St. John's College, Oxford. He entered the Board of Education's inspectorate in 1902, rising to senior chief inspector in 1926. After his retirement in 1933, Richards maintained his interest in education, serving in a number of different capacities including governor of Stowe School, Mill Hill School, and Hertford Grammar School and chairman of the Conference of Educational Associations.

William Arthur Robinson, CB (1915), CBE (1918), KCB (1919), GCB (1929), GBE (1941). Born 1874. Robinson attended Appleby School and Queen's College,

Oxford. He entered the Colonial Office in 1897 after placing first in the Class 1 examination. Robinson rose to the rank of assistant secretary of the Ministry of Works in 1912 and permanent secretary of the Air Ministry in 1917. In 1920 Robinson replaced Robert Morant as permanent secretary of the Ministry of Health, a position he held until 1935.

A.G.L. Rogers. Born 1864. Rogers entered the Board of Agriculture in 1898.

Lewis Amherst Selby-Bigge, CB (1905), KCB (1913), BT (1919). Born 1860. Selby-Bigge attended Winchester and Christ Church, Oxford. He entered the Board of Education in 1902, succeeding Sir Robert Morant as permanent secretary in 1911. He retired from the Board in 1925 but maintained an active interest in educational policy.

Russell Edwin Stanley, MBE. Born 1884. Stanley entered the Board of Agriculture and Fisheries in 1905. He was finally promoted from the Second Division to the rank of principal in 1938.

Andrew Denys Stocks, CBE (1919), CB (1932). Born 1884, the son of John Edward Stocks, archdeacon of Leicester and canon of Peterborough. Stocks became a solicitor in the Board of Customs and Excise in 1910. After serving in the Solicitors' Department of the Treasury from 1914 until 1920, Stocks entered the Ministry of Agriculture as an assistant legal adviser. He was promoted to legal adviser of the Ministry of Agriculture in 1925 and served in that capacity until after the Second World War.

Arthur William Street, MC, CIE (1924), CMG (1933), CB (1935), KBE (1938), KCB (1941). Born 1892. Street attended Sandown County School and King's College, London. Street entered the Ministry of Agriculture in 1919 as private secretary to the minister. He became an assistant secretary in 1929, a principal assistant secretary in 1932, and second secretary in 1936. He left the Ministry of Agriculture for the Air Ministry in 1938 where he served as permanent secretary.

Ernest John Strohmenger, CB (1919), KBE (1927), GBE (1937). Born 1873. Strohmenger entered the civil service in 1893. In 1912 he was appointed principal at the National Health Insurance Commission. Upon the formation of the Ministry of Health in 1919, Strohmenger became accountant-general, a role he held until 1930. After serving as the Ministry of Health's deputy secretary from 1930 until 1932, Strohmenger became undersecretary at the Treasury, and he then served as deputy chairman of the Unemployment Assistant Board from 1934 until his retirement in 1937.

Aubrey V. Symonds, CB (1916), KCB (1919). Born 1874. Symonds attended Bedford School and University College, Oxford. Symonds served the bulk of his career at the Local Government Board, which he entered in 1897 after placing eighty-third on the Class 1 examination that year. He became second secretary in the newly formed Ministry of Health in 1920, and he succeeded Selby-Bigge as permanent secretary of the Board of Education in 1926. His career was cut short by his death in 1931.

Charles John Howell Thomas, KCB (1928), KCMG (1934), Kt. (1927), CMG (1925). Born 1874. Thomas had been chief valuer at the Board of Inland Revenue before his appointment as permanent secretary of the Ministry of Agriculture, a position he held from 1927 until 1936. He left Agriculture to become chairman of the Tithe Redemption Commission in 1936.

Robert John Thompson, CB (1923), OBE. Born 1867. Thompson served as an assistant secretary in the Ministry of Agriculture until his retirement in 1929. He served as president of the Agricultural Economics Society in 1929 and 1930 and published several articles in the *Journal of the Royal Statistical Society*.

Frank Newton Tribe, OBE (1919), CBE (1930), CB (1938), KBE (1941). Born 1893. Tribe attended Clifton College and Trinity College, Oxford. After passing the 1919 Reconstruction examination, Tribe entered the Ministry of Labour where he reached the rank of assistant secretary in 1934, principal assistant secretary in 1937, and deputy secretary in 1940. Tribe became permanent secretary of the Ministry of Fuel and Power in 1945.

Herbert Brough Usher, CB (1948). Born 1892. Usher attended Haileybury and Trinity Hall, Cambridge. He was an assistant editor of the *Westminster Gazette* in 1919 and stood as a candidate for the Labour party in 1924 and 1929. Usher served as the prime minister's personal private secretary from 1929 until 1935. He entered the Treasury in 1936 and reached the rank of assistant secretary in 1940.

John Ballingall Forbes Watson, Kt. (1939), MA, LL.B. Born 1880. Forbes Watson attended Dollar Academy, Edinburgh University; the École de Droit and the École des Sciences Politiques, Paris; the universities of Göttingen and Heidelberg. A barrister, Watson was director of the National Confederation of Employers' Organizations. He also served as the British Employers' delegate at the 1929 International Labour Conference.

Griffith Goodland Williams, CB, KBE. Born 1890. Williams attended Westminster and Christ Church, Oxford. Williams attained the rank of assistant secretary in 1939 and reached the rank of deputy secretary of the Ministry of Education by 1950.

Horace John Wilson, CBE (1918), CB (1920), KCB (1924), GCMG (1933), GCB (1937). Born 1882. Wilson attended Kurnella School, Bournemouth, and the London School of Economics. Best known as one of Neville Chamberlain's most trusted advisers during the appeasement period, Wilson had a long and distinguished career at the Ministry of Labour before his forays into foreign policy. Wilson entered the civil service by appointment to the Board of Trade in 1900. He became permanent secretary of the Ministry of Labour in 1921, a position that he held until 1930 when he became chief industrial adviser to the government, a position he held until 1939. Wilson also served as Neville Chamberlain's adviser from 1935 until his appointment as permanent secretary of the Treasury and head of the civil service in 1939.

Robert Stanford Wood, CB (1939), KBE (1941). Born 1886, the son of Reverend John Roskruge Wood. Wood attended City of London School and Jesus College, Cambridge. Wood entered the Board of Education in 1911. He served as Eustace Percy's principal private secretary from 1926 until 1928, after which he served as the Board's director of Establishments until 1936. He became principal assistant secretary of the Technical Branch in 1936 and deputy secretary in 1940.

Sydney Herbert Wood, MC, CB, (1943). Born 1884. Wood attended Stanley House, Margate, and University College, London. From 1908 until 1910 he was warden at University College, Hull. He entered the Board of Education in 1910 and reached the rank of principal assistant secretary in 1944. He served as secretary to the 1926 Royal Commission on the University of London and the 1936 Royal Commission on the University of Durham.

Notes

Unpublished Sources, Locations, and Abbreviations

Private Papers
Christopher Addison Papers (Bodleian Library, Oxford University)
Noel Buxton Papers (McGill University Library, Montreal, Canada)
Nevile Chamberlain Papers (Birmingham University Library)
H.A.L. Fisher Papers (Bodleian Library, Oxford University)
Sir Edward Hilton Young, Kennet Papers (Cambridge University Library)
Sir George Newman Papers (Library of the Wellcombe Institute of the History of Medicine, London)
Sir Robert Arthur Sanders Papers (Conservative Research Department, London)
Sir Arthur Steel-Maitland Papers (Scottish Record Office, Edinburgh)
C. P. Trevelyan Papers (Library of the University of Newcastle-upon-Tyne)

Sources from the Public Record Office (PRO)
Board of Education: ED
Cabinet Papers: CAB
Ministry of Agriculture: MAF
Ministry of Health: MH
Ministry of Housing and Local Government: HLG
Ministry of Labour: LAB
Treasury: T

Introduction: The English Civil Service and Social Policy

1. Robert Graves's *Good-bye to All That* (Garden City, N.Y.: Doubleday, 1957) remains the most famous expression of this feeling. Vera Brittain, after serving as a nurse for nearly four years, wrote of her return to Oxford in 1919: "Once again, as in 1915, Oxford from Carfax to Summertown was warm and sweet with lilac and wallflowers and may; it seemed unbearable that everything should be exactly the same when all my life was so much changed." Vera Brittain, *Testament of Youth* (London: Victor Gollancz, 1933; rpt. Wideview Books, 1980), 477. The epigraph is from R. W. Harris, *Not So Humdrum: The Autobiography of a Civil Servant* (London: John Lane, 1939), 270.

2. Keith Middlemas, in *Politics in Industrial Society: The Experience of the British System Since 1911* (London: A. Deutsch, 1979), argues that the development of a "corporate bias" provided the key to this success story. His work commands respect for its scope and comprehensiveness although it has been criticized in detail. See Rodney Lowe, "The Ministry of Labour: Fact and Fiction," *Bulletin of the Society for the Study of Labour History* 4 (1980): 23–27.

3. For an example, see Mark Swenarton, " 'An Insurance Against Revolution': Ideological Objectives of the Provision and Design of Public Housing in Britain After the First World War," *Bulletin of the Institute of Historical Research* 54 (May 1981): 92–95.

4. See James E. Cronin, "Coping with Labour, 1918–1926," in *Social Conflict and the Political Order in Modern Britain,* ed. James E. Cronin and Jonathan Scheer (London: Croom Helm, 1982), 113–45; and Christopher J. Nottingham, "Recasting Bourgeois Britain? The British State in the Years Which Followed the First World War," *International Review of Social History* 31 (1986): 227–47, for different scenarios of how this was accomplished. Cronin refines and elaborates his analysis in "The British State and the Structure of Political Opportunity," *Journal of British Studies* 27 (July 1988): 199–231.

5. Hugh Dalton, *Call Back Yesterday,* vol. 1, *Memories, 1887 to 1931* (London: Frederick Mallen, 1953), 301; Oswald Mosley, *My Life* (New Rochelle, N.Y.: Arlington House, 1968), 237.

6. Robert Skidelsky, *Politicians and the Slump: The Labour Government of 1929–1931* (London: Macmillan, 1967), 391; A.J.P. Taylor, *English History, 1914–1945* (Oxford: Oxford University Press, 1965), 210.

7. H. E. Dale, *The Higher Civil Service of Great Britain* (Oxford: Oxford University Press, 1941), 118–19; J. Donald Kingsley, *Representative Bureaucracy* (Ohio: Antioch Press, 1944), 282.

8. See David Rubinstein, "Ellen Wilkinson Re-considered," *History Workshop Journal* 7 (spring 1979): 161–69. D. W. Dean, in "Planning for a Postwar Generation: Ellen Wilkinson and George Tomlinson at the Ministry of Education, 1945–51," *History of Education* 15 (June 1986): 95–117, gives a more detailed and nuanced account of the development of education policy during the postwar Labour government. R. H. Crossman, *The Diaries of a Cabinet Minister* (New York: Holt, Rinehart, and Winston, 1975). See vol. 1, 614–22, for Crossman's evaluation of the civil service.

9. See Sir John Hoskyns, "Whitehall and Westminster: An Outsider's View," *Parliamentary Affairs* 36 (spring 1983): 137–47, for a Thatcherite prescription for civil service reform. Geoffrey K. Fry surveys these recent developments in *The Changing Civil Service* (London: Allen and Unwin, 1985), 9–35; "The British Career Civil Service Under Challenge," *Political Studies* 34 (1986): 533–55; and "The Thatcher Government, the Financial Management Initiative, and the 'New Civil Service,' " *Public Administration* 66 (spring 1988): 1–20. See Richard A. Chapman, "The Rise and Fall of the CSD," *Policy and Politics* 11, no. 1 (1983): 41–61, for an account of one especially dramatic episode in the Thatcher government's attempts to bring the civil service under its control.

10. Max Beloff, "The Whitehall Factor: The Role of the Higher Civil Service, 1919–39," in *The Politics of Reappraisal, 1919–1939,* ed. Gillian Peele and Chris Cook (New York: St. Martin's Press, 1975), 210; R. Davidson and R. Lowe, "Bureaucracy and Innovation in British Welfare Policy, 1870–1945," in *The Emergence of the Welfare State in Britain and Germany, 1850–1950,* ed. W. J. Mommsen with Wolfgang Mock (London: Croom Helm, 1981), 263–64; R. Lowe, "Bureaucracy Triumphant or Denied? The Expansion of the British Civil Service, 1919–1939," *Public Administration* 62 (autumn 1984): 291–310.

11. Ivan Reid in *Social Class Difference in Britain: A Sourcebook* (London: Open Books, 1977), 15, baldly states the first view: "Social class is a grouping of people into categories on the basis of occupation." This perspective provides a straightforward foundation for the empirical tradition in sociology. Reid's book is essentially a compendium of empirical studies. This stance toward class is inherently static and cannot speak to the processes that form, maintain, and modify the occupational structure. An important systematic exposition of the second view has been developed by Anthony Giddens: " 'Class' is a phenomenon of the totality, in the sense in which, in a capitalist society, it expresses a system of exploitative domination cohered in terms of a definite alignment of economy and policy sanctioned by the state." *Studies in Social and Political Theory* (New York: Basic Books, 1977), 208. Here he expresses concisely the core of

the theory he elaborated in his *Class Structure of the Advanced Societies* (New York: Harper and Row, 1973). Giddens develops his views in *The Constitution of Society* (Berkeley and Los Angeles: University of California Press, 1984). His notion of the duality of social process—the simultaneity of social structure and individual action, which he tries to express by using the term *structuration*—strikes me as compelling. For a brief discussion of class, see T. B. Bottomore, *Classes in Modern Society* (New York: Vintage Books, 1966). Ralf Dahrendorf's *Class and Class Conflict in Industrial Society* (Stanford, Calif.: Stanford University Press, 1959), remains a modern classic on the subject of class. Dahrendorf departs substantially from the views of class cited above, defining "class" in terms of access to or exclusion from authority (204).

12. T. J. Jackson Lears, in an essay on the concept of hegemony, has underlined this pitfall. See "The Concept of Cultural Hegemony: Problems and Possibilities," *American Historical Review* 90 (June 1985): 587–88.

13. E. P. Thompson's example inspired a large and fruitful literature but one largely confined to the history of labor and the working class. David Cannadine in his ambitious *Decline and Fall of the British Aristocracy* (New York: Doubleday, 1990) brings a sensibility informed by Thompson to the study of England's aristocratic elite (see 1–25 for Cannadine's discussion).

14. Giddens, *Class Structure of the Advanced Societies,* 51.

15. J. Saville, "The Welfare State: An Historical Perspective," in *Social Welfare in Modern Britain,* ed. Eric Butterworth and Robert Holman (Glasgow: Collins, 1975), 65. This essay first appeared in the *New Reasoner* 3 (winter 1957–1958): 5, 6, 11, 12–17, 20–24.

16. See Victor George and Paul Wilding, "Social Values, Social Class, and Social Policy," *Social and Economic Administration* 6 (1972): 236–48, for a clear definition of this approach to the study of social policy. Norman Ginsburg in *Class, Capital, and Social Policy* (London: Macmillan, 1979) uses just such a Marxist theoretical perspective to analyze the development of social security and housing policy in postwar England.

17. Peter Taylor-Gooby, "The State, Class Ideology, and Social Policy," *Journal of Social Policy* 10 (Oct. 1981): 433. This essay provides a good critical analysis of this approach to the study of social policy.

18. George and Wilding, "Social Values, Social Class, and Social Policy," 240. Ralph Miliband has taken a similar view, stressing the homogeneous social origin of those who hold high position in the governments of advanced capitalist societies, in *The State in Capitalist Society* (London: Weidenfeld and Nicolson, 1969), 66–67, 123–24.

19. Elite theory derives from the work of Vilfredo Pareto *(The Mind and Society)* and Gaetano Mosca *(The Ruling Class)*. For a brief critical summary of elite theory, see T. B. Bottomore, *Elites and Society* (London: Penguin, 1966). Ezra N. Suleiman, *Elites in French Society* (Princeton: Princeton University Press, 1978), is a good example of an empirical study based on elite theory conducted by a political scientist.

20. Lewis J. Edinger and Donald O. Searing have established the contingent nature of the relationship between social background and the values espoused by elite groups. They did not address the processes that might have enhanced or mitigated such a relationship between social origin and beliefs. "Social Background in Elite Analysis: A Methodological Inquiry," *American Political Science Review* 61 (June 1967): 428–45.

21. Anthony Giddens, "Elites in the British Class Structure," in *Elites and Power in British Society,* ed. Philip Stanworth and Anthony Giddens (Cambridge: Cambridge University Press, 1974), 4.

22. Richard N. Adams, *Energy and Structure: A Theory of Social Power* (Austin: University of Texas Press, 1975), 4–10. Adams's work represents a trend toward the application of anthropological theory to the study of complex societies. Adams links the development of cultural forms to changes in the material environment. For a different approach to materialist explanations of cultural forms, see Marvin Harris, *The Rise of Anthropological Theory: A History of Theories of Culture* (New York: Crowell, 1968), and *Cultural Materialism: The Struggle for a Science of Culture* (New York: Random House, 1979). See also Steve Lukes, "Power and Struc-

ture," in *Essays in Social Theory* (New York: Columbia University Press, 1977), for a concise discussion of the issues raised by any attempt to formulate a concept of power.

23. Giddens, *Constitution of Society*, 257.

24. Lowe, "Bureaucracy Triumphant or Denied?" 292.

25. Harold Perkin, *The Origins of Modern English Society, 1780–1880* (London: Routledge and Kegan Paul, 1969), 291–301. Scholars recognize and lament the shortcomings of employing such a limited range of information as a surrogate for social origins and identity, but they continue to do so rather than give up such studies altogether. For recent studies that utilize this methodology, see Kevin Theakston and Geoffrey K. Fry, "Britain's Administrative Elite: Permanent Secretaries, 1900–1986," *Public Administration* 67 (summer 1989): 129–47; William Gibson, "The Social Origins and Education of an Elite: The Nineteenth-Century Episcopate," *History of Education* 20 (June 1991): 95–105; and June Burnham and G. W. Jones, "Advising Margaret Thatcher: The Prime Minister's Office and the Cabinet Office Compared," *Political Studies* 41 (June 1993): 299–314.

26. Joseph Melling, "Welfare Capitalism and the Origins of Welfare States: British Industry, Workplace Welfare, and Social Reform, c. 1870–1914," *Social History* 17 (Oct. 1992): 457.

27. Anthony Giddens, in one schematic elaboration of his theory of structuration, stresses that human agency necessarily entails having power (power understood as the capacity to make a difference in the world). He also points out that individuals may engage in actions that are understandable in light of class relationships without being conscious of themselves as members of a class or as acting on behalf of class interests. Anthony Giddens, "Power, the Dialectic of Control, and Class Structuration," in *Social Class and the Division of Labour: Essays in Honour of Ilya Neustadt*, ed. Anthony Giddens and Gavin MacKenzie (Cambridge: Cambridge University Press, 1982), 30–31, 40. Although it does not utilize any explicit theoretical model, Victor M. Batzel's study of the work of John Smith, who served as the first inspector-general of the Department of Companies Liquidation at the Board of Trade in the late nineteenth century, shows how one civil servant developed a normative model upon which to base his interpretation of policy, as well as how his conduct made a difference. " 'The General Scope of the Act': A Study of Law, Moralism, and Administration in England, 1844–1910," *Canadian Journal of History* 22 (Dec. 1987): 349–66.

1. The Civil Service and the Social Calculus of English Education

1. See C. H. Dodd, "Recruitment to the Administrative Class, 1960–1964," *Public Administration* 45 (spring 1967): 55–80. Civil servant rebel Clive Ponting made this point again in *Whitehall: Tragedy and Farce* (London: Hamish Hamilton, 1986), 73–77. The epigraph is taken from R. K. Kelsall, "Selection and the Social Background of the Administrative Class: A Rejoinder," *Public Administration* 34 (summer 1956): 170–71.

2. See Brian Simon, *Education and the Labour Movement, 1870–1920* (London: Lawrence and Wishart, 1965), 97–120, and Olive Banks, *Parity and Prestige in English Secondary Education* (London: Routledge and Kegan Paul, 1955), 13–30, 61–71, for a discussion of these developments in the scholarship ladder. See G.A.N. Lowndes, *The Silent Social Revolution* (London: Oxford University Press, 1937), for an overall history of English education by a former official of the Board of Education. See J. L. Gray and Pearl Moshinsky, "Ability and Opportunity in English Education," and David V. Glass and J. L. Gray, "Opportunity and the Older Universities," in *Political Arithmetic*, ed. Lancelot Hogben (London: Allen and Unwin, 1938), 334–76, 418–70, for an analysis of the situation as it stood in the 1930s.

3. D. V. Glass, ed., *Social Mobility in Britain* (London: Routledge and Kegan Paul, 1954). See also D. V. Glass and J. R. Hall, "A Description of a Sample Inquiry into Social Mobility in Great Britain," in ibid., for a detailed description of how the survey was conducted. See also A. H. Halsey, *Change in British Society* (Oxford: Oxford University Press, 1978), 112, 116, for an indication of Glass's influence. Alan Little and John Westergaard carry the analysis of educa-

tional opportunity into the postwar period, finding only a small increase. "The Trends of Class Differentials in Educational Opportunity in England and Wales," *British Journal of Sociology* 15 (1964): 301–16.

4. Jean Floud, "The Educational Experience of the Adult Population of England and Wales as at July 1949," in Glass, *Social Mobility in Britain* (see esp. appendix 1; table 1, 124; table 19, 138–39).

5. Floud, "Educational Experience," table 2, 120–21; R. K. Kelsall, *Higher Civil Servants in Britain* (London: Routledge and Kegan Paul, 1955), 52.

6. A. H. Halsey, John Sheehan, and John Vaisey, "Schools," in *Trends in British Society Since 1900,* ed. A. H. Halsey (London: Macmillan, 1972), table 6.28, 189.

7. Guy Routh, *Occupation and Pay in Great Britain, 1906–1910* (Cambridge: Cambridge University Press, 1965), 6. See also W. D. Rubinstein, "Education and the Social Origins of British Elites, 1880–1970," *Past and Present* 112 (1986): 163–207, esp. 169–70 and 170, n. 11. Rubinstein argues that the social origins of English elite groups bespeak a meritocratic system of social mobility, although his own work shows that this system functioned to serve the middle classes, broadly defined, and excluded the working class, at least until after the Second World War. William Gibson has come to similar conclusions about the role of education in limiting access to the meritocratic ladder to the middle and upper classes in his study of the careers of Anglican bishops during the nineteenth century. "The Social Origins and Education of an Elite: The Nineteenth-Century Episcopate," *History of Education* 20 (June 1991): 95–105.

8. University Grants Committee, *Report,* 1929–30 to 1934–35 (London: HMSO, 1935).

9. Ibid.

10. Halsey et al., "Schools," table 6.5, 167.

11. Ibid., table 6.21, 182.

12. Ibid., table 6.2, 154. Beginning in 1907, the Board of Education published figures on the enrollment of schools—but only for those schools that the Board inspected, and the Board inspected private schools only if invited to do so. To make matters more complex, the Board kept records only on those schools that, upon inspection, were found to be either eligible for a grant from the state or certifiable as "efficient." The schools that were not inspected, as well as those failing to pass inspection, do not appear on either list (neither the list of schools eligible for grant nor the list of schools certified as efficient) published by the Board of Education. This lacuna in the records makes difficult even an aggregate analysis of secondary school enrollment, especially for the early years of the twentieth century.

13. In addition to the list of well-known schools used by Kelsall in *Higher Civil Servants in Britain* and cited below, see David Boyd, *Elites and Their Education* (Windsor: NFER Publishing, 1973), 41, for a similar list of well-known schools. J. R. de S. Honey has challenged the use of such lists as anachronistic in *Tom Brown's Universe* (New York: Quadrangle, 1977), 273–82.

14. It is estimated that in 1895 there were between 65,000 and 75,000 boys in grammar schools of various sorts and perhaps another 34,000 students in proprietary schools. There were 3,600 students at the "inner seven" of the Clarendon schools—Eton, Harrow, Westminster, Winchester, Charterhouse, Rugby, Shrewsbury. Allowing for an additional thousand boys at the two great London day schools also regarded as Clarendon schools (St. Paul's and Merchant Taylors'), these institutions would represent approximately 4 percent of the total enrollment in secondary schools at the end of the nineteenth century. There were about a hundred schools in the Headmasters' Conference in 1902. Assuming an average enrollment of 400 boys per school (almost certainly an overestimate, as the average was 405 in 1930), then the Clarendon schools would represent about 10 percent of the boys in Headmasters' Conference schools. Boys in Headmasters' Conference schools would, however, represent some 40 percent of all boys enrolled in secondary schools, a much higher proportion than obtained in 1930. F. Musgrove, "Middle-Class Education and Employment in the Nineteenth Century: A Rejoinder," *Economic*

History Review, 2d ser., 14 (1961): 322–23; Honey, *Tom Brown's Universe*, 143–44, 249; Lowndes, *The Silent Social Revolution*, 45–55, 261–66. This estimate appears reasonable in light of the trend shown by Board of Education figures on secondary school enrollment during the early years of the twentieth century. Between 1913 and 1933, the proportion of secondary school pupils enrolled in public schools gradually declined (from 34 to 22.5 percent). Glass and Gray, "Opportunity and the Older Universities," table 3, 425.

15. In 1929, 51.2 percent of those who held high rank had attended Oxford, 18.2 percent had attended Cambridge, only 5.8 percent had attended the University of London. Approximately 4 percent of this group had attended a Scottish university, and 2.7 percent had not attended any university at all. In 1939, 43.5 percent had attended Oxford, 22.2 percent had attended Cambridge, 7.3 percent had attended London, 6.7 percent had attended a Scottish university, and 2.9 percent had not attended any university. In each of these two years, only one person had attended an English or Welsh university other than Oxford, Cambridge, or London. Among open competition entrants to the home civil service between 1909 and 1939 (those who qualified for the civil service by examination), 45.6 percent had attended Oxford, 36.8 percent had attended Cambridge, 6.1 percent had attended a Scottish university, only 1.7 percent had not attended any university. For the period from 1909 to 1914 (prior to the time when the Board of Education or the Board of Agriculture began to receive open competition recruits), 53.3 percent of the open competition entrants had attended Oxford, 26.9 percent had attended Cambridge, 7.5 percent London, 4.8 percent a Scottish university, and 2.2 percent had not attended any university. Kelsall, *Higher Civil Servants*, table 22, 138; table 23, 139. (I have combined Kelsall's categories of "Oxford" with "Oxford and other," and "Cambridge" with "Cambridge and other.")

16. Ibid., table 13, 123.

17. Ibid., 120. Kelsall's "best-known" schools include Charterhouse, Cheltenham, Clifton, Eton, Fettes, Haileybury, Harrow, Loretto, Malvern, Marlborough, Oundle, Radley, Repton, Rossall, Rugby, Sedbergh, Sherborne, Shrewsbury, Uppingham, and Winchester.

18. Ibid., table 15, 125; table 17, 129.

19. The "missing" category in table 2 and those that follow includes all those individuals whose educational experience I could not identify. The missing category can be thought of as an "other" category because—thanks to the nature of the sources (the many published registers of universities and public schools)—I could determine both that these individuals did not attend Oxford or Cambridge and that they probably did not attend one of the well-known secondary schools.

20. See John Chandos, *Boys Together: English Public Schools, 1800–1864* (New Haven: Yale University Press, 1984), 320–51, for a recent capitulation of this transformation.

21. For the peccadillo, see David Newsome, *Godliness and Good Learning* (London: John Murry, 1961), 45. For changing behavior, see Harold Perkin, *The Origins of Modern English Society, 1780–1880* (London: Routledge and Kegan Paul, 1969), 297–98. See also Martin J. Wiener, *English Culture and the Decline of the Industrial Spirit, 1850–1980* (Cambridge: Cambridge University Press, 1980), 16–24.

22. First two quotations are from Rupert Wilkinson, *Gentlemanly Power* (London: Oxford University Press, 1964), 21, 18. Sir Stephen Tallents, *Man and Boy* (London: Faber and Faber, 1943), 163.

23. T. H. Huxley, "A Liberal Education; and Where to Find It," in *Victorian Culture and Society*, ed. Eugene C. Black (New York: Harper and Row, 1973), 442. See Edward C. Mack, *Public Schools and British Opinion Since 1860* (Westport, Conn.: Greenwood Press, 1971), 50–90, for a detailed discussion of the controversy over the proper place of science in the public school curriculum.

24. Mack, *Public Schools*, 35; Wilkinson, *Gentlemanly Power*, 64. See Honey, *Tom Brown's Universe*, 126–38, for a discussion of the curriculum taught in public schools.

25. Wilkinson, *Gentlemanly Power*, 64.

26. Mack, *Public Schools,* 339. See also Sheila Fletcher, "Co-education and the Victorian Grammar School," *History of Education* 11 (1982): 87–98.

27. Arnold quoted in Vivian Ogilvie, *The British Public School* (London: B. T. Batsford, 1957), 145. See Newsome, *Godliness and Good Learning,* for a definitive discussion of the transition from piety to manliness as desired attributes. Gary McCulloch, in *Philosophers and Kings: Education for Leadership in Modern England* (Cambridge: Cambridge University Press, 1991), examines the development of the public school tradition in terms of its role in developing the character of its pupils to take on positions of leadership in English society. His discussion of the public school in the nineteenth and early twentieth centuries (see 14–22) is among the most recent to cover this ground.

28. Thomas Hughes, *Tom Brown's School Days* (New York: A. L. Burt, n.d.), 68–69. This well-worn phrase is quoted by (among others) Ogilvie in *British Public School,* 145.

29. Matthew Arnold, "An Eton Boy," *Fortnightly Review* 37 (June 1882): 695–97.

30. Tallents, *Man and Boy,* 76.

31. See Honey, *Tom Brown's Universe,* 104–17, for an account of the development of the games cult. See also Spencer Leeson, "The Public Schools Question, 1938 to 1947," in *The Public Schools Question and Other Essays* (London: Longmans, Green, 1948), 5; and Wilkinson, *Gentlemanly Power,* 21, 31, 81.

32. J. Donald Kingsley, *Representative Bureaucracy* (Ohio: Antioch Press, 1944), 151–55. Wilkinson, *Gentlemanly Power,* 21.

33. John Wakeford, *The Cloistered Elite* (New York: Frederick Praeger, 1969), 143.

34. Ian Weinberg, *The English Public Schools* (New York: Atherton Press, 1967), 122.

2. Recruitment and Promotion in the Social Service Ministries

1. The MacDonnell Commission was one of a series of important studies of the civil service carried out by royal commissions and select committees. Evidence presented to the commission provides a detailed portrait of the civil service immediately before the First World War. See E. N. Gladden, *Civil Services of the United Kingdom, 1855–1970* (London: Frank Cass, 1967), 18–40, for a brief discussion. Richard Chapman and J. R. Greenaway situate the MacDonnell Commission in the development of a movement to reform the civil service. *The Dynamics of Administrative Reform* (London: Croom Helm, 1980), 58. The epigraph is from H. E. Dale, "Agriculture and the Civil Service" in *Agriculture in the Twentieth Century* (Oxford: Clarendon Press, 1939), 13.

2. See Jenifer Hart, "The Genesis of the Northcote-Trevelyan Report," in *Studies in the Growth of Nineteenth-Century Government,* ed. Gillian Sutherland (Totowa, N.J.: Rowman and Littlefield, 1972), 63–81, and Geoffrey K. Fry, *Statesmen in Disguise* (London: Macmillan, 1969), 67–83, for general discussions of these developments. See Jill Pellew, *The Home Office, 1848–1914* (Rutherford, N.J.: Fairleigh Dickinson University Press, 1982), esp. 183–205, for a discussion of their impact on one department.

3. See Fry, *Statesmen in Disguise,* 69–71, for a discussion of the development of the examination before the First World War, and 77–80, for the changes made in the examination after the First World War.

4. United Kingdom. Parliament. Royal Commission on the Civil Service [MacDonnell Commission]. *Fourth Report,* 21–25. Cd. 7338. 1914. Hereafter referred to as MacDonnell Commission.

5. Established in 1855 to supervise the examination of new recruits to the civil service, the Civil Service Commission constituted the first concrete reform achieved by the Trevelyan-Northcote report of the previous year. Gladden, *Civil Services,* 20–21; Fry, *Statesmen in Disguise,* 68.

6. Civil Service Commission, *Report,* 1939.

7. MacDonnell Commission, *Appendix to Third Report, Minutes of Evidence.* Testimony of F. B. Jevons, University of Durham, 226; Prof. W. J. Ashley, University of Birmingham, 244;

Edward Gonner, University of Liverpool, 272; C. E. Vaughn, University of Leeds, 265. Cd. 6740. 1913.

8. Fry, *Statesmen in Disguise,* 95. In 1916 Leathes chaired a committee charged with the evaluation of the Class I examination. The subsequent revisions of the examination required candidates to show competence in a modern language and the social and natural sciences as well as in written English. In addition, a viva voce (or personal interview) became part of the selection procedure. Ibid., 77–78.

9. MacDonnell Commission, *Appendix to Third Report, Minutes of Evidence.* Testimony of Dudley J. Medley, University of Glasgow, 206; Richard Lodge, University of Edinburgh, 213; John Burnet, University of St. Andrews, 276. Cd. 6740. 1913.

10. Ibid., Testimony of Lodge, 214; Burnet, 276; Reichel, 235.

11. Fry, *Statesmen in Disguise,* 80–81. Hilda Martindale in *Women Servants of the State, 1870–1938* (London: Allen and Unwin, 1938), 167, has pointed out how the interview disadvantaged outstanding women candidates. R. K. Kelsall in *Higher Civil Servants in Britain* (London: Routledge and Kegan Paul, 1955), 82–84, has shown how graduates of boarding schools surpassed the performance of the graduates of local education authority schools in the 1938 competition.

12. MacDonnell Commission, *Appendix to First Report, Minutes of Evidence.* Appendix II, 126. Cd. 6210. 1912. A. P. W[aterfield], "Note B by the First Civil Service Commission for the Vice-Chancellors' Sub-Committee on Post-War Recruitment to the Civil Service," Table I, Oct. 30, 1941 (PRO ED 136/327). The proportions reported in the text are my calculations based on the data contained in these documents.

13. See Richard A. Chapman, *Leadership in the British Civil Service* (London: Croom Helm, 1984), 17, for several examples of the prevailing view of Oxford and Cambridge in the civil service. Chapman's study of the development of the Civil Service Selection Board shows how this view continued to influence official behavior after the Second World War.

14. A. P. W[aterfield], "Note B by the First Civil Service Commissioner for the Vice-Chancellor's Sub-Committee on Post-War Recruitment to the Civil Service," Oct. 30, 1941 (PRO ED 136/327). A. P. W.[aterfield], Oct. 30, 1941.

15. Calculations based on data provided by "Administrative Class of the Home Civil Service Examination" of 1936 and 1937, n.d. (PRO T162/480/115742).

16. Ibid.

17. The Civil Service Commission's ranking of secondary schools for the purposes of this analysis sheds light on the question of the contemporary hierarchy of prestige among the various public schools. Comparing the list of "well-known" schools employed by Kelsall (the Clarendon schools plus Bradfield, Cheltenham, Clifton, Fettes, Haileybury, Loretto, Malvern, Marlborough, Oundle, Radley, Repton, Rossall, Sedbergh, Sherborne, Uppingham, and Wellington) to the superior Headmasters' Conference schools attended by the 1936 and 1937 open competition candidates shows that only one of Kelsall's schools (Loretto) did not appear on at least one of the two lists. On the other hand, both lists include many more schools than did Kelsall. Schools in the 1936 list that Kelsall did not recognize as well known include Beaumont, Christ's Hospital, City of London, Downside, Dulwich, Edinburgh Academy, Gresham's School, Highgate, Lancing, Manchester Grammar School, Merchant Taylors' (Liverpool), Merchant Taylors' (Northwood), Mill Hill, Monkton Combe, Stonyhurst, Stowe, Tonbridge, University College School, Victoria College (Jersey); additional schools on the 1937 list not listed in 1936 and not recognized as well known by Kelsall include Aldenham, Ampleforth, Bedford, George Watson's College, Giggleswick, King's School (Canterbury). These lists do not represent a comprehensive survey of all Headmasters' Conference schools because no school would appear on either the 1936 or the 1937 list unless one of its alumni attempted the examination. Officials understood the problematic nature of any such ranking, characterizing the lists of schools as "sub-divisions of alleged importance." Mennell to Parker (PRO T162/480/E3646).

18. MacDonnell Commission, *Appendix to Second Report, Minutes of Evidence,* 241, 242, 246. Cd. 6535. 1912.

19. MacDonnell Commission, *Appendix to the First Report, Minutes of Evidence,* appendix 2, 126–27. Cd. 6210. 1912.

20. Ibid., Cd. 6210; ibid., appendix 12, table 3. Cd. 6535. 1912.

21. MacDonnell Commission, *Appendix to Second Report, Minutes of Evidence.* Testimony of Selby-Bigge, 260. Cd. 6535. 1912.

22. Ibid., Testimony of Phipps, 264. Cd. 6535. 1912.

23. MacDonnell Commission, *Appendix to Third Report, Minutes of Evidence.* Testimony of Waterfield, 144, 147. Cd. 6740. 1913.

24. Mr. H. A. Roberts informed the MacDonnell Commission that the Cambridge Appointments Board had handled 380 appointments to business firms between 1907 and 1912 (ibid., 251). In contrast, the Oxford Appointments Committee had placed only fourteen men in business positions in 1911 (ibid., 144).

25. See Sheldon Rothblatt, *Revolution of the Dons* (New York: Basic Books, 1968), 262–65, for a discussion of the formation of the Cambridge Appointments Board. Waterfield quoted in MacDonnell Commission, *Appendix to Third Report, Minutes of Evidence,* Cd. 6740, 142. See David Cannadine, *The Decline and Fall of the British Aristocracy* (New York: Anchor Books, 1990), 240, for a few relevant examples of patronage appointments to the home civil service in the years before the First World War.

26. MacDonnell Commission, *Appendix to Second Report, Minutes of Evidence.* Testimony of Selby-Bigge, 265. Cd. 6535. 1912.

27. MacDonnell Commission, *Appendix to First Report, Minutes of Evidence.* Testimony of Elliott, 218. Cd. 6535. 1912.

28. Ibid., 220.

29. Ibid., 221–24, quotation 221.

30. Ibid., 229.

31. MacDonnell Commission, *Fourth Report,* 39. Cd. 7338. 1914.

32. Civil Service Commission, *Reports,* 1925–1939. These annual reports are the texts I used to compile details concerning the education and appointment of the civil servants who staffed the departments under study.

33. "Assistant Principles Analysed into Groups According to Recruitment," (PRO T162/141/E 20151, 1928).

34. MacDonnell Commission, *Appendix to Second Report, Minutes of Evidence.* Testimony of Elliott, 251–59. Cd. 6535. 1912.

35. MacDonnell Commission, *Fourth Report,* 65. Cd. 7338. 1914.

36. Ibid., 68.

37. J.A.M. Caldwell, "The Genesis of the Ministry of Labour," *Public Administration* 37 (winter 1959): 367. See also Roger Davidson, "Llewellyn Smith, the Labour Department, and Government Growth, 1886–1909," in Sutherland, *Studies in the Growth of Nineteenth-Century Government,* 227–62.

38. MacDonnell Commission, *Appendix to Third Report, Minutes of Evidence.* Testimony of Beveridge, 43. Cd. 6740. 1913.

39. Ibid. Testimony of Beveridge, 42–43. See also José Harris, *William Beveridge: A Biography* (Oxford: Clarendon Press, 1977), 157.

40. Caldwell, "Genesis of the Ministry of Labour," 370.

41. Special competitions, geared to the problem of absorbing demobilized veterans, governed civil service recruitment until the ordinary process of open competition examination resumed in 1925.

42. See Paul R. Wilding, "The Genesis of the Ministry of Health," *Public Administration* 45 (summer 1967): 149–68, and Frank Honigsbaum, *The Struggle for the Ministry of Health,*

1914–1919, Occasional Papers on Social Administration, no. 37 (London: G. Bell, 1970) for detailed accounts of the formation of the Ministry of Health.

43. Honigsbaum, *Struggle for the Ministry of Health,* 55.

44. MacDonnell Commission, *Appendix to Second Report, Minutes of Evidence.* Testimony of Monro, 174. Cd. 6535. 1912.

45. In his autobiography R. W. Harris recalled his isolated situation as one of the few officials from the NHIC to have an assistant secretary–level position at the newly created Ministry of Health. *Not So Humdrum: The Autobiography of a Civil Servant* (London: John Lane, 1939), 155–56, 203.

46. Although the bulk of those appointed as examiners in the Board of Education prior to 1914 did not possess credentials sufficiently meritorious to justify the retention of patronage appointments, they did have among their ranks two eminent literary scholars, A. J. Butler and E. K. Chambers; a biographer, J. W. MacKail; a historian, C. L. Kingsford; and an expert in English eighteenth-century philosophy, L. A. Selby-Bigge. The postwar recruits produced by the Class 1 examination did not include anyone with the intellectual stature of these men. Gillian Sutherland, "Administrators in Education After 1870: Patronage, Professionalism, and Expertise," in Sutherland, *Studies in the Growth of Nineteenth-Century Government,* 267.

47. The following analysis draws upon career records of individual civil servants traced through the annual listings of ministerial staff published by the *Imperial Calendar and Civil Service List* (London: HMSO) and *Whitaker's Almanac* (London: J. Whitaker).

48. Table 6, "Years of Service in Assistant Principal Grade of Assistant Principal, Principals Promoted to Principal Grades" (PRO T162/141/E20151, 1928). It seems that 40 percent of the 192 promotions authorized between 1920 and 1928 took place after six, seven, or eight years of service. One-third of the promotions occurred after less than six years of service; only 23.9 percent of those promoted had served nine or more years. During this eight-year period, the Board of Education promoted twenty-two men, the Ministry of Health promoted seven, the Ministry of Labour promoted eight, and the Ministry of Agriculture, only two.

49. The proportions reported in this paragraph are based on an aggregate analysis of the promotion experience of the civil servants who staffed the four social service ministries under study here. Overall, 54 percent of assistant principals won at least one promotion. At both the principal and the assistant secretary levels, 32 percent succeeded in securing a promotion. Although this gives us a retrospective view of what expectations a civil servant might have reasonably entertained about his or her career prospects, this information lay in the future for individuals whose professional records form the raw material for the analysis here. Even so, officials showed themselves acutely aware of the economic vicissitudes of the time, which threatened the smooth operation of the promotion ladder.

50. Overall, 50 percent of assistant principals were promoted. Clarendon schools alumni (at 34.8 percent promoted) fell well below this average, in contrast to Headmasters' Conference old boys (54.5 percent) and all others (53.8 percent), who experienced a somewhat higher than average success rate. Looking at university education again shows a narrower range (from a low of 48.1 percent for Cambridge graduates to a high of 51.3 percent for non-Oxbridge graduates) and a promotion rate of exactly 50 percent for Oxford graduates.

51. PRO MH 78/18 1493.

52. H. E. Dale, himself a former civil servant, thought that the similar backgrounds of ministers and civil servants made their relationships easier, and that drawing officials from a lower class might result in a loss of this mutual confidence. *The Higher Civil Service of Great Britain* (Oxford: Oxford University Press, 1941), 118–19, 194.

53. The essays in Roy MacLeod, ed., *Government and Expertise: Specialists, Administrators, and Professionals, 1860-1919* (Cambridge: Cambridge University Press, 1988), document the rich variety of experts in the English civil service. Meta Zimmeck explicitly raises the issue of the implications of the different presuppositions that might define expertise in "The 'New

Woman' in the Machinery of Government: A Spanner in the Works?" in MacLeod, *Government and Expertise,* 185–86.

54. See Philippa Levine, "History in the Archives: The Public Record Office and Its Staff, 1838–1886," *English Historical Review* (1986): 20–41, for an example of the development of one department's identity within the constraints of open competition recruitment during the nineteenth century. See June Burnham and G. W. Jones, "Advising Margaret Thatcher: The Prime Minister's Office and the Cabinet Office Compared," *Political Studies* 41 (June 1993): 299–314, for an analysis of the contemporary civil service that links recruitment with departmental style and point of view.

3. The Board of Education: Defining Secondary Education

1. R. H. Tawney, *Equality* (1931; rpt. New York: Capricorn Books, 1961), 153–58 (157). For an account of Tawney's influence on the development of education policy within the Labour party, see J. R. Brooks, "Labour and Educational Reconstruction, 1916–1926," *History of Education* 20 (Sept. 1991): 245–59.

2. Anthony Giddens, "Elites in the British Class Structure," in *Elites and Power in British Society,* ed. Philip Stanworth and Anthony Giddens (Cambridge: Cambridge University Press, 1974); Anthony Giddens, *The Class Structure of the Advanced Societies* (New York: Harper and Row, 1973), 120–23.

3. Bentley Gilbert has observed: "in education after the evisceration of the Fisher Act, there is little to write about. When the political leaders of both major parties are unable to redeem a 20-year-old promise to increase the school leaving age beyond 14, a nation can hardly be said to have a deep concern with public education." *British Social Policy, 1914–1939* (London: B. T. Batsford, 1970), viii. Although the essential elements of Gilbert's assessment remain unchallenged, a great deal has been written about the development of educational policy between the First and Second World Wars. See Brian Simon, *The Politics of Educational Reform, 1920–1940* (London: Lawrence and Wishart, 1974), for a comprehensive account of educational policy during this period, and Gary McCulloch, *Philosophers and Kings: Education for Leadership in Modern England* (Cambridge: Cambridge University Press, 1991), for a more recent consideration of the period. For H.A.L. Fisher and the development of the Fisher Act, see D. H. Akenson, "Patterns of English Educational Change: The Fisher and the Butler Acts," *History of Education* (summer 1971): 143–56; D. W. Dean, "H.A.L. Fisher, Reconstruction and the Development of the 1918 Education Act," *British Journal of Educational Studies* 18 (1970): 259–76; E. W. Jenkins, "The Board of Education and the Reconstruction Committee, 1916–18," *Journal of Educational Administration and History* 1 (1973): 42–51, and "The Thomson Committee and the Board of Education, 1916–22," *British Journal of Educational Studies* 21 (Feb. 1973): 76–87; G. E. Sherington, "The 1918 Education Act: Origins, Aims, and Development," *British Journal of Educational Studies* 24 (Feb. 1976): 66–85, and "H.A.L. Fisher and the Teachers—Further Notes," *British Journal of Educational Studies* 24 (June 1976): 171–76; D. W. Thoms, "The Emergence and Failure of the Day Continuation School Experiment," *History of Education* 4 (spring 1975): 36–50; J. R. Brooks, "Labour and Educational Reconstruction, 1916–1926," *History of Education* 20 (Sept. 1991): 245–59. For the period after the passage of the Fisher Act, see D. W. Dean, "Conservatism and the National Educational System, 1922–40," *Journal of Contemporary History* 6 (1971): 150–65; M. Hyndman, "Multilateralism and the Spens Report: Evidence from the Archives," *British Journal of Educational Studies* 24 (Oct. 1976): 242–53; R.J.W. Selleck, "The Hadow Report: A Study in Ambiguity," *Melbourne Studies in Education* (1972): 143–84; Jennifer Firmager, "The Consultative Committee under the Chairmanship of Sir Henry Hadow: The Education of the Adolescent," *History of Education* 10 (1981): 273–81; and Joan Simon, "The Shaping of the Spens Report on Secondary Education 1933–38: An Inside View; Part I and Part II," *British Journal of Educational Studies* 25 (Feb. and June 1977): 63–80, 170–85; R. A. Lowe, "Eugenicists, Doctors, and the Quest for

National Efficiency: An Educational Crusade, 1900–1939," *History of Education* 8 (Dec. 1979): 293–306; D. W. Thoms, "Curriculum Innovation in Technical Education: London, 1918–1939," *History of Education* 8 (Dec. 1979): 307–19; Bill Bailey, "The Development of Technical Education, 1934–1939," *History of Education* 16 (March 1987): 49–66; Gary McCulloch, " 'Spens v. Norwood': Contesting the Educational State?" *History of Education* 27 (June 1993): 163–80; Peter Gosden, "From Board to Ministry: The Impact of the War on the Education Department," *History of Education* 18 (Sept. 1989): 183–94. And this listing, although full, is not by any means comprehensive.

4. Alfred T. Davies, *The Lloyd George I Knew* (London: Henry E. Walton, 1948), 52–54.

5. L. A. Selby-Bigge, *The Board of Education* (London: G. P. Putnam's Sons, 1927), 73–77.

6. Ibid., 123–26.

7. E. K. Chambers, July 20, 1917 (PRO ED 24/270).

8. John Dover Wilson, *Milestones on the Dover Road* (London: Faber and Faber, 1969), 68, 72, 74, 92, 93.

9. L. A. Selby-Bigge, Nov. 14, 1922; E. H. Pelham, Jan. 9, 1923 (both in PRO ED 24/1660).

10. Pelham, "Fees and Free Places," Jan. 28, 1924 (PRO ED 24/1647).

11. "[Memorandum on the Organization of] Post-Primary Education," July 30, 1937 (PRO ED 10/273).

12. H.A.L. Fisher, May 23, 1921 (PRO ED 12/328); Pelham, Jan. 28, 1924 (PRO ED 24/1647).

13. Pelham, Jan. 20, 1922 (PRO ED 12/328), and Jan. 16, 1922 (PRO ED 24/1644).

14. On the Geddes Committee and its impact on the spending departments see: Andrew McDonald, "The Geddes Committee and the Formulation of Public Expenditure Policy, 1921–1922," *Historical Journal* 32, 2 (1989): 643–74.

15. Chambers, Oct. 20, 1921 (PRO ED 24/2077).

16. H. W. Orange, Jan. 29, 1924; Pelham, Feb. 5, 1924; Selby-Bigge, Feb. 6, 1924 (all in PRO ED 24/1647).

17. M. G. Holmes, Sept. 23, 1929 (PRO ED 24/1651), and "Notes on Fees and Free Places," April 21, 1932 (PRO ED 24/1652).

18. Board of Education, Nov. 23, 1933 (PRO ED 24/1395).

19. Holmes, "Notes on Fees and Free Places," April 21, 1932 (PRO ED 24/1652).

20. Pelham, "School Fees and Free Places in LEA Secondary Schools," April 27, 1932 (PRO ED 24/1652).

21. Note of a Meeting of the Committee on Secondary School Fees, July 13, 1932 (PRO ED 12/353).

22. N. D. Bosworth-Smith, July 14, 1932 (PRO ED 12/353).

23. R. S. Wood, July 26, 1932 (PRO ED 12/353).

24. Holmes, Sept. 3, 1932; Pelham, Sept. 3, 1932 (both in PRO ED 12/353).

25. Holmes, Sept. 6, 1932; H. Ramsbotham to Irwin (Vt. Halifax), Sept. 8, 1932; Irwin to Holmes, Sept. 8, 1932 (all in PRO ED 12/353).

26. R. S. Wood, "Post-Primary Education," July 30, 1937; "Memorandum on the Organization of Post-Primary Education," n.d. (both in PRO ED 10/273).

27. Ross Terrill, *R. H. Tawney and His Times: Socialism as Fellowship* (Cambridge, Mass.: Harvard University Press, 1973), 63–64.

28. Pelham, Oct. 1, 1927; Percy, Nov. 3, 1927; Pelham, n.d. (all in PRO ED 24/1539).

29. See Selleck, "The Hadow Report," 143–84, for a detailed analysis. See also Firmager, "Consultative Committee Under the Chairmanship of Sir Henry Hadow," 273–81.

30. H. E. Mann, "Raising the School-Age to Fifteen," n.d.; D. du B. Davidson, July 18, 1929, both in PRO ED 24/1543). C. P. Trevelyan, Note on Conference, July 30, 1929;

H. Richards, Note of Discussion, "The School Leaving Age," July 24, 1929; H. Richards, Conference of Divisional Inspectors, Oct. 2, 1929 (all in PRO ED 24/1542).

31. Eustace Percy to Winston Churchill, Oct. 1, 1928 (PRO ED 24/1389).

32. PRO ED 24/1543; PRO ED 24/1541; quotation from "Note of Discussion," Oct. 14, 1937 (PRO ED 10/273); Holmes, Nov. 28, 1938 (PRO ED 136/160).

33. See correspondence between Leeson and Holmes (PRO ED 136/129).

34. These same officials, particularly Holmes, played a decisive role in seeing that multilateralism was not included among the reforms of the 1944 Education Act. R. G. Wallace, "The Origins and Authorship of the 1944 Education Act," *History of Education* 10 (1981): 283–90. See Brian Simon, "The Politics of Comprehensive Reorganization: A Retrospective Analysis," *History of Education* 21 (1992): 355–62, for a brief overview of the fortunes and vicissitudes of this concept.

35. Morgan Jones, Sept. 11, 1929 (PRO ED 24/1651); Labour Party Research Department, Nov. 7, 1929 (PRO ED 24/1393).

36. Holmes, Aug. 2, 1929; S. H. Wood, Aug. 14, 1929 (both in PRO ED 24/1393); Stead, Oct. 1, 1929 (PRO ED 24/1651); quotation from Report of Conference of Divisional Inspectors, Oct. 2, 1929 (PRO ED 24/1542).

37. See Hyndman, "Multilateralism and the Spens Report," 242–53, for a discussion of the consideration of the idea of comprehensive education by the Consultative Committee of the Board of Education during the 1930s. See also David Rubinstein and Brian Simon, *The Evolution of the Comprehensive School, 1926–1972* (London: Routledge and Kegan Paul, 1973).

38. These views summarized in Note of Discussion, Oct. 14, 1937 (PRO ED 10/273).

39. On Williams's views and status within the Board of Education, see Wallace, "The Origins and Authorship," 284–85.

40. Quotation in Note of Discussion, Oct. 14, 1937; Williams, Oct. 18, 1937; Duckworth, n.d. (all in PRO ED 10/273).

41. R. S. Wood, Oct. 28, 1937; Williams, Nov. 15, 1937; F. Duckworth, Nov. 24, 1937 (all in PRO ED 10/273).

42. Notes on Meeting, Nov. 29, 1937; Wood, Nov. 11, 1937; "Organization of Post-Primary Education," n.d. (all in PRO ED 10/273); Bailey, "The Development of Technical Education, 1934–1939," 49–66. See also Keith Burgess, "Education Policy in Relation to Employment in Britain 1935–45: A Decade of 'Missed Opportunities'?" *History of Education* 22 (1993): 365–90, and "Youth Employment Policy During the 1930s," *Twentieth Century British History* 6 (1995): 23–55, for detailed accounts of the Board's efforts on behalf of technical education.

43. "Summary of Oral Evidence given by Holmes and Duckworth, Chief Inspector of Secondary Schools" (PRO ED 10/151).

44. R. S. Wood, "Post-Primary Education," July 30, 1937 (PRO ED 10/273).

45. The close relationship between Fisher and his official advisers has not gone unnoticed. See Sherington, "The 1918 Education Act," 66–85, and L. O. Ward, "H.A.L. Fisher and the Teachers," *British Journal of Educational Studies* 22 (1974): 191–99. Sherington has elaborated his views on Fisher in *English Education, Social Change, and War, 1911–1920* (Manchester: Manchester University Press, 1981), 73–84. D. W. Dean details Fisher's personal contribution to obtaining the passage of the 1918 Education Act in "H.A.L. Fisher, Reconstruction and the Development of the 1918 Education Act," 259–76.

46. Selby-Bigge to Fisher, Dec. 4, 1920; Fisher to Selby-Bigge, Dec. 7, 1920; Selby-Bigge to Fisher, Dec. 11, 1920; Fisher to Herbert Lewis, Dec. 12, 1920; Fisher to Selby-Bigge (telegram), Dec. 14, 1920 (all in PRO ED 24/1443). For an important part of this story, see Thoms, "The Emergence and Failure of the Day Continuation School Experiment," 36–50 (esp. 44–46, 48–49), which further illustrates the way Fisher and Selby-Bigge worked together.

47. Selby-Bigge to Fisher, Dec. 4, 1920 (PRO ED 24/1443). Formed in March 1919,

the Middle Classes Union was dedicated to the preservation of the middle-class way of life. To achieve this end they opposed increased taxation. London *Times,* March 7, 1919.

48. E.J.R. Eaglesham, "The Centenary of Sir Robert Morant," *British Journal of Educational Studies* 12 (Nov. 1963): 5–18; David Ogg, *Herbert Fisher, 1869–1940* (London: Edward Arnold, 1947), 20–21; Duchess of Atholl, *Working Partnership* (London: Arthur Barber, 1958), 143; Wilson, *Milestones,* 87–88, 92, 93, 94.

49. Chambers to Percy, Nov. 3, 1925 (PRO ED 24/1198).

50. Eustace Percy, *Some Memories* (London: Eyre and Spottiswoode, 1958), 97.

51. Simon, *Politics of Educational Reform,* 108–15.

52. G.A.N. Lowndes, *The Silent Social Revolution* (London: Oxford University Press, 1937), 324.

53. Gosden, "From Board to Ministry," 188.

54. W. R. Davies to Selby-Bigge, July 16, 1917; Chambers, July 20, 1917 (both in PRO ED 24/720).

55. Percy, Statement to Deputation, Nov. 3, 1927 (PRO ED 24/1539).

56. Heath, July 20, 1929; Mann, "Raising the School Age to Fifteen," n.d.; Davidson, July 18, 1929; Maxwell-Lyte, July 17, 1929 (all in PRO ED 24/1543).

57. Selby-Bigge to Trevelyan, Nov. 23, 1930 (Trevelyan Papers, CPT 139); L. A. Selby-Bigge, "Voluntary Schools," *Nineteenth Century* 110 (1931): 8–20.

58. Symonds quoted in "Note of a Discussion on 19th June 1929" (PRO ED 24/1542).

59. D. W. Dean in "The Difficulties of a Labour Educational Policy: The Failure of the Trevelyan Bill, 1929–31," *British Journal of Educational Studies* 16 (1969): 286–300, argues that the key to Trevelyan's failure to achieve the passage of his bill lay in his inability to engineer a compromise among the various groups interested in state-funded education.

60. E. B. Phipps, June 24, 1929 (PRO ED 24/1542).

61. N. F. Lawson Fisher to Trevelyan, Nov. 20, 1930 (Trevelyan Papers, CPT 139); Symonds to Trevelyan, March 3, 1931 (CPT 142).

62. Simon, *Politics of Educational Reform,* 1974.

63. See Gary McCulloch, " 'Spens v. Norwood,' " 163–80, for a salutary reminder of the problematic and contingent aspects of the policy process.

64. Stephen Gould notes the relationship between contemporary scientific opinion, IQ, and educational policy in England during this period. In his analysis he argues that the scientific view was itself informed by class bias and social prejudice. Stephen Jay Gould, *The Mismeasure of Man* (New York: Norton, 1981), 292–99. Gillian Sutherland shows that these ideas, although pervasive, did not have a uniform impact on the actual administration of the schools, in *Ability, Merit, and Measurement: Mental Testing and English Education, 1880–1940* (Oxford: Oxford University Press, 1984). Lowe, in his "Eugenicists, Doctors, and the Quest for National Efficiency," 293–306, shows how a eugenic point of view gradually came to predominate within the Board of Education by the end of the 1930s.

4. The Ministry of Agriculture: Friend to the Worker

1. Reg Groves, *Sharpen the Sickle! The History of the Farm Workers Union* (London: Porcupine Press, 1949; rpt. New York: AMS Press, 1976), 164, 172, 207–08; Charles Loch Mowat, *Britain Between the Wars, 1918–1940* (Boston: Beacon Press, 1971), 252–53. The epigraph is from C.L.M., "The Ministry of Agriculture and Fisheries," in Sir Francis L. Floud, *The Ministry of Agriculture and Fisheries* (London: G. P. Putnam's Sons, 1927), p. 321, reprinted from *Punch,* April 20, 1927.

2. See Edith H. Whetham, "The Agriculture Act, 1920 and Its Repeal—the 'Great Betrayal,' " *Agricultural History Review* 22 (1974): 36–49, for a complete account of this episode. See also Kenneth O. Morgan, *Consensus and Disunity: The Lloyd George Coalition Government, 1919–1922* (Oxford: Clarendon Press, 1979), 157–59, 337, for an analysis of the political sig-

nificance of the repeal of the 1920 Agriculture Act. Andrew Fenton Cooper, *British Agricultural Policy, 1912–36: A Study in Conservative Politics* (Manchester and New York: Manchester University Press, 1989), 42–63, takes a very different view of this episode, arguing that it did not constitute a "betrayal" but rather relieved the farmer of the burden of government interference in the conduct of agriculture.

3. This does not constitute an exhaustive list of the Ministry's responsibilities for formulating and administering government policy regarding the position of labor in the agricultural community. See Daniel A. Pigott, "Agricultural Scholarships for Rural Youth in England and Wales, 1922–58," *History of Education Quarterly* 30 (spring 1990): 17–45, for an account of the scholarship program that provided talented children of agricultural workers opportunities to continue their education at secondary school and university.

4. Sir John Winnifrith, *The Ministry of Agriculture, Fisheries, and Food* (London: Allen and Unwin, 1962), 22–25; H. E. Dale, "Agriculture and the Civil Service," in *Agriculture in the Twentieth Century* (Oxford: Clarendon Press, 1939), 3–4.

5. H. E. Dale, *Daniel Hall: Pioneer in Scientific Agriculture* (London: John Murray, 1956), 108–09; Whetham, "The Agriculture Act, 1920," 39–40.

6. Dale, "Agriculture and the Civil Service," 10; Floud, *Ministry of Agriculture and Fisheries*, 39–48.

7. Dale, "Agriculture and the Civil Service," 7–8.

8. Edith H. Whetham, *The Agrarian History of England and Wales, 1914–1939* (Cambridge: Cambridge University Press, 1985), 88.

9. United Kingdom. Parliament. Ministry of Agriculture and Fisheries, *The Agricultural Output of England and Wales, 1925*. Table 30, p. 152. Cmd. 2815. 1927.

10. Ibid.

11. R. E. Stanley, Jan. 16, 1923 (PRO MAF 47/25).

12. Sanders Diaries, Oct. 25, 1923. Sir Robert Sanders (1867–1940) served as minister of agriculture for the 1922–1924 Conservative government.

13. Stanley, Dec. 21, 1923; R. J. Thompson, "Notes to Be Considered in Establishing a Wages Board," Jan. 21, 1924; Stanley, quotation from "Wages Board Bill Possible Points of Contention," March 31, 1924 (all in PRO MAF 47/26).

14. Thompson, "Memorandum on the Desirability of Including a Statutory Minimal Wage of 30s/per Week," n.d.; Stanley, "Statutory Minimum of 30s," March 21, 1924 (both in PRO MAF 47/26).

15. Sir Francis Floud, "Agricultural Wages," Feb. 8, 1924; A.G.L. Rogers, "Low Wages in Gloucestershire," May 23, 1924; Stanley, "Low Wages," July 21, 1924 (all in PRO MAF 47/26).

16. Groves, *Sharpen the Sickle!* 207–08.

17. Whetham, *Agrarian History*, 156–57, 236–37.

18. Floud, "Agriculture and Unemployment" (PRO MAF 53/62).

19. Sir Arthur Griffith-Boscawen recorded a positive evaluation of the permanent officials who served him during his tenure as minister of agriculture. *Memoirs* (London: John Murray, 1925), 233.

20. Dobson, June 23, July 13, 1922 (PRO MAF 47/2).

21. The Ministry of Agriculture calculated that between 1921 and 1922 the state spent £400,000 on drainage schemes; 90 percent of this sum went for labor, and projects employed from 1,600 to 7,870 men. "Description of Operation of Drainage Schemes," n.d. (PRO MAF 47/2). I. A. Richmond, *Roman Britain* (London: Jonathan Cape, 1963), 102–03.

22. Kenneth O. Morgan, *Portrait of a Progressive: The Political Career of Christopher, Viscount Addison* (Oxford: Clarendon Press, 1980), 197; Floud, *Ministry of Agriculture and Fisheries*, 261; United Kingdom. Parliament. *Final Report of the Unemployment Grants Committee*, appendix 2, 33. Cmd. 4354. 1933.

23. United Kingdom. Parliament. *Report of the Committee on Unemployment Insurance in Agriculture,* Cmd. 1344, 1921.

24. H. L. French, Jan. 15, 1931; French to P. Y. Blunden, Feb. 11, 1931; J.F.G. Price to French, Feb. 13, 1931; Floud to H. B. Usher, March 10, 1931 (all in PRO MAF 47/15). (See appendix for biographical details for French, Thomas, and Usher.)

25. See J. D. Tomlinson, "Women as 'Anomalies': The Anomalies Regulations of 1931, Their Background and Implications," *Public Administration* 62 (winter 1984): 423–37, for a discussion of the passage of this measure and its significance for the position of women in the unemployment insurance system.

26. This revision led to legislation that created the Unemployment Assistance Board. The issue of the position of agricultural workers with respect to unemployment relief and unemployment insurance constituted a relatively minor subplot in the larger drama of conflict and controversy surrounding this attempt to achieve a definitive solution to the problem of large-scale unemployment relief. For the full story, see Frederic M. Miller, "National Assistance or Unemployment Assistance? The British Cabinet and Relief Policy, 1932–33," *Journal of Contemporary History* 9 (1974): 163–84; "The Unemployment Policy of the National Government, 1931–1936," *The Historical Journal* 19 (1976): 453–76; "The British Unemployment Crisis of 1935," *Journal of Contemporary History* 14 (1979): 329–52; Eric Briggs and Alan Deacon, "The Creation of the Unemployment Assistance Board," *Policy and Politics* 2 (Sept. 1973): 43–62; Bentley B. Gilbert, *British Social Policy, 1914–1939* (London: B. T. Batsford, 1970), 162–92.

27. Miller, "National Assistance," 175; Gilbert, *British Social Policy,* 182, n. 1.

28. French, July 3, 1933; Record of Discussion, Aug. 4, 1933 (both in PRO MAF 47/15).

29. See Andrew Fenton Cooper, *British Agricultural Policy, 1912–36: A Study in Conservative Politics* (Manchester: Manchester University Press, 1989), 160–83, for an account of Walter Elliot's career as minister of agriculture.

30. French, Aug. 17, 1933; Minister, Aug. 18, 1933; Nathan to Blunden, Aug. 22, 1933 (all in PRO MAF 47/15).

31. Miller, "National Assistance," 180.

32. Betterton to Elliot, Sept. 26, 1933 (PRO MAF 47/15).

33. Nathan, Oct. 7, 1933 (PRO MAF 47/15).

34. Floud, Oct. 9, 1933 (PRO MAF 47/15).

35. Note of Discussion, Oct. 17, 1933 (all in PRO MAF 47/15).

36. Stanley, Nov. 7, 1938; E. L. Mitchell, Nov. 9, 1938 (both in PRO MAF 47/22).

37. Secretary, Nov. 16, 1938; Minister, Nov. 31, 1938; "Memorandum Sent to Unemployment Insurance Statutory Committee on Agricultural Unemployment Insurance," Dec. 19, 1938; "Notes on the Agricultural Account of the Unemployment Insurance Fund," Nov. 17, 1939; "Agriculture Unemployment Insurance: Observations by the Ministry of Agriculture and Fisheries," Jan. 9, 1940 (all in PRO MAF 47/22).

38. Whetham, *Agrarian History,* 47–48; United Kingdom. Parliament. *Report of the Inter-Departmental Committee on Agricultural Tied Cottages, 1932,* 5, 20–21. Cmd. 4148. 1932.

39. Stanley, Nov. 18, 1929 (PRO MAF 48/207).

40. Ibid.

41. Thomas, Nov. 18, 1939; A. D. Stocks, Nov. 30, 1929; French, Dec. 6, 1929 (all in PRO MAF 48/207).

42. Thomas, Dec. 10, 1929; N. Buxton to A. Greenwood, Dec. 23, 1929 (both in PRO MAF 48/207).

43. French, Jan. 1, 1930; Stocks, Jan. 6, 1930; French, Jan. 8, 1930; Stocks, Jan. 9, 1930 (all in PRO MAF 48/207).

44. Meeting, Jan. 10, 1930 (PRO MAF 48/207).

45. United Kingdom. Parliament. *Report of Inter-Departmental Committee on Agricultural Tied Cottages, 1932,* 32. Cmd. 4148. 1932.

46. Lord Addison, *A Policy for Agriculture* (London: Victor Gollancz, 1939), 52.

47. Peter Self and Herbert J. Storing, *The State and the Farmer: British Agricultural Policies and Politics* (Berkeley and Los Angeles: University of California Press, 1963), 173–74. See also F. D. Mills, "The National Union of Agricultural Workers," *Journal of Agricultural Economics* 16 (1964–1965): 244.

48. Enfield, "The Economic Position of Agriculture (Part 3) Domestic Farming Conditions," 18–26, draft forwarded to Secretary, Dec. 2, 1936; A. W. Street, Dec. 18, 1936 (both in PRO MAF 38/50). See also observations by Stanley, Dec. 23, 1937 and Mitchell, Jan. 4, 1937 (both in PRO MAF 38/77).

49. "Economic Position of Agriculture; Labour Aspect, 1937" (PRO MAF 47/3).

50. Ibid. This was not a new complaint. See Pamela Horn, "The Employment of Elementary Schoolchildren in Agriculture, 1914–1918," *History of Education* 12 (1983): 204.

51. Thompson to Floud, n.d.; Floud to Thompson, Aug. 30, 1922 (both in PRO MAF 53/58).

52. Sir Daniel Hall, Aug. 31, 1922; Thompson to Floud, Sept. 1, 1922; Floud to Hall, Sept. 1, 1922 (all in PRO MAF 53/58).

53. Floud, "Notes on Proposals for the Relief of Agriculture," Sept. 18, 1922; A. Griffith-Boscawen to Lloyd George, n.d. (all in PRO MAF 53/58).

54. Floud to Minister, Nov. 7, 1922 (PRO MAF 53/59).

55. Floud, "The Agricultural Situation," Feb. 25, 1925 (PRO MAF 53/62).

56. Sir Daniel Hall, "Note on Agricultural Policy," n.d. (PRO MAF 53/62).

57. Ibid.

58. Floud to Minister, Sept. 25, 1925; Bledisloe to Floud, Sept. 26, 1925; Wood to Floud, Sept. 25, 1925 (all in PRO MAF 53/62).

59. United Kingdom. Parliament. *Agricultural Policy.* Cmd. 2581. 1926; A. W. Ashby, "Agricultural Conditions and Policies, 1910–38," in *Agriculture in the Twentieth Century* (Oxford: Clarendon Press, 1939), 67–68. Whetham, *Agrarian History,* 165.

60. Dale, *Daniel Hall,* 134. Floud, May 18, 1927; Meiklejohn, May 31, 1927 (both in PRO T 162/325/E 17190). Whenever the Treasury questioned this arrangement, the Ministry of Agriculture put up a vigorous defense of Hall, enabling him to stay on the government payroll until 1935. Hall's biographer, H. E. Dale (who himself served in the Agriculture Ministry until his retirement in 1935), was promoted to principal assistant secretary in 1927 to take over a portion of Hall's duties.

61. Lord Ernle (R. E. Prothero), *English Farming Past and Present* (London: Heinemann, 1961). Originally published in 1912 this work still forms the basis for research in the history of English agriculture. See, for example, E. L. Jones, "The Changing Basis of English Agricultural Prosperity, 1853–73," in *Agriculture and the Industrial Revolution,* ed. E. L. Jones (Oxford: Basil Blackwell, 1974), 191.

62. Dale, *Daniel Hall,* 109, 119–20.

63. Mosea Anderson, *Noel Buxton: A Life* (London: Allen and Unwin, 1952), 112–20. Morgan, *Portrait of a Progressive,* 165–66.

64. Henry Roseveare, *The Treasury* (New York: Columbia University Press, 1969), 266.

65. Floud, *Ministry of Agriculture and Fisheries,* 210–11.

66. See Stanley Baker, *Milk to Market: Forty Years of Milk Marketing* (London: Heinemann, 1973), for an account of the operation of marketing boards in the dairy industry. Baker credits Sir Arthur Street, head of the Ministry of Agriculture's Marketing Division, with a major role in developing marketing boards in agriculture. Street drafted the 1931 Marketing Act (67–68). See also Cooper, *British Agricultural Policy, 1912–35,* 160–83, for an account of Conservative party agricultural policy during the 1930s.

67. Morgan, *Portrait of a Progressive,* 199–201.

68. See for example Dale, *Daniel Hall,* 128–30. When Hall gave evidence to the 1919 Royal Commission on Agriculture he was called upon to explain his supposed view that most farmers were "deficient in brains and capital." Hall did not accept this as a totally accurate description of his views, but he did not reject it either. He observed philosophically in reply: "you have to take people, including farmers, as you find them. If you want the land cultivated, they are the only people who can cultivate it. You have not another race of heaven-made farmers to put in their place." United Kingdom. Parliament. Royal Commission on Agriculture, *Minutes of Evidence,* 11. Cmd. 345. 1919. Colin J. Holmes, in "Science and the Farmer: The Development of the Agricultural Advisory Service in England and Wales, 1900–1939," *Agricultural History Review* 36 (1988): 77–86, documents efforts to provide farmers with the most up-to-date scientific information. Holmes also delineates the impediments to success these efforts encountered, including the hostility and skepticism with which many farmers viewed such advice.

69. Winnifrith, *Ministry of Agriculture, Fisheries, and Food,* 144.

70. Graham Cox, Philip Lowe, and Michael Winter, "From State Direction to Self Regulation: The Historical Development of Corporatism in British Agriculture," *Policy and Politics* 14 (1986): 475–90; Graham Cox, Philip Lowe, and Michael Winter, "The Origins and Early Development of the National Farmers' Union," *Agricultural History Review* 39 (1991): 30–47. See also Martin J. Smith, "Changing Agendas and Policy Communities: Agricultural Issues in the 1930s and the 1980s," *Public Administration* 67 (summer 1989): 155–57. These developments formed the foundation for the consensus about agricultural policy that held sway for almost forty years after the Second World War. J. K. Bowers, "British Agricultural Policy Since the Second World War," *Agricultural History Review* 33 (1985): 66–76.

5. The Ministry of Labour: Accentuating the Negative

1. Unemployment figures are reprinted in many places. They vary slightly from source to source, but they all follow this pattern. See B. R. Mitchell and Phyllis Deane, *Abstract of British Historical Statistics* (Cambridge: Cambridge University Press, 1962), 67. The epigraph is from Ministry of Labour, *Report on National Unemployment Insurance to July 1923* (London: HMSO, 1923), 16.

2. Alan Bullock, *The Life and Times of Ernest Bevin,* vol. 2, *Minister of Labour, 1940–1945* (London: Heinemann, 1976), 119.

3. Rodney Lowe, "The Ministry of Labour, 1916–1924: A Graveyard of Social Reform," *Public Administration* 52 (1974): 415–38. See also Rodney Lowe, *Adjusting to Democracy: The Role of the Ministry of Labour in British Politics, 1916–1939* (Oxford: Clarendon Press, 1986), 15–21.

4. Whitley councils were named for J. H. Whitley, Liberal MP from 1900 until 1928 and Speaker of the House from 1921 until 1928. In 1916 Lloyd George had appointed Whitley to chair a committee to investigate labor relations. The committee recommended the formation of industrial councils in each industry to include representatives of both workers and employers to discuss a wide range of issues in addition to wages and hours. The government embraced this idea with far more enthusiasm than trade unions, and most of the councils formed operated for only a short period. Charles Loch Mowat, *Britain Between the Wars, 1918–1940* (Chicago: University of Chicago Press, 1955), 37. See also Leonard D. White, *Whitley Councils in the British Civil Service: A Study in Conciliation and Arbitration* (Chicago: University of Chicago Press, 1933).

5. United Kingdom. Parliament. *Report on the Committees Appointed to Investigate the Staffing and Methods of Work of the Ministry of Labour . . .* , 2–3. Cmd 1069. 1920.

6. J.A.M. Caldwell, "The Genesis of the Ministry of Labour," *Public Administration* (1959): 367–91.

7. At the end of June 1920, the total staff of the Ministry of Labour equaled 11,995.

United Kingdom. Parliament. *Report of . . . Ministry of Labour . . .*, appendixes 3, 6, pp. 13, 15. Cmd. 1069. 1920.

8. Lowe, *Adjusting to Democracy,* 52.

9. Rodney Lowe, "Bureaucracy Triumphant or Denied? The Expansion of the British Civil Service, 1919–1939," *Public Administration* 62 (autumn 1984): 294–97.

10. R. H. Tawney had a longstanding interest in both the state's provision for education and the question of juvenile employment. R. Szreter, "A Note on R. H. Tawney's Early Interest in Juvenile Employment and Misemployment," *History of Education* 19 (Dec. 1990): 375–82.

11. Percy to A. Steel-Maitland, Oct. 17, 1927; Note on Tawney's Paper, n.d.; A. B., Oct. 27, 1927 (all in PRO LAB 2/1328, EDJ 1036/28). First quotation from "Note;" second from A. B. and Lowe-Watson.

12. Quotation from Lowe-Watson, n.d.; Phillips to Wolfe, Nov. 5, 1927; Steel-Maitland to Percy, Nov. 10, 1927 (all in PRO LAB 2/1328, EDJ 1036/28).

13. See W. R. Garside, "Juvenile Unemployment and Public Policy Between the Wars," *Economic History Review,* 2d ser., 30 (1977): 322–39, and "Unemployment and the School-Leaving Age in Inter-War Britain," *International Review of Social History* 26 (1981): 159–70. See also the entertaining exchange between W. R. Garside, Daniel K. Benjamin, and Lewis A. Kockin, in Benjamin and Kockin, "What Went Right with Juvenile Unemployment Policy Between the Wars: A Comment," *Economic History Review,* 2d ser. 32 (Nov. 1979): 523–28; W. R. Garside, "Juvenile Unemployment Between the Wars: A Rejoinder," *Economic History Review,* 2d ser. 32 (Nov. 1979): 529–32.

14. Blunden, Jan. 31, 1930 (PRO LAB 2/1372, ET 1996/1930, A23, 1930).

15. Allen to Marsh, Feb. 3, 1930 (PRO LAB 2/1372, ET 1996/1930, A23/1930).

16. Instructions to Blunden and Allen in Conference of Heads of Departments, Jan. 29, 1930; Phillips to Minister, Feb. 21, 1930; Allen, Blunden, Phillips, March 31, 1930 (all in PRO LAB 2/1372, ET 1996/1930, A23/1930). See also Lowe, *Adjusting to Democracy,* 218–19, for a survey of various proposals for alternative uses of the unemployment insurance fund entertained by Labour officials during the 1930s.

17. Susan Howson and Donald Winch, *The Economic Advisory Council, 1930–1939* (Cambridge: Cambridge University Press, 1977), 17–29.

18. Eady to Phillips, July 3, 1930 (PRO LAB 2/1377, ET 5286/1930, A45/1930).

19. Ibid.; quotation from Eady to Acting Secretary, July 18, 1930 (PRO LAB 2/1377, ET 5286/1930, A45/1930).

20. Accountant-General (Bowers) to Emmerson, July 21, 1930 (PRO LAB 2/1377, ET 5286/1930, A45/1930).

21. E. A. Hitchman to G. H. Ince, Feb. 17, 1939 (PRO LAB 8/250, EMA 624/1939).

22. In responding to this simple request, the Ministry of Labour bogged down in a stereotypical bureaucratic tangle. The Prime Minister's Office wrote Hitchman asking what reply to make to the TUC. After receiving no response they sent another letter three weeks later. At this point, a Labour official remarked: "I cannot help feeling that we ought to send them some sort of reply fairly soon in order not to aggravate them further!" (May 6, 1939 [PRO LAB 8/253, EMA 1559/1939]). In the ensuing discussion Ince expressed the view that the prime minister did not need to meet the TUC delegation, but that they should meet the minister of labour and the president of the Board of Trade instead. F. W. Leggett disagreed, arguing that he doubted the TUC would be content with anyone less than the prime minister. The secretary agreed with Leggett, and the minister elected to follow their advice. Hitchman wrote to the Prime Minister's Office telling them George Brown recommended that the delegation be received. The Prime Minister's Office responded by requesting that the Ministry of Labour prepare a note for the use of the prime minister, George Brown, and the Chancellor of the Exchequer. Responsibility for the actual preparation of the note was passed down a chain of command through Leggett and T. S. Chegwidden to R. M. Gould, acting assistant secretary of the Employment Department (G. H. Ince, April 21, 1939; F. W. Leggett, May 4, 1939; Secretary to Minister, May 5, 1939;

Hitchman to Prime Minister's Office, May 6, 1939; T. S. Chegwidden to R. M. Gould, May 10, 1939 [all in PRO LAB 8/253, EMA/1559/1939]).

23. TUC Economic Committee on Unemployment, Mar. 7, 1939 (PRO LAB 8/253, EMA 1559/1939).

24. "Note on Memorandum Prepared by the Economic Committee of the Trade Union Congress," n.d.; Leggett to secretary, Sept. 18, 1939; to minister, Sept. 19, 1939 (all in PRO LAB 8/253, EMA/1559/1939).

25. Allen, Aug. 11, 1930 (PRO LAB 2/1377, ET 5286/1930, A45/1930).

26. Floud quoted by Allen, Aug. 11, 1930 (PRO LAB 2/1377, ET 5286/1930, A45/1930).

27. Keynes's influence on Treasury officials made itself felt through his membership on the Economic Advisory Council. Howson and Winch, *Economic Advisory Council,* 108–09.

28. During the interwar period, the Treasury gained enormous control over the policy-making process of the government bureaucracy. See John R. Greenaway, "Warren Fisher and the Transformation of the British Treasury, 1919–1939," *Journal of British Studies* 23 (fall 1983): 125–42, and G. C. Peden, "The Treasury as the Central Department of Government, 1919–1939," *Public Administration* 61 (winter 1983): 371–83. It was widely believed then (and now) that Treasury hegemony crippled the development of innovative approaches to the social problems England faced during the 1920s and 1930s. Keith Middlemas, *Politics in Industrial Society: The Experience of the British System Since 1911* (London: Andre Deutsch, 1979), 228–29. See G. C. Peden, "The 'Treasury View' on Public Works and Employment in the Interwar Period," *Economic History Review,* 2d ser., 37 (May 1984): 167–81, for a survey of the literature on the subject. See Robert Self, "Treasury Control and the Empire Marketing Board: The Rise and Fall of Non-Tariff Preference in Britain, 1924–1933," *Twentieth Century British History* 5 (1994): 153–82, for an especially vivid example of the power of the Treasury to inhibit the development of innovative policy.

29. See K. J. Hancock, "The Reduction of Unemployment as a Problem of Public Policy, 1920–29," *Economic History Review,* 2d ser. 15 (Dec. 1962): 334–35.

30. Steel-Maitland to Churchill, July 17, 1926; P. J. Grigg to F. N. Tribe, July 21, 1926 (both in PRO LAB 2/1211, ED 11770/2, A44/1926).

31. Tribe, July 23, 1926; Eady to Phillips, July 27, 1926; Tribe to Steel-Maitland, July 31, 1926 (all in PRO LAB 2/1211, ED 11770/2, A 44/1926).

32. Steel-Maitland to Churchill, Aug. 5, 1926 (PRO LAB 2/1211, ED 11770/2, A 44/1926). Eveline M. Burns, *British Unemployment Programs, 1920–1938* (Washington: SSRC Committee on Social Security, 1941), 133, 134. In the view of R. C. Davison (see appendix), public works were retained in the 1920s for political reasons only. Davison was himself very critical of the use of public works to relieve unemployment, pointing out that a worker aided through the UGC cost the government £324 per year, whereas a worker aided by unemployment insurance cost only between £46 and £75. *The Unemployed: Old Policies and New* (London: Longmans, Green, 1929), 44–46, 52.

33. See Alan Anderson, "The Labour Laws and the Cabinet Legislative Committee of 1926–27," *Bulletin of the Society for the Study of Labour History* 23 (1971): 37–54, for a detailed description of the 1927 Trade Disputes Act. For more general accounts see Melvin C. Shefftz, "The Trade Disputes and Trade Unions Act of 1927: The Aftermath of the General Strike," *Review of Politics* 29 (1967): 387–406, and G. A. Phillips, *The General Strike: The Politics of Industrial Conflict* (London: Weidenfeld and Nicolson, 1976), 274–79.

34. Sir John Corcoran, July 21, 1926; Notes on Deputation, Oct. 12, 1926 (both in PRO LAB 10/4, IR 801/27/1926).

35. H. J. Wilson to J. Forbes Watson, Feb. 4, 1927 (PRO LAB 2/1207, IR 801/36, A37/1926). See Terence Rodgers, "Employers' Organizations, Unemployment and Social Politics in Britain during the Inter-war Period," *Social History* 13 (Oct. 1988): 315–41, for a discussion

of the role of organizations such as the NUM and the NCEO in the development of government policy toward unemployment.

36. M. A. Bevan, "Note on Strikes and Lockouts Officially Recorded During the Years 1898–1913, Inclusive," Oct. 23, 1926 (PRO LAB 2/1207, IR 801/36, A37/1926).

37. H. J. Wilson to J. Forbes Watson, Feb. 4, 1927 (PRO LAB 2/1207, IR 801/36, A37/1926).

38. Overseas Section, Statistics Division, "Memo on Right of Association, Right to Strike . . . in Various Countries" (PRO LAB 2/1238, IR 759, A78/1926). H. J. Wilson to Barlow, Dec. 16, 1926; H. J. Wilson, March 10, 1927; Chief Conciliation Officers, regional reports, Jan. 1927 (all in PRO LAB 10/5, IR 801/57/1926). Quotations from reports on Scotland and the northwest area.

39. Both quotations from "Memo on Trade Union Act Amendment Bill," n.d. (PRO LAB 2/882, IR 1169).

40. Neville Chamberlain Papers, "Political Diaries," May 11, 1926 (NC 2/21); Steel-Maitland, Nov. 22, 1926 (CP [Cabinet Papers] 394 [26]), reproduced in Anderson, "Labour Laws and the Cabinet Legislation Committee of 1926–27," 54.

41. H.B.W. to Minister, Oct. 28, 1926; Ince, "Victimization by Trade Unions," Oct. 29, 1926; Minister of Labour to Cabinet, "Victimization by Trade Unions" (all in PRO LAB 2/1206, IR 742/211/1926, A37/1926).

42. For an overview of the Ministry of Labour's record on industrial relations, see Lowe, *Adjusting to Democracy,* 76–113. During the negotiations between miners and mine owners that followed the collapse of the General Strike, Steel-Maitland believed that Churchill took too strong a stand in support of the miners' demand for a national agreement. Martin Gilbert, *Winston S. Churchill: Prophet of Truth, 1922–1939,* vol. 5 (Boston: Houghton Mifflin, 1977), 199–200.

43. Steel-Maitland, Oct. 3, 1926; Bircham to Price, Nov. 8, 1926; Blunden, Dec. 2, 1926 (all in PRO LAB 8/53, ED 4546/1926).

44. Eady, March 16, 1933 (PRO LAB 2/1474/ET 1750/1933, A103/1933).

45. For the full story, see Frederic Miller, "National Assistance or Unemployment Assistance? The British Cabinet and Relief Policy, 1932–33," *Journal of Contemporary History* 9 (1974): 163–84; "The British Unemployment Assistance Crisis of 1935," *Journal of Contemporary History* 14 (1979): 329–52; "The Unemployment Policy of the National Government, 1931–1936," *Historical Journal* 19 (1976): 453–76; Eric Briggs and Alan Deacon, "The Creation of the Unemployment Assistance Board," *Policy and Politics* 2 (Sept. 1973): 43–62; B. Gilbert, *British Social Policy, 1914–1939* (London: B. T. Batsford, 1970); Lowe, *Adjusting to Democracy,* 154–67.

46. Eady, March 16, 1933 (PRO LAB 2/1474/ET 1750/1933, A103/1933).

47. Miller, "National Assistance or Unemployment Assistance?"

48. "Allocation of government contracts so as best to alleviate unemployment," n.d.; Ministry of Labour Council, Minutes of Meeting, Nov. 14, 1919; F. Philips (Treasury) to Bowers (Labour), Nov. 19, 1919; Bowers, Dec. 1, 1919; Conference between Ministry of Labour and Contracting Departments, Minutes, Feb. 4, 1920 (all in PRO LAB 2/493, ED 70081/1919, A196/1919).

49. Eady, "Unemployment and the Insurance Fund," Aug. 25, 1926 (PRO LAB 2/1248, ED 36802/1927, A20/1927).

50. Eady, "Unemployment and the Insurance Fund," Aug. 25, 1926 (LAB 2/1248, ED 36802/1927, A20/1927).

51. Steel-Maitland to Secretary, July 19, 1927 (PRO LAB 2/1248, ED 36802/1927, A20/1927).

52. Eady, "Tendencies of Employment and Unemployment Since 1921," Nov. 3, 1926 (PRO LAB 2/1215, ED 48401/1926, A63/1926).

53. Ibid.

54. Ibid.

55. Eady to H. D. Hancock, Feb. 17, 1927; Eady to Secretary, July 14, 1927 (PRO LAB 2/1215, ED 48401/1926).

56. Eady, "Employment Aspect," March 16, 1933 (PRO LAB 2/1474, ET 1750/1933, A103/1933). These articles appeared in March 1933 and were later published as a pamphlet entitled *The Means of Prosperity.* In them Keynes elaborated the concept of the multiplier effect, the most important theoretical justification of public works and deficit spending as the proper response of government to depression. R. Skidelsky, "Keynes and the Treasury View: The Case For and Against an Active Unemployment Policy, 1920–1939," in *The Emergence of the Welfare State in Britain and Germany, 1850–1950,* ed. W. J. Mommsen with Wolfgang Mock (London: Croom Helm, 1981), 183–84.

57. Eady, "Employment Prospects: Memorandum on Possible Policy," March 20, 1933 (PRO LAB 2/1474/ET 1750/1933).

58. The MacMillan Report was the final report of the Committee on Finance and Industry that appeared in 1931. Appointed by the Labour government in 1929 this committee, chaired by Lord MacMillan, included among its members J. M. Keynes and Ernest Bevin. It was in his testimony before this committee that Sir Richard Hopkins of the Treasury elaborated the "Treasury view." Mowat, *Britain Between the Wars,* 260–62; A. J. Youngson, *Britain's Economic Growth, 1920–1966* (London: Allen and Unwin, 1967), 295–96.

59. Eady, "Employment Prospects," March 20, 1933 (PRO LAB 2/1474/ET 1750/1933).

60. Ibid.

61. In an effort to marshal support for his analysis, Eady noted that F. W. Leggett, principal assistant secretary of the General Department, agreed with his views and that Horace Wilson shared his concern (ibid.).

62. In a letter to J.C.C. Davison in September 1926, Patrick Gower commented: "One cannot help feeling sorry for Steel-Maitland because he has borne much of the burden during the past six months. But on the other hand, he seems to be more nervy than usual and hardly in a fit state to take charge of the negotiations. In some ways it is almost a pity that his doctor does not advise him to take a few weeks holiday." Robert Rhodes James, *Memoirs of a Conservative: J.C.C. Davison's Memoirs and Papers, 1910–1937* (London: Weidenfeld and Nicolson, 1969), 256–57.

63. Howson and Winch, *Economic Advisory Council,* provides a detailed account of the Economic Advisory Council's activities during the 1930s.

64. Miller, "National Assistance or Unemployment Assistance?" 176–77, 180–83.

65. Rodney Lowe, in "Bureaucracy Triumphant or Denied?" 307–09, takes great pains to distinguish between the views of Ministry of Labour and Treasury officials.

66. See Ronald C. Davison, *The Unemployed: Old Policies and New* (London: Longmans, Green, 1929), 52–58, for a clear example of the Ministry of Labour's view of public works. For the crucial importance of the multiplier effect as a justification for public works, see Donald Winch, *Economics and Policy: A Historical Study* (New York: Walker and Company, 1969), 156; Michael Stewart, *Keynes and After* (London: Penguin, 1967), 94; and Ross McKibbon, "The Economic Policy of the Second Labour Government, 1929–1931," *Past and Present* 68 (Aug. 1975): 107–08.

67. Malcolm Mansfield, "Labour Exchanges and the Labour Reserve in Turn of the Century Social Reform," *Journal of Social Policy* 21 (Oct. 1992): 435–68. See Alan Deacon, *In Search of the Scrounger,* Occasional Papers on Social Administration, no. 60 (London: G. Bell and Sons, 1976), for an account of the Ministry of Labour's administration of unemployment benefits.

68. Hardman, "Control of Employment: Notes on TUC Memorandum," June 16, 1939 (PRO LAB 8/248, EMC 69).

69. Ibid.; Meeting, June 28, 1939; Hardman, July 25, 1939 (all in PRO LAB 8/248, EMC 69).

70. R. Davison and R. Lowe, "Bureaucracy and Innovation in British Welfare Policy, 1870–1945," in Mommsen with Mock, *Emergence of the Welfare State in Britain and Germany,* 263–95 (see esp. 264–69 where Davison and Lowe delineate the connection of recruitment and social origins to the development of innovative policy). On Horace Wilson, see Rodney Lowe and Richard Roberts, "Sir Horace Wilson, 1900–1935: The Making of a Mandarin," *Historical Journal* 30, no. 3 (1987): 641–62.

6. The Ministry of Health: Fiscal Versus Social Responsibility

1. The epigraph is from William A. Ross, "Local Government Board and After: Retrospect," *Public Administration* 34 (1956): 18.

2. The principle of "less eligibility" embodied by the 1834 Poor Law held that receiving relief must be a less attractive prospect than going out to work. Rates of relief, therefore, must be kept at a level below that of the lowest wage rates. This Benthamite principle dominated the administration of poor relief in England for one hundred years (Oliver MacDonagh, *Early Victorian Government, 1830–1870* [London: Weidenfeld and Nicolson, 1977], 101–02).

3. Kenneth O. Morgan, *Consensus and Disunity: The Lloyd George Coalition Government, 1918–1922* (Oxford: Clarendon Press, 1979), 87.

4. Paul R. Wilding, "The Genesis of the Ministry of Health," *Public Administration* 45 (summer 1967): 149–50.

5. For comprehensive accounts of the creation of the Ministry of Health, see Bentley Gilbert, *British Social Policy, 1914–1939* (London: B. T. Batsford, 1970), 98–132; Frank Honigsbaum, *The Struggle for the Ministry of Health, 1914–1919,* Occasional Papers of Social Administration, no. 37 (London: G. Bell and Sons, 1970); and Paul R. Wilding, "The Genesis of the Ministry of Health," *Public Administration* 45 (summer 1967): 149–68.

6. G. R. Searle, *The Quest for National Efficiency: A Study in British Politics and Political Thought, 1899–1914* (Berkeley and Los Angeles: University of California Press, 1971), 238–42.

7. Gilbert, *British Social Policy,* 102. Honigsbaum cites the slogan coined by leaders of the infant mortality campaign: "It was more dangerous to be a baby in England than a soldier in France." *Struggle for the Ministry of Health,* 13. See Jane Lewis, *The Politics of Motherhood: Child and Maternal Welfare in England, 1900–1939* (London: Croom Helm, 1980), 61–113, for an account of the efforts to reduce infant mortality in England.

8. See Kenneth D. Brown, "John Burns at the Local Government Board: a Reassessment," *Journal of Social Policy* 6 (1977): 157–70 for a discussion of Burns's tenure at the Local Government Board.

9. Wilding, "Genesis of the Ministry of Health," 150–57.

10. Morant, n.d. (PRO MH 79/377).

11. Kenneth O. Morgan, *Portrait of a Progressive: The Political Career of Christopher Viscount Addison* (Oxford: Clarendon Press, 1980).

12. Sir Arthur Newsholme, *The Last Thirty Years in Public Health* (London: Allen and Unwin, 1936), 47.

13. See chapter 2 on recruitment to the Ministry of Health. Of the two hundred men who represented the top ten successful Class 1 candidates to join the home civil service between 1896 and 1914, fifty (one-quarter) chose the Admiralty or the War Office. Another twenty-two chose the Treasury. The Colonial Office was comparatively popular, attracting twenty-five of this group. The Board of Trade and the LGB each attracted only fifteen men from the group, but the Board of Trade made free use of special appointments to supplement recruitment by competitive examination.

14. P. A. Ryan, " 'Poplarism,' 1894–1930," in *The Origins of British Social Policy,* ed. Pat Thane (London: Croom Helm, 1978), 72–78. Francis quoted in Ryan " 'Poplarism,' " 72.

See also the account of this episode from Chamberlain's point of view in David Dilks, *Neville Chamberlain,* vol. 1, *Pioneering and Reform, 1869–1929* (Cambridge: Cambridge University Press, 1984), 518–20.

15. Hervey to Lowry, Dec. 6, 1922; Lowry to Francis, Dec. 8, 1922; Francis to Symonds, Jan. 12, 1923; Hervey to Francis, Jan. 22, 1923 (all in PRO MH 57/120). In 1795, after a succession of bad harvests, Berkshire justices met at the village of Speenhamland and agreed upon a plan to supplement low wages out of the poor rates. This approach to poor relief, while it simultaneously prevented starvation and purchased a measure of social peace, subsidized the low wages paid by farmers to their workers. The scandal of the Speenhamland system constituted one of the components in the campaign for the 1834 Poor Law and the principle of "less eligibility" that it embodied. R. K. Webb, *Modern England* (New York: Harper and Row, 1980), 140, 247.

16. Francis to Robinson, Jan. 8, 1929 (PRO MH 79/304).

17. Ibid.

18. Ibid.

19. For another example of the stringency routinely adopted by Ministry of Health officials, see Maureen Turnbull, "Attitude of Government and Administration towards the 'Hunger Marches' of the 1920s and 1930s," *Journal of Social Policy* 2 (1973): 131–42.

20. M. A. Crowther, "The Later Years of the Workhouse, 1890–1929," in Thane, *Origins of British Social Policy,* 51–53; M. A. Crowther, *The Workhouse System, 1834–1929: The History of a Social Institution* (Athens: University of Georgia Press, 1981), 110.

21. Crowther, *The Workhouse System,* 264.

22. M. A. Crowther, "Family Responsibility and State Responsibility in Britain Before the Welfare State," *Historical Journal* 25 (1982): 131–45.

23. John Macnicol, "Family Allowances and Less Eligibility," in Thane, *Origins of British Social Policy,* 173–202 (Strohmenger quoted 182). John Macnicol, *The Movement for Family Allowances, 1918–1945: A Study in Social Policy Development* (London: Heinemann, 1980), 55. Charles Webster, "Health, Welfare and Unemployment During the Depression," *Past and Present* 109 (Nov. 1985): 218. Webster focuses on local administration of social services, showing the impact that the lack of positive leadership had on their provision. See also Madeleine Mayhew, "The 1930s Nutrition Controversy," *Journal of Contemporary History* 23 (1988): 445–64.

24. On this point, contrast J. M. Winter, "Infant Mortality, Maternal Mortality, and Public Health in Britain in the 1930s," *Journal of European Economic History* 8 (fall 1979): 439–62 and Noel Whiteside, "Counting the Cost: Sickness and Disability among Working People in an Era of Industrial Recession, 1920–39," *Economic History Review,* 2d ser. 40 (1987): 228–46.

25. The Anderson Committee had two unusual characteristics: its members were all drawn from the civil service and it lacked a representative from the Treasury. See Gilbert, *British Social Policy,* 242; Macnicol, *Movement for Family Allowances,* 110–11.

26. Eady quoted in Macnicol, *Movement for Family Allowances,* 116.

27. Deputation to Ministry of Health, Oct. 31, 1928; Robinson to Chamberlain, Nov. 1, 1928 (both in PRO HLG 30/63).

28. Robinson to Chamberlain, Nov. 1, 1928 (PRO HLG 30/63).

29. Lowry to Robinson, Dec. 4, 1928 (PRO MH 79/304).

30. Note to Forber, Jan. 23, 1928; Report on Durham by Mr. Batterbury to Francis, Feb. 6, 1928; Report on South Wales by Jones Evans to Francis, Feb. 13, 1928; Report of Special Committee on Distress in South Wales, March 8, 1928 (all in PRO HLG 30/47).

31. Notes of Conference of Heads of Departments on Unemployment, July 9, 1931 (PRO HLG 30/27).

32. Robinson and Gibbon, Oct. 11, 1930; Meetings with Mr. Davidge, Oct. 28 and Nov. 12, 1930 (all in PRO HLG 30/27).

33. Hilton-Young, May 22, 1933; Note to Robinson, June 1, 1933; Robinson, June 2, 1933 (all in PRO HLG 30/1).

34. E. J. Strohmenger to Treasury, Aug. 15, 1931; Strohmenger to Greenwood, Aug. 17, 18, 1931; Greenwood to Snowden, Aug. 20, 1931 (all in PRO HLG 68/35).

35. Strohmenger to Hurst, Aug. 28, 1931; Strohmenger, Aug. 31, 1931; Strohmenger to Greenwood, Sept. 4, 1931 (all in PRO HLG 68/35).

36. For a full discussion of housing policy, see Marion Bowley, *Housing and the State* (London: Allen and Unwin, 1945); Gilbert, *British Social Policy;* Paul Johnson, *Land Fit for Heroes* (Chicago: University of Chicago Press, 1968); Mark Swenarton, *Homes Fit for Heroes: The Politics and Architecture of Early State Housing in Britain* (London: Heinemann Educational Books, 1981).

37. Deputation, March 28, 1933; Robinson to Hilton-Young, March 27, 1933 (both in PRO HLG 30/43).

38. "Equalisation of Poor Rates," n.d. (PRO HLG 30/43).

39. Chamberlain to his sister quoted in Iain MacLeod, *Neville Chamberlain* (New York: Atheneum, 1962), 164. Hilton-Young to Neville Chamberlain, n.d. (PRO HLG 30/3).

40. Note, Dec. 15, 1932 (PRO HLG 30/3).

41. Meetings between Hilton-Young, Robinson, Lowry, Francis, Maude, Jan. 30–31, 1933 (PRO HLG 30/3).

42. Frederic Miller, "National Assistance or Unemployment Assistance? The British Cabinet and Relief Policy, 1932–33," *Journal of Contemporary History* 9 (1974): 163–84.

43. Note to Sir Arthur Lowry, Aug. 8, 1933 (PRO HLG 30/5).

44. See chapter 5 for a discussion of the Ministry of Labour's view of this disagreement.

45. Note to Sir Arthur Lowry, Oct. 23, 1933 (PRO HLG 30/5).

46. See Frederic Miller, "The British Unemployment Assistance Crisis of 1935," *Journal of Contemporary History* 14 (1979): 329–51.

47. For a discussion of how the expectations of Poor Law administration could conflict with professional standards of conduct, see M. A. Crowther, "Paupers or Patients? Obstacles to Professionalization in the Poor Law Medical Service Before 1914," *Journal of the History of Medicine and Allied Sciences* 39 (Jan. 1984): 33–54.

48. Dilks, *Chamberlain,* 405–21.

49. Addison to Churchill, March 26, 1920; Churchill to Addison, March 29, 1920 (Addison Papers, Box 53, file 684).

50. Ross, "Local Government Board," 21–22.

51. Gilbert, *British Social Policy,* 195.

52. Neville Chamberlain, Political Diaries, Nov. 1, 1928 (Neville Chamberlain Papers, NC 2/22). Robinson to Chamberlain, June 28, 1929 (NC 7/11/22/25), and March 12, 1934 (NC 7/11/27/28).

53. Keith Feiling, *The Life of Neville Chamberlain* (London: Macmillan, 1946), 314 (quotation from exchange of letters, 405).

54. Veale to Chamberlain, June 7, 1929 (Neville Chamberlain papers, NC 7/11/22/32); quotation from Veale to Chamberlain, n.d. (NC 7/11/26/39); Veale to Chamberlain, Nov. 24, 1935 (NC 7/11/28/45); Veale to Mrs. Chamberlain, Nov. 11, 1940 (NC 7/11/30/48).

55. Dilks, *Chamberlain,* 328–35, 412–13, 560. Chamberlain, Oct. 4, 1926 (Neville Chamberlain Papers, NC 1/26/372).

56. Hilton-Young to his wife, Sept. 14, 1932, quotation from Feb. 1934; Neville Chamberlain to Hilton-Young, Jan. 30, 1933 (Kennet Papers).

57. Hilton-Young to Chamberlain, June 26, 1935 (Neville Chamberlain papers, NC 7/11/28/49); Neville Chamberlain to Hilton-Young, June 7, 1935 (Kennet Papers).

Conclusion: The Influence of the Civil Service

1. The epigraph is from John Rex, "Capitalism, Elites, and the Ruling Class," in *Elites and Power in British Society,* ed. Philip Stanworth and Anthony Giddens (Cambridge: Cambridge University Press, 1974), 210.

2. This pattern has continued to hold, down to the present day, keeping alive concerns about the social representativeness and social biases of the higher levels of the civil service. See Kevin Theakston and Geoffrey K. Fry, "Britain's Administrative Elite: Permanent Secretaries, 1900–1986," *Public Administration* 67 (summer 1989): 129–47, for another study confirming the persistence of this pattern. See Andrew Gray, "The Civil Service and Parliament: Eleventh Report of the Expenditure Committee, 1976–77," *Parliamentary Affairs* 32, 1 (winter 1979): 42, and F. F. Ridley, "The British Civil Service and Politics: Principles in Question and Traditions in Flux," *Parliamentary Affairs* 36, 1 (winter 1983): 31–32, for additional contemporary commentaries. See also Sophie Watson, "Producing the Right Sort of Chap: the Senior Civil Service as an Exclusionary Culture," *Policy and Politics* 22 (July 1994): 211–22, for a discussion of these issues with respect to their relevance to providing equal opportunity for women in the civil service.

3. Charles Douie, "Can England Afford Her Public Schools: I," *Journal of Education* 71 (July 1939): 471; "Can England Afford Her Public Schools: II," *Journal of Education* 71 (Aug. 1939): 547; Charles Douie, *So Long to Learn* (Oxford: George Ronald, 1951), 73. Douie discusses his civil service career and the Board of Education, 73–79. See also Charles Douie, *Beyond the Sunset* (London: John Murray, 1935), 30–90.

4. C.E.M. Joad, *Under the Fifth Rib: A Belligerent Autobiography* (London: Faber and Faber, 1932), 10, 63.

5. Ibid., 289; Jan. 25, 1927 (PRO LAB 2/1991, S and E 980/1931); Treasury officials did not expect Joad would ever receive a promotion; they consequently regarded his retirement as desirable since that would enable them to fill his position with a younger man (Norman to Foyle, Nov. 28, 1929 [PRO T164/83/26]). A.J.P. Taylor, *English History, 1914–1945* (Oxford: Oxford University Press, 1965), 362, n. 1. Joad was not the only one to depart. See Rodney Lowe, "Bureaucracy Triumphant or Denied? The Expansion of the British Civil Service, 1919–1939," *Public Administration* 62 (autumn 1984): 294.

6. See also Gary McCulloch, " 'Spens v. Norwood': Contesting the Educational State?" *History of Education* 22 (June 1993): 163–80, for another example of interdepartmental disagreement.

7. Anthony Giddens used two central factors in his typology of elites: "elite formation" and "issue-strength." Homogeneity, as a product of recruitment and social integration, represents a crucial element in his delineation of elite formation. *The Class Structure of the Advanced Societies* (New York: Harper and Row, 1973), 118–27, esp. 120.

8. For a more detailed treatment of these developments, see Richard A. Chapman and J. R. Greenaway, *The Dynamics of Administrative Reform* (London: Croom Helm, 1980), 71–119.

9. William A. Ross, "Local Government Board and After: Retrospect," *Public Administration* 34 (1956): 22.

10. C. K. Munro, *The Fountains in Trafalgar Square: Some Reflections on the Civil Service* (London: William Heinemann, 1952), 158. Under the name of C. K. MacMullan, Munro entered the civil service by competitive examination in 1912. He served first in the Board of Trade and then in the Ministry of Labour, where he attained the rank of assistant secretary in 1939. He ultimately rose to the position of undersecretary. At the same time, MacMullen carried on an active literary career as a playwright and essayist under the name of Munro.

11. George Newman to Mr. Pumphrey, April 7, 1921 (Newman Papers).

12. On the other hand, for a particularly vivid example of the aggressiveness with which the Treasury could act, see Robert Self, "Treasury Control and the Empire Marketing Board: The Rise and Fall of Non-Tariff Preference in Britain, 1924–1933," *Twentieth Century British History* 5 (1994): 153–82. Detailing examples of the Treasury's various successes and failures will not, by itself, settle the more general question of the nature and extent of the Treasury's power during this period, and the study that delivers a definitive and authoritative judgment on "Treasury control" during the interwar period has yet to be written. Andrew McDonald has begun a promising line of analysis that stresses how conflict and disagreement within the Trea-

sury undercut the implementation of a rigorously consistent Treasury view. See his "The Geddes Committee and the Formulation of Public Expenditure Policy, 1921–1922," *Historical Journal* 32 (1989): 643–74. On the more general point, see also Keith Middlemas, *Politics in Industrial Society* (London: Andre Deutsch, 1979), 228. I found the interplay between the spending departments and the Treasury to be very similar to the one, described in Maurice Wright, "Treasury Control, 1854–1914," in *Studies in the Growth of Nineteenth-Century Government,* ed. Gillian Sutherland (Totowa, N.J.: Rowman and Littlefield, 1972), 195–226, which obtained in the years prior to 1914. See also Henry Roseveare, *The Treasury* (New York: Columbia University Press, 1969), 242–57. For a discussion of the Treasury's role in the development of the civil service during the interwar period see John Greenaway, "Warren Fisher and the Transformation of the British Treasury, 1919–1939," *Journal of British Studies* 23 (fall 1983): 125–42.

13. Gary McCulloch's *Philosophers and Kings: Education for Leadership in Modern England* (Cambridge: Cambridge University Press, 1991), discusses the ongoing modification of the public school tradition during the twentieth century, showing both the continuity and the flexibility of that tradition.

14. United Kingdom. Parliament. Royal Commission on Agriculture, *Minutes of Evidence,* 2. Cmd 345. 1919.

15. Joseph Melling, in the course of a general discussion of different approaches to the study of the welfare state, stresses the importance of understanding the role such systems of values play in the development of welfare politics. "Welfare Capitalism and the Origins of Welfare States: British Industry, Workplace Welfare, and Social Reform," *Social History* 17 (Oct. 1992): 457.

16. I am thinking here of the dual nature of the social structure, which simultaneously confines and enables the individual. Anthony Giddens, "Power, the Dialectic of Control, and Class Structuration," in *Social Class and the Division of Labour: Essays in Honour of Ilya Neustadt,* ed. Anthony Giddens and Gavin MacKenzie (Cambridge: Cambridge University Press, 1982), 30.

Index